Ringside Gamble

Praise for *Ringside Gamble*:

"An exciting and realistic depiction of the underworld of Muay Thai and what it takes to be a Muay Thai fighter."

Aphidet Joy Chaithet, former Muay Thai Champion, National Coach Singapore and Head Trainer, BXG Boxing and Fitness

"The story of childhood friends and boxing rivals Nong and Sert will stay with you for a long time."

Diana Campillo, Owner, Rawai Muay Thai, Thailand

"S. J. Clarke's *Ringside Gamble* is a must-read, seamlessly blending myth, magic, and the cultural significance of Thai boxing. The characters come alive, drawing readers into the heart of Thai culture and martial arts. It offers an educational and emotional journey suitable for all ages and genders. Clarke's storytelling skilfully captures the essence of national heroism and generational pride associated with this discipline.

Dr. Budi Miller, Actor, Artist, Teacher and Co-Artistic Director, Theatre of Others

"A well-known line reminds us that the size of the fight in the dog is more relevant than the size of the dog in the fight, and there's plenty of fight in S. J. Clarke's *Ringside Gamble*. Here is a coming-of-age story of Muay Thai boxers that never stoops to being a mere coming-of-rage story. Like many of our fights, the hero's real battles here are those in his own uneasy heart."

Professor Darryl Whetter, author of the climate-crisis novel *Our Sands* (from Penguin)

"In *Ringside Gamble*, S.J. Clarke weaves an enthralling world, skillfully blending the brutal beauty of Muay Thai with the serene mystique of Thai culture. This gripping saga invites readers into the heart of stifling arenas and sacred temples, where the line between the natural and the mystical becomes hazy. Clarke expertly delves into the close-knit community supporting the solitary fighter in the ring, shedding light on the sacrifices and triumphs that pave the way to glory."

Adam Marple, Assistant Professor of Directing at The American University in Cairo

ISBN 978-1-7384419-0-7 (paperback)
ISBN 978-1-7384419-1-4 (ebook)

Cover photograph by Josef Hlávka.

Typeset and published by Michelle Emerson.
www.michelleemerson.co.uk.

Ringside Gamble

S. J. Clarke

For those who teach

ACKNOWLEDGEMENTS

I would like to thank Professor Darryl Whetter, author and editor, for reviewing an early draft and making *Ringside Gamble* better. He is a brilliant editor as well as an educator and an aspiring writer's best friend. Playwright and dramaturg Steven Gaultney provided keen insights as well as mentorship and contributed to the editing of this book along with Michelle Emerson, who undertook the management of this book's publication and final editing stages.

Ringside Gamble is the story of many fighters' struggles and dreams of success. In Thailand, I have had the honour of training with fighters from the golden age of Muay Thai. Most notably, Chanchai Sor Tamarangsri, and I attended training camps in Chiang Mai, Koh Lanta, Phuket, and Khao Lak. I spent many weeks at Rawai Muay Thai over ten years where Tuk (whose boxing name is Sakedao Sor Ayupinda) and Diana Campillo the owners, have built one of the premier Muay Thai gyms in Thailand. Their students have won numerous stadium trophies, as well as the World Muay Thai Council (WMC) and the World Professional Muay Thai Federation (WPMF) titles. Their teaching style follows the traditional methods passed on from generation to generation. *Kru* Aphidet Joy Chaithet, former professional boxer, previous Singapore National coach and trainer at BXG Boxing and Fitness, introduced me to the spirit of what it means to be a Muay Thai fighter, and I thank him for his coaching over these last twelve years. As well as BXG owner/trainer Joe Yeo Ying Han and team Joy Lim Shu Zhen and Lawrence Lau Guo Jin, who have made such a tremendous difference to so many people and their contribution to the performance of Singapore's Muay Thai athletic community cannot be overstated. I wholeheartedly thank such wonderful members of the Muay Thai community for critiquing and improving early versions of my manuscript.

Elaine Ng, Julie Cutting, Kitty Mulligan, Victoria Silberbauer and Dr Budi Miller deserve special thanks for giving me the confidence to continue writing. Andrew Mulligan, my husband, best friend and Muay Thai travel buddy—it really is the journey and not the destination. Thank you. My sister Nancy Morris for providing invaluable feedback, and my brothers Simon and Max. Lastly, my amazing parents, Robert and Marjorie Clarke, I thank you for being you.

Chapter One

NONG and Klapet's muscular bodies tensed, oiled skin glistening beneath the twirling Chiang Mai stadium spotlights. The referee's black sleeve sliced downwards. The shouts of the crowd caused such a cacophony that the referee's order to fight was inaudible to everyone, except the slim Thai boys facing one another at the centre of the boxing ring.

Nong moved forwards in a southpaw stance, feet a hip-distance apart, right foot in front. He knocked Klapet's left upper arm with his right glove, judging the distance between them. Klapet did the same in reverse, tapping Nong with his left glove. Weaving from side-to-side, the fighters alternately tested reactions and distances, measuring where they needed to be when they committed to a strike. They tapped their leading foot on the ground, feigning front kicks or *teeps*. Light-footed, they circled one another, each fighter as perfectly balanced as a world-class ballet dancer. Only in their mid-teens, they already showcased the years of extensive training and technique required to be a professional boxer.

Klapet probed Nong's speed with a quick left jab followed by a cross. Nong leant back, easily avoiding the strike and defending the side of his head with his left well-worn boxing glove as he twisted his body to the right. Shifting his weight to his back left leg, Nong struck out with his right leg, aiming a low roundhouse kick at Klapet's left thigh. Then Nong took two steps back before advancing to *teep* Klapet in the stomach with his left foot.

They recovered their stances. Nong, the faster of the two, attacked first. He attempted to hit Klapet with a lightning-low kick but missed and his foot glided through the air. Klapet, spotting an opening in Nong's defences, retaliated with a left kick but failed to connect. Cursing, Klapet rebalanced, raising his gloves to protect his face. Nong feigned a jab and then slammed his arm across Klapet's chest, forcing him backwards and driving his left knee into Klapet's right quadricep. The crowd roared as Klapet stumbled, tripped over his own feet and crashed to the floor. Nong swaggered, arms above his head, as he grinned triumphantly to encourage the cheers of the crowd whilst his opponent clambered onto his feet. Adrenaline-fuelled, Nong charged Klapet before he had even stood upright, causing the referee to shove him in the chest and issue a warning. The crowd, eager for action, egged Nong on, applauding and shouting his name.

"Continue," commanded the referee. Immediately, Klapet attempted a roundhouse kick to Nong's head, but it was too low and Nong caught his leg in an underarm grip. Nong twisted his right arm around Klapet's leg, lifting it up under the crook of his arm, and punched him hard several times in the face. Klapet fought back to escape Nong's grip, red patches that would soon turn purple and black sprouting on his jaw and cheek. Furiously, he pushed and pulled but Nong was too strong. Nong released Klapet's leg and bounced back a step to better assess where to make the killing blow. Spotting a weakness in Klapet's upper defences, he whipped round his left leg and struck Klapet in the neck. Nong's foot found its mark, but Klapet lessened the force of the impact by leaning to his right, his face grimacing in pain.

"Whooooo. Yes!" screamed the crowd in appreciation as the ringside musicians played at an even more frantic pace. This was a standard of boxing not witnessed in Chiang Mai for years, especially between two youngsters, each fighter being only fifteen. Nong flashed a confident grin at his corner team, hitched up his shorts and faced Klapet. The perspiring fighters circled. Swiftly, Klapet hit Nong with a low right kick to his outer left thigh. Nong responded with a jab and left kick.

"Oh-hoy!" "Oy!" and "Ohh-Wee!" encouraged the crowd.

Klapet attempted to grab Nong's left leg but failed as Nong wriggled free. The boxers reset their stances. A jab from Nong and a *teep* from Klapet. Nong struck again with his devasting left kick, but Klapet escaped just in time, crouching down and forcing Nong to sweep the air and receive the punishment for overreaching in the form of a swift kick to his inner left thigh.

Enjoying the fight as much as the crowd, the endorphin-high boys tapped gloves, fully engaged in this battle that tested their skills. They settled into their stances, gloves up as they sought an opening. Nong stood on one spot, switching his feet back and forth and weaving in an attempt to confuse Klapet and misdirect his defences. Pressing forwards, he *teeped* at Klapet, who barely managed to parry him away. Resetting, Nong moved back within striking distance, just far away enough for Klapet to be tempted to attack with a roundhouse kick, which he did. Nong caught his left leg under his arm and leaned to his right, avoiding Klapet's frenzied jabs. Enraged, he aimed a low kick at Klapet's inner right thigh and made contact, then released him. Standing back, arms by his side, Nong smirked at Klapet as if to say, "you were lucky this time."

The bell sounded. They clapped each other on the back, raising their arms to claim victory, and returned to their respective corners. Nong's crew's advice rained like the water from their sponges, but each syllable dripped away unnoticed. He turned to smile at the well-loved faces and simply nodded as, bruised and cut, he mentally steeled himself for round two.

* * *

Unlike the large city boxing arenas in places such as Bangkok and Chiang Mai, where Nong fought in later years, the one in his hometown was not high-tech. It was not an air-conditioned sports centre with digital screens, plush changing rooms, restaurants, and well-stocked bars offering premium drinks, nor was it well-known. It was a local stadium, and that meant rough.

The cement floor was perpetually littered with cigarette butts, and the stench of stale beer and sweat hung in the air. On the walls, behind the small bar, large grimy mirrors hung. Their metallic grey surfaces reflected the glow of the naked lightbulbs, which also illuminated the bottles of cheap spirits.

On this night, beneath the corrugated iron fencing marking the perimeter of the stadium, the bare feet of children were just visible and their small faces peered through the gaps between the panels fastened together by weathered blue fishing ropes. The children waved to their friends playing near those parents with enough baht to buy a ticket. Their excited hands fluttered like swiftlets clinging to a rock face. One of the smallest children spying through the fence appeared to be wearing a macaque mask.

The *farangs* (non-Thais) complained. Everything was wrong: the humidity, the smell, the locals puffing away as if it were the 1920s, and the plastic coating on the blue and white padded VIP ringside seats that caused them to sweat in the tropical heat. Before the start of the evening's fight card, Thais loitered near the stadium entrance or clambered up to the upper tiers of wooden benches. The locals knew that the tourists seated in the ringside VIP area would have to crane their necks and would soon be showered in blood.

sweat and spittle.

"Five minutes please, five minutes please," croaked the wizened, brown-toothed barman across the tannoy. "Eight p.m. fight start. Bar open. Tiger, Singha, Heineken, whisky, chips."

The night's fighters, Nong and Prasert (whom everyone called Sert), both just eight-year-old boys, sat on opposite sides of the stadium beside leather punching bags covered in a mesh of masking tape scars, waiting for their fathers' signals.

* * *

Nong and Sert started learning Muay Thai, the ancient Thai martial sport known as 'the art of eight limbs' when they were six. A practitioner of Muay Thai is known as a *nak muay*. Western practitioners were sometimes called *nak muay farang* ('foreign boxer'). Unlike Western boxers who use only their fists, Muay Thai fighters have an arsenal of weapons: punches, kicks, elbow and knee strikes. Eight 'points of contact' as opposed to two.

Sert was a happy-go-lucky boy who preferred to spend time reading or playing football rather than learning Muay Thai. In July, when the temperatures reached the mid-thirties, and he managed to escape his father, Sert swam in the natural rock pools greened by the overhanging forest canopy with the other village children. Released from the confines of the classroom, they would clamber onto bicycles in the late afternoon and hurtle down the stony paths bordered by ancient trees. Younger children rode on the handlebars or behind the older children on the saddles whilst the bicycle owners pedalled standing up.

On weekends, Nong and Sert played volleyball or football with their friends on the white stretches of sand fringing the Andaman Sea. When the sand burnt the soles of their feet, they swam in the bath-warm turquoise water, far away from the tourists. Until, salt-covered and spent, they headed for a shady spot beneath the coconut trees to half-doze in a heap like puppies, idly gossip and dream.

Nong would often lie on his back, his feet buried in the sand, gazing at the lotus blue sky, boasting to Sert that he would represent Thailand in a Muay Thai international championship and knock out a Burmese boxer on world television screens. Sert, only half-listening to his friend's daydreams, would re-live his favourite fantasy of becoming a pop star, winning *Asia's Got Talent* and performing in front of millions of fans shouting his name.

Sert frequently complained about his father, Warit. A trainer and former professional boxer, he entertained great hopes that his son would achieve what he had been unable to: The *Sports Writers of Thailand Fighter of the Year Award* and the Lumpinee, Thailand and Rajadamnern championship titles. Like most Muay Thai aficionados, Warit did not care about sanctioned belts from organisations such as the World Boxing Championships or the World Boxing Association, which he felt held little credibility or prestige.

Sert's neighbours never watched reality TV. Why would they when, outside their concrete shacks, they could often enjoy the Warit and Sert drama live? Early each morning, aunts, uncles and neighbours would wander out with sleepy eyes, drinking a coffee or Milo, gossiping and sharing plans. Warit would appear, chasing Sert with a newly torn slim tree branch, threatening him with a thrashing for missing training. The *kampong* hens would scatter along with his formerly sleepy son. Knowing looks would be shared. On occasion, neighbours would even bet on whether Sert would be caught. Sert's aunt even complained when her nephew complied with Warit's demands. Because not only did she enjoy the amateur dramatics, but she also relished seeing her normally taciturn brother driven to anger, cursing, and shouting. Sert's uncles welcomed the charades too, punting on how long it would take between Warit's shouts of "Get up!" and the disgruntled pair leaving for Dragon's Gym boxing camp.

Only two mornings ago, Warit and Sert had yet another set-to when the sun was barely up. Sert groaned as his mother Neuy called "breakfast" for the third time, slamming his book down. "She's really angry now," Sert muttered, rolling his eyes. With a sigh, he turned on his side and pulled the thin cotton bedsheets over his matted brown hair. Then, the scrape of his father's old metal front porch chair against the concrete floor caused his pulse to race. Adrenaline pumped into his muscles as he prepared to scarper. Footsteps approached.

"Out!" commanded Warit, yanking back the bedsheets and waving a freshly torn switch above his head. Sert leapt from the bed, ducked beneath his father's muscled arm, sprinted the four metres to the front entrance and through the open door. The bright sun momentarily blinded him.

"Good morning, Aunty, morning Gai," he said with a grin and wave as he looked around the yard. He could hear that his father was still in the house. The sing-song of his parents chatting in the kitchen let him know he had a few moments to catch his breath before Act II. The middle-aged ladies waved back from their ringside seats, the flashing sequins of their fake Gucci and Chanel t-shirts causing them to resemble a pair of disco balls.

"Stop wasting time," his aunt shouted, taking a drag on her cigarette and winking at her friend sipping coffee. Both of them strategically sat under the fragrant frangipani tree that provided shade as well as a good view of the much-anticipated show.

"Sert, where are you? If you're not in that shower by now, I'll…"

"Here comes your father!" warned Gai with a kind smile as she leaned back in her sun-faded, orange, rickety deckchair that had been salvaged from a nearby beach last summer.

Doing his best Usain Bolt impression, Sert bent down on one knee, placed his palms flat down on the ground, and sprinted as if he could feel the breath of rabid street dogs on his heels.

"Run, Sert. Faster. Run! Or you're going to get it this time," his neighbours encouraged from where they loitered on porches and dusty front yards under clouds of cheap tobacco.

As he disappeared behind the house, he disturbed scavenging dogs and cats luxuriating in the early morning sun. Thin, brown chickens flew onto the highest branches of the frangipani tree, squawking in fright.

"Come here, you little sod," Warit roared with false fury, brandishing his now wilted stick. As Warit chased his eel-quick son, he lunged forwards, stretching out his left hand to make a grab for Sert as he slithered by. But Sert dropped from his grasp like a piece of overripe mango from a fork.

"I'm getting too old for this game," Warit said as he leaned forward, resting his veined hands on his sinewy thighs. Catching sight of one of his neighbours, he signalled with two fingers against his lips for a cigarette.

Drawing in the dry tobacco, he shook his head. Ruefully, he thought, *the boy is never going to be a boxer. But he's going to learn what it means to stand up and fight. That he needs to know.* As he took his last draw, he contemplated Sert darting through the banana trees dotting the yard, and a secret smile crossed his heart. *Ahh, how I'd like to not have a care in the world,* he mused as Sert whizzed by again just out of reach, his outstretched arms imitating an airplane whooshing through a bright blue sky.

"Enough!"

That tone brought Sert's plane back to land.

"But—"

"But nothing," snapped Warit.

"But I want to read. Boxing is boring," Sert said pleadingly, looking up with his best I'm-a-great-son expression. He knew, though, that it was futile to beg. The fight with Nong was going to take place whatever he said or however he pleaded.

"There's no money in superhero comics. Now stop it with your stories! Get showered, fetch your gloves and let's go. The other boys will already have finished their run by now and be skipping." Warit was steadfast in his belief that he, and only he, knew what was in the boy's best interest. Sert might be young, but Warit was the same age when he first fought.

Sert made a great show of slouching in the direction of the outhouse, where the yellow hose pipe with the garden sprinkler attachment that served as a shower was. Accepting the inevitable, he continued playing to the gallery, dragging his feet as he walked and hanging his head. Sert decided to have one last attempt at putting off training and hunched his shoulders slightly to see if any sympathy could be extracted from his mother standing in the front doorway. But Neuy only smiled and gave a small shrug as if to say, you know your father.

"Get a move on! Don't be such a child!" shouted

Warit, hands on his hips, shaking his head.

Sert stood upright, threw an angry look at his father and stomped off to the shower. *All that effort for nothing,* he thought, as the neighbours went back to the business of breakfasting, gossiping, and gathering their belongings for the wet market. The fishing boats would have returned. Years ago, the fisherman sold an amazing variety of fish and the market stalls had had fresh mollusc and crustaceans of all sizes and varieties: glistening prawns, squid, parrot fish, and sometimes larger fish such as mackerel, barracuda, snapper, and bill fish. As overfishing took its toll, the catches shrunk. Eventually, even the bamboo sharks could not find enough fish to eat and had disappeared to hunting grounds near less populated coastal areas.

Neuy smiled as she watched Sert doing his protest march. She was an attractive, slim woman in her mid-thirties. Well-liked, Neuy had an open, honest face and a warm character. Once her boy had closed the rickety outhouse door behind him, she went to the kitchen to retrieve his breakfast.

She paused at the small altar on one side of the kitchen wall, picked up a banana from the fruit bowl and put it on the plate at the feet of the Buddha statue. She prayed for Sert's safety as well as Nong's. Only last week, her neighbour's nine-year-old boy had received a vicious jab to his left eye. The doctors said it was too early to tell if there was any permanent damage. But what to do? This was the way of things, and her husband insisted Sert fight. Neuy pressed her palms together again, beseeching the gods to protect her son.

Prayers done and food collected, she went outside to kiss Warit goodbye, hand over Sert's lunch of sticky rice topped with green curried chicken and remind her husband to collect some pork from the market for dinner.

Moments later, a soggy Sert, still damp from the shower, wearing faded rose, gold-fringed Muay Thai shorts and an old Spider-Man t-shirt, emerged from the house. Still sulking, he kissed her on the cheek whilst pointedly ignoring his father.

"Come on with you! Give me your gloves. HERE, hold your lunch!" snapped Warit as he hung Sert's gloves around his own neck before mounting the red and black Honda 125cc. He pushed back the kickstand, turned the engine over and let the bike warm-up for about forty-five seconds. Sert rode pillion with his feet resting on the foot pedals, one arm wrapped around his father's taut stomach, and his other holding tight onto his lunch. His father let out the clutch lever until the bike started to roll forward, pulling back on the throttle slightly to prevent the bike from stalling whilst releasing the clutch. The ride to Dragon's Gym avoided the main road, so they did not worry about the police fining them 500 baht for not wearing helmets.

Sert dismounted the motorbike outside the training centre, accepting his gloves in silence as he rubbed a piece of grit from his eye. "Thanks," he muttered, his young face sullen. *Well, here we go*, he thought.

Another boring two hours of training. Sert could not help but feel all this time spent training was a waste. He would never be a champion. Would he ever even win a match? Peering into the gloom of the gym, he spotted his best friend Nong inside and felt better. Preparing himself for the habitual teasing from the older boys, he trudged in the direction of the gym, his bottom lip sticking out.

"Ok, Champ! Get to it. I'll see you inside in a minute. We've got a trainer's meeting for five minutes. Warm-up and then practice throwing your left knee. As I've told you a million times, in Muay Thai, you're dead if you're lazy. Go!" said his father, heading to clock-in at reception, a smile flitting across his face.

Sert stuck his tongue out at his father's back before side-stepping round the black and tan mongrel dogs. At the two-metre gap in the cement wall that served as a gym entrance, he kicked off his dusty red flip-flops on top of the pile of rubber shoes and worn trainers. He gave a slight bow before stepping on the freshly washed blue training mats with their pungent aroma of bleach.

Thud, thud, thud went the skipping ropes of the other Thai boys. They had already heard that Sert had received another scolding that morning and teased him into smiling.

A perennially cheerful Nong greeted him, joking, "Thanks for choosing us over your books."

Sert acknowledged Nong with a thump to his upper arm and quietly said, "One more day," as he retrieved a thin yellow plastic skipping rope from a rusted wall hook.

After tying several knots to shorten the rope, he began to skip beside Nong, who he knew would be bursting to talk about Saturday's fight. Both boys were relieved they were battling each other and not a stranger, but pride stopped them from saying so. It wouldn't do to appear weak.

"Last night, I had the best dream," said Nong.

"Huh, I've had the worst morning," puffed Sert, his voice rising and falling in time with his skipping.

"I saw myself kneeling down in front of my mum and handing her the prize money."

"Whatever," retorted Sert, promising himself he would make sure this fight would be his last and not caring to respond to Nong's baiting.

The two friends faced the old, full-length training mirrors. In addition to the two skipping boys, the mirrors reflected two small square boxing rings of four-point-five metres. Each ring extended outside the ropes by fifty centimetres, with padded posts at each of the four corners. There were no stairs at the opposite corners of the ring for the boxers to use, as no matches were fought at the camp. Open to the elements, the total floor area was 2,000 metres. There was a three-foot-high wall on two sides constructed with unpainted cement blocks. Between the ceiling edge and the top of the wall, there was a gap of one-point-five metres, through which the sun's rays and rain poured through. The constant flow of wind kept the gym ventilated. Red punching bags hung from the lowest metal roof beams near one wall. One could tell they had been patched together many times by the shiny strips of sun-bleached masking tape, which ran like scars across the leather.

Between the gym and the road, there was about fifteen square metres of land where everyone parked. A special space under the trees was reserved for the bosses. When the rain was torrential during the wet season, this area turned into a sea of mud. Surrounding the gym were residential bungalows that housed up to fifty guests. Accommodations for the trainers and their families dotted the village and the camp. However, only paying guests could use the swimming pool and laundry services. In the training centre, there was a weight room with an assortment of well-used black kettlebells, hand weights, medicine balls, a running machine, and a fixed bike. It was the only part of the gym that was air-conditioned. When not in use by boxers or camp residents, this doubled up as a kindergarten for the trainers' children. There was also a stark but clean shower and locker room. Patrons soon learned to bring their own lavatory roll.

Photographs depicting the *krus,* or 'instructors', title fight wins hung on the back wall below a gunmetal grey shelf that held the gold and silver trophies, many of which were dressed in tattered ribbons in the red, white and blue colours of the Thai national flag. Championship weight belts were also crammed onto the shelf, emblazoned with the names of each boxing competition, along with the sponsors of regional championships, *Xtreme Muay Thai*, local tournaments, and international awards. Black and white photographs, news clippings and framed certificates on the wall were a Muay Thai sports historian's dream.

Unlike Sert, who had no interest in boxing histories, myths or folklore, Nong loved the bedtime stories his father told. Again and again, he asked to hear the famous tale of the Thai fighter, Nai Khanom Tom. He never tired of the part when the Burmese captured Khanom Tom during the sacking and burning of Thailand's ancient capital, Ayutthaya, in 1767 with its three palaces and more than 400 temples. He joined his father in cursing the people who razed this wonderous ancient city, with its population of over one million, nearly to the ground.

Joi, Nong's father, was typically a reserved man. But when he narrated the tales of ancient heroes, his voice became animated, especially when he told of Nai Khanom Tom's famous 1774 defeat of the ten best Burmese fighters by knockout during a tournament. Nong dreamt about his father's legends of warriors, the protectors of Thai kings and the country, picturing himself with his hands and forearms wrapped in old-fashioned hemp rope to both safeguard his fists from injury and make each strike deadlier for his opponent.

On 17 March, which Thais celebrate as Boxers Night, all the boxers at the gym, along with the villagers, honoured Nai Khanom Tom. Every stadium in the country dedicated fights in his honour, celebrating his valour. Joi had often spoken of his wish to visit the Nai Khanom Tom festival held in the beautiful ancient capital city of Ayutthaya. For the Thai people, this historical figure illustrated the best attributes of the Muay Thai athlete and the country's people. These were attributes Nong had been raised to always remember: the indomitable will to win for an honour other than his own and the readiness to face any odds in defence of the fighting art.

Displayed under lock and key in a glass cabinet within the training camp office were the prestigious national championship belts. After training, Nong went to see if he could smile his way to a free drink from the receptionist and take one last look at the title fight belts before his first real boxing match against Sert.

Chapter Two

STONEY faced, his skin glistening with oil and menthol, and his chin tilting upwards, Nong listened to Joi as he stretched his arms in front of him, clenching and unclenching his bony fists.

"Sirachai," said Joi, using his son's full name, "You begged me for this opportunity. Remember? So you've got to win tonight. I paid the promoter 5,000 baht. Don't rush. Don't worry about your punches. Cover your head. Keep your hands up."

"Yep. But stop, please, putting all that Vaseline in my hair. I'll never get it out," complained Nong, moving his head away to one side. "It makes me look stupid with a greasy face."

"Stop whinging, will you?" remonstrated Joi, adding another big dollop. He couldn't stand anyone moaning. Least of all his son. He believed complaining reflected badly on the whole family. He himself tried to always keep a neutral expression to show he was not impacted by life's events.

"You've worked harder than Sert. I know he's your friend but show him your goods. Don't pull your striking elbow too far back. But don't throw it a 100 per cent either. Remember: step and kick, step and KICK! The point of this match is to gain experience in the ring."

"Yep. Thank you, Father," said Nong with a barely concealed puff of impatience, submitting himself to more Vaseline lathering. The referee would later wipe the ointment from his face but not from the back of his neck, which his father coated to make it more difficult for his opponent to clinch (wrestle) him.

"Defend yourself with *teeps*," Joi told him, describing the front kicks to the stomach that would act as an electrical fence around Nong, shocking his opponent whenever he attacked. "And find a space for an uppercut elbow followed by a side elbow, but again, not too hard. If you can help it. He IS your neighbour and best friend, " said Joi as he roughed up Nong's hair with an encouraging smile and reminded him that this match was not meant to be fought at full strength, and each side would expect the other to hold back. They were there to gain experience, not draw blood for the hungry masses.

"Lastly, remember, your body is both a weapon and a shield," said Joi.

"I will, Father," said Nong, impatiently nodding in time to Joi's advice, advice that he had heard as often as the lullabies his mother sang. Joi had been a Thai Southern champion and was now a *kru.* He held the position of head trainer at Dragon's Gym, where he managed a team of ten ex-professional boxers, including Warit. Joi and his team trained the amateur boxing tourists residing at the boxing camp as well as the locals and four boys sponsored by the gym. Joi was happiest when sparring with other Thais but earned his money teaching group classes and private sessions to the *farangs*, as did the other trainers. However, he did not waste his time on the *farang* students who showed no heart or commitment to the honour of Muay Thai, deeming them unworthy of his time.

As a toddler, Nong had played on the stadium's dusty floor wearing his father's cast-off red leather boxing gloves, the white ties wrapped just below his elbow. A chubby, round cherub with a toothy grin, he could do little that was not forgiven. He helped give boxers drinks of water between rounds, photobombed the post-match pictures, and made a loveable nuisance of himself. His mother, Gan, chided him but even then, he was incorrigible. She could only ever settle him for a few minutes before, like a jack-in-the-box, he would spring up again. Chasing pigtails, pulling the boxers' shorts or clamouring for his father's attention. Other boys needed to be punished for not training hard enough, but Nong was kicking the bags, imitating leg blocks and trying to skip with a too-long rope before he could even ride a bicycle.

Nong had not run this morning because he needed to reserve his energy for this evening's match. In response to Joi's encouragement, he had begun to search for a place of balance, slowing down his breathing and sharpening his focus. There were seven fights of five rounds each lasting two minutes on the billing, with the three adult bouts scheduled last. Around the ring, Nong and Sert, separately, shadow-boxed, stealing glances across the room at one another.

Their fight was first, at 8 p.m.

Four musicians, a five-litre paint bucket filled with Changi beer at their feet, were there to heighten the intensity of the fight and followed the lead of the brass cymbal or *Ching.* Being masters of their art, each musician could improvise and required no sheet music. The cymbal player-come-car-mechanic moved his cigarette between stained teeth as he set the tempo for the rest of the group. The shortest musician, dressed in a black shirt and jeans, played the main instrument, the *Pi Java*, or 'Javanese clarinet', which sounded like Scottish bagpipes. Another musician played a pair of *Klong Kaak* (set of drums) while the other drummer played the *Kong Mong* (heavy drum).

Shouts of "*chok dee*" or 'good luck' followed Nong as he climbed the steps to his corner seat. His skinny legs, dangling from beneath his father's red and gold, worn boxing shorts, gave him the appearance of an agile gibbon in garish pantaloons. He had turned over the waistband of the shorts, which he wore for good luck, several times, and the hems still brushed his knees. He sat on a white plastic stool centred on a thin metal disc designed to catch any water or sweat. On the referee's hand signal, Nong and Sert stood and stepped away from the stools and metal trays, which their coaches removed from the ring. Both boys asked for their parents' blessing before commencing the *Wai Kru Ram Muay*, the ancient dance in which students show respect and gratitude to their teachers, parents and ancestors. Unlike Sert, who had not yet learnt all the steps, Nong bowed his head three times in salutation to Buddha, Rama and the Sangha of monks. Nong held on to the top rope, his yellow *Mongkhon* or 'headband' firmly in place for good luck. On his upper arm, he had tied a piece of his mother's sarong. Walking in an anti-clockwise direction, he trailed his right hand on the top rope, pausing at each corner to bow and tap the post thrice in upward movements with his right hand.

Nong prayed for good luck and protection whilst walking before moving into the middle of the ring to sit on his knees facing his corner. Joi studied the scene, still as a tiger watching its prey, his expression a mixture of pride and steel. Placing his old red gloves together, Nong bowed to perform prayers. Sert, facing his corner, also kowtowed to thank his *kru*. Nong paid homage to his teacher, to his camp and to his forefathers. After the *Wai Kru*, Nong started the *Ram Muay* dance. The *Ching* struck a slow rhythm as the musicians marked the time of this solemn pre-fight ritual. Nong felt calmer as he moved around the ring, raising one knee each time and returning it to the floor while maintaining the boxing stance. Every third step, Nong would draw his back foot through and forwards, standing in the opposite stance, switching to southpaw. He used dance movements that indicated his home province of Thailand, unlike others who simply added their own moves. Nong flowed through the dance as he pictured himself floating in the river behind his parents' house with the clear water refreshing his mind.

The final stage of the dance was a modern version

of the *Ram Muay* called the 'Swan's Flight' (*Hong Hern*). Nong moved to each side of the ring and conducted a series of movements reminiscent of a bird flapping its wings slowly while kneeling on one leg in a lunge position and shifting his weight back and forth. His back foot tapped in time to the music. After one minute, he stood up and gave a final bow to Joi before walking in his direction for the performance of the final rite. Joi placed both hands on the *Mongkhon*, pausing to bless Nong before removing it and placing it on the corner pole. Next, he dabbed holy water on Nong's forehead and cheeks before handing him his mouthguard.

"Son, fight with heart," said Joi as he crushed Nong in an embrace.

The music increased in tempo and volume, signalling the fight was due to start. People sat up in their seats, put down their mobile phones and shifted to a more comfortable position for better viewing.

Cheers and shouts of "Come on! Hands up! Courage!" rang out across the stadium. The children outside, hearing the noise, scrabbled back to their spy holes in the fence. The referee called the boys to the ring centre, indicating that they should stand facing one another and two feet apart opposite one another. Nong and Sert stood oiled from head to foot, two miniature boxers smiling.

Although the Khao Lak stadium was a small regional affair, the ever-present hard-faced gamblers circulated. Many of these men and women felt no love for Thailand's national sport, nor did they care if the boxers were injured. Just anger and frustration when they lost. They often attempted to goad a boxer to continue fighting by screaming insults or waving fistfuls of baht or dollars. The more aggrieved ones who stood the most to lose would hurl insults at beaten athletes with serious cuts and, in some cases, broken bones and head injuries. At times, the gamblers even followed boxers into the changing rooms hurling insults.

Officially, gambling was prohibited in Thailand, other than betting on horse races or the government-sponsored Thai lottery. Yet, both before and during the fight, like traders in an old, open outcry system, the gamblers communicated the fighters' stock price using verbal bids and offers as well as hand signals to convey trading information, intentions, and acceptance. It was all part of an orchestrated ritual, at times just as watched as the fight in the ring.

From the side ropes, schoolmates, boxing gym brothers and sisters and their extended families continued to clap and whistle.

"Come on. Don't run. There're no banana trees now for you to hide behind," shouted Sert's sister, Natcha, earning her a slap around the back of her head from her mother.

"My money's on Nong," muttered Sert's oldest uncle, getting up to place a bet with a sleazy-looking fifty-year-old man in a black and white fake Adidas t-shirt and crimson red shorts.

"At least if Sert does lose, we can give money to my sister and help pay the medical bills," agreed his broad wife. "They could do with the money. But just don't make a show of it. She's a superstitious one. She'll think your betting against her son will bring bad luck."

"Listen to me at all times, boys!" instructed the referee. "Now START!"

As the music became more frenetic, the boys weaved across the black tarpaulin mat, feet forwards, facing each other at an angle. Their feet were a hip's width apart, elbows tucked in, chins down, and fists held up.

Sert struck out first. Shifting his weight to his left foot, he attacked Nong with a low right kick to his outside left thigh. Nong blocked the kick, raising his left knee to the inside of his elbow and twisting his shin slightly so Sert hit bone rather than muscle. Retaliating, Nong landed on his left foot, swinging his right leg around to hit Sert's upper thigh. Sert attempted to block the kick in return with his left leg, but Nong was too fast, and Sert's leg felt the full impact of his kick. Pain shot across the muscle.

The enthusiastic crowd encouraged the boys from the ringside, recognising each strike with an "Oh-hoy!" "Oy!" or "Ohh-Wee!" The supporters of the boys tried to outdo each other, making as much noise as possible in an attempt to sway the three judges' opinions.

The boys bobbed as they ducked and weaved, jabbed and feinted, searching for gaps in each other's defence. Sert advanced. But Nong countered – punishing him with a toe jab. It impacted him 10 centimetres below the sternum. Winded, Sert staggered back. Nong took two steps forwards, then kneed him in the right side, followed by a right straight elbow. Boom. Blood poured down Sert's head, his face a macabre crimson and white child's mask as he collapsed. Nuey screamed in horror, her hands covering her mouth as she clambered between the ropes to get to her son. Confused, asynchronous shouts and gasps came from the crowd. No-one expected a blow of such force, not in this match.

"Stop," instructed the referee, rushing to stand between Nong and Sert.

"Yesssss," shouted Nong raising his arms in the air and running around the perimeter of the ring, jumping on ropes to celebrate his win. Furious, Joi grabbed his son, pulling him off the ropes and sharply turning him to face Sert.

"Still feel like celebrating?" he growled.

Horrified at himself, Nong broke free of his father and rushed to kneel by his friend's side and bow. Blood from the elbow strike to Sert's forehead seeped through the compress held down by the local midwife, who doubled up as medical support. Beside him crouched Warit. Standing next to him was Neuy, her head buried in her daughter's embrace.

"He's not to be moved," said the midwife. "Get the ambulance."

Natcha, frown lines creasing her brow as tears welled up in her eyes, released her mother and started dialling.

Sert stirred with a groan and tried to sit up, but the midwife forced him to lie still with a firm hand on the centre of his chest. “The ambulance’s coming,” she soothed.

“I lost. I’m fine. I lost. Where’s Nong?”

“Here!” exclaimed Nong, ashamed of himself for his boastful behaviour. “Are you OK?”

“Err, no.”

“I wish you a fast recovery and blessings,” Nong replied, bowing, using the formal words Joi had taught him.

“Sert’s fine. Shocked but fine,” said the referee, raising Nong’s arm in acknowledgement of the judges’ score. The musicians began to play as the crowd cheered and shouted at the sight of Sert sitting up. Relief spread through the rows of the stadium.

Several tourists left aghast at the sight of children hurting one another. Mutters of “It shouldn’t be allowed” and words such as “barbaric” could be heard as people walked out. Nong bowed to Sert’s coach, then the crowds on each side of the boxing ring and finally Sert. He scanned the crowd for his mother, but she was nowhere to be seen.

“Come here, mate,” said a tall Londoner sweating in a black Nike singlet and stained cargo trousers. His hair was scraped back into a ponytail. Not speaking English, Nong just nodded. Food was all he could think about.

“Father, I’m hungry. Please, let’s go.”

"Stay."

"But I'm hungry."

The more persistent *farangs* waved bank notes to attract Nong's attention; their desperation for social media-worthy photographs irritating Joi.

"Where's Mother?"

"She's at home, waiting."

Joi didn't want to let Nong know that Gan was furious at him for allowing the fight to go ahead. The only winds that would blow away that particular storm were those of time and change. Joi understood her anger. Gan's father-in-law had been a boxer too, quite well-known in his day. But now all he did was sit around smoking and drinking cheap beer. And Gan threatened to go without food rather than see Nong follow in his or her husband's footsteps. Tourists thrust money in Nong's direction, and Joi had no choice but to hold his hands out and accept with a polite smile.

In high season, from November to March, his monthly family income was $500 and less than half that for the rest of the year. Nong would earn $200 with all the tips and the extra from the promoter for the knockout. Joi encouraged Nong, who was still bouncing like a puppy, to acknowledge the gifts. Together, they suffered five more minutes of niceties before Joi signalled the end to the selfie frenzy by hoisting Nong onto his shoulders for a piggyback and heading for the exit.

Joi wanted his son to become a Muay Thai champion but would never voice that opinion as it was not for him to decide, and he knew how difficult the life of a professional fighter could be. The majority of Muay Thai fighters did not earn a high salary and accepted as many fights as they could. It was not unusual to compete every fortnight. Most of the trainers at the gym had fought at least 250 fights. A mid-ranked fighter might make around 6,000 baht per month. Top-level fighters more at around 12,000 baht a month, equating to around $370.

Outside the boxing arena, children skipped, kicked footballs and chased one another between the parked cars, *tuk-tuks*, motorbikes and street food stalls selling cold drinks, sliced fruit and a variety of meat skewers. The smell of the food mingled with petrol fumes. People sat in cars with the engines running and the air-conditioning on full blast. Some of the children re-enacted the fight's final moments. Being southern Thailand, some of the girls wore headscarves in an array of brightly coloured prints. Joi set Nong down so he could go and play with his friends.

Traversing the car park took ten minutes. Joi accepted the congratulations and well wishes while Nong capered in the dark with what looked like the ugliest child he had ever seen. The poor thing had bandy legs and long, long, thin arms. *It must be that little kid I saw peering through the fence earlier*, Joi thought. *Where did Nong meet him?* The light made it difficult for him to keep track of Nong as he ran into the tropical vegetation fringing the edge of the car park, chasing a new friend who appeared to be making rude gestures and, to Joi's eyes, moved more like a macaque than a boy. Joi shouted to Nong to come back as he had plenty of time to relive the match during tomorrow's training and it was not just his son that had not eaten.

Chapter Three

WITHIN ten minutes of arriving home, Joi had demonstrated to Nong that his right elbow was not at the correct angle when he struck Sert and that he could have raised his knees higher when blocking. Nong was also not forward enough and—

"Shh." Frowning, Gan shushed Joi as she noted Nong's downcast face and hunched shoulders. "Come, let's eat." She guided Nong towards the dinner table, where she placed sharing plates of steaming jasmine rice and her son's favourite dish of Thai yellow chicken curry with potatoes.

Gan knew her son well and could see that she was not the only one upset by Joi's critiques. Indeed, the disappointment of finding himself deprived of the celebratory mood he had dreamt of after a victory so affected Nong that he could barely muster the energy to shoo his friend Monkey's tail under the table.

"Your knee angle wasn't right," Joi continued. "You need to bring it in more, closer to your body. Not sticking out like the arm of a ladyboy with her hand on her hip. Look at me!"

"Stop! Now!" Gan snapped, shooting Joi a warning look. "Can't you see he's had enough? What more can he do this evening to make you happy? Spare us the demonstrations and sit down. This is not the place for boxing training but for eating!"

Gan's raised voice sent Monkey scurrying out of the room, once again disappearing before Nong could determine if anyone other than he could see the macaque. That very night after the fight, he'd chased Monkey into the forest when he had brazenly appeared right in front of his father and anyone else who cared to see.

Digesting Gan's words and pursing his lips, Joi pulled out the dark wood dining chair, centring the hand-embroidered seat cover that his wife had woven to protect the wood. Gan knew what it took to be the best at Muay Thai. She had trained in Muay Thai as a child, despite the protestations of her mother that it was unseemly for girls.

Joi gave a nod to let Gan know she was right: supper was not the right time to continue Nong's training, cursing under his breath for not telling Nong where he was going wrong BEFORE entering the house.

Misreading his wife's calm expression, Joi asked for a Changi beer. The thunderstorm returned to Gan's eyes as she slammed down the water jug in front of him.

"Thanks," muttered Joi, glumly taking his punishment.

In the kitchen, they ate all their family meals, caught up on the day's events and made important decisions. Once Nong had gone to sleep, it was here that his parents would discuss the best course of action for his future. Nong was already behind the other boxers his age, most of whom had fought at least twenty matches. Gan and Joi could not forestall the decision any longer. Nong loved boxing more than anything, but was it the right path in life for their boy?

Joi ate contemplatively while Gan washed the large steel wok and plain white serving bowls. He pondered whether it would be possible for Nong to fast-track his way to the top by entering a number of key competitions. The challenge was how to combine an intense training programme with studies. But what did Nong want?

"Hurry up with your dinner, Nong, and stop playing with your watermelon," Gan chided.

Wearily, Nong looked up. "Can I leave it?"

"Sure," Gan said, concerned.

Nong put down his spoon and fork, then stood to give his parents a goodnight hug. Gan tapped her husband under the table with her left foot, just hard enough to wake him from his introspection.

"Goodnight, Nong," Joi murmured, not looking up from his plate, another kick to his shin prompting a, "Well done, boy."

"Sleep well, my love," said Gan before kissing Nong's cheek. In silence, she waited until she heard the creak of Nong's bed before turning to Joi.

"Look, I cry for him with a mother's heart. I want to support you both. But how? Does Nong only box because he wants to impress you and the other men and boys at the gym? Did he get into that ring tonight because he wanted to? Or did you force him?"

"My love, you've been trying to get him to sit and read for ten years. He wants to fight! But hush. Let the boy go to sleep."

"It's my fault now that he's tired!" Gan rolled her chestnut eyes. "Tomorrow, then. We'll talk about his future tomorrow."

"Let's do that," replied Joi wearily.

The weight between them plunged the kitchen into silence.

* * *

Chaos greeted Nong in his bedroom. Monkey was re-enacting key parts of the fight while Tiger sat upright on his bed, her head tilted to one side, contemplating his antics. Tiger's enormous size covered the mattress completely, and only the rough-hewn wooden legs of Nong's bed showed. If she had been fully in the physical plane, the single bed his father had made would have broken. The end of her tail twitched as her amber eyes tracked Monkey's antics. Back and forth, back and forth, the white tip flicked against the crumbling ceiling paint. The movement was as delicate as a Chinese watercolourist's brush on mulberry paper but still caused fragments to drift down like snowflakes.

Elephant stood at the window, her leathery grey trunk gently swaying. Her trunk served as a nose, a hand, an extra foot, a signalling device and a tool for gathering food, siphoning water, dusting, digging and more. Right now, it was engaged in moving in time to Monkey's cheers as he celebrated every roundhouse kick against an imagined opponent.

The physical buzzing in Nong's chest told him Elephant was making low-frequency sounds, signifying happiness. She withdrew her trunk from the window, and then there was a loud crunching of foliage as she knelt down outside and put one side of her face to the window so she could see Nong. A small, maternal, dark-brown, heavily lashed eye set in skin as dry and cracked as the small stream running alongside the village at the end of the hot season regarded the bedroom occupants.

Nong slumped on the floor at the end of the bed opposite the window, blocking a right hook from Monkey as he did so with a tired left arm. He looked around the small room, wishing that Monkey would leave. He had heard the end of the conversation his parents were having. He had hoped there would have been a bit more of a celebration, given his win. *I'm never going to be good enough for him*, thought Nong. *Ever.* Sighing, he began to pick at the cotton threads at the edge of the worn, white bed sheet.

"You were lucky. You almost missed. Come on, stand up. What ya got?" challenged Monkey, drawing himself up to his full height of two feet and shifting his weight between his back left and right paws. In his right fist, there was a mangled bit of banana, which he took bites from between shouting taunts at Nong, only breaking his diatribe to demonstrate his jab, cross, right hook, and uppercut drills. Along with gifts of food and booze, Monkey craved attention.

"All right. All right. Come here!" relented Nong with a sigh, reaching out his arms to Monkey, who changed his mind and bounced away up onto a small study table.

Tiger chuffed through her closed jaws, pushing air through her nostrils. This was the nearest she ever got to laughing. She lifted her left forepaw, the size of a fourteen-ounce boxing glove, with its ten-centimetre talons fully retracted. Nong felt her warmth as a paw the size of his head rested on his left shoulder.

"Monkey desist," commanded Tiger.

"I'm not pissed."

"Muuun…KEY!"

Monkey began to reveal his sharp, yellow canines. Then, seeing Tiger's warning glare, shut his mouth quickly, blinked several times, waggled his eyebrows, swallowed the last piece of banana and made a show of inspecting the soft grey fur on his lower abdomen.

Now that the audience better suited her temperament, Tiger addressed the issue at hand. "Cub. Sert will be fine. Stop worrying about him. Soon you're going to face the question of which road to travel. Your destiny is influenced by your parents, but only you can decide what's best for you. Your father will paint an either-or option, and your mother is torn. She'll love you no matter what you decide."

Nong nodded, listening as intently as exhaustion would permit. When Tiger spoke, it was wise to give her your fullest attention.

She continued, “Your father delayed your first fight till tonight. Many boys have already had twenty fights, so if you want to be a boxer, you must start now. And think what is best for the family: if you’re not going to be a fighter, it is better that you say so. When Joi trains you, others who also need his support suffer. Don’t be selfish. Many of your boxing brothers would welcome your father’s schooling.”

“Khun Tiger, Khun Elephant, I want to be a boxing champion. And yes, I love my brothers, but… but… I’m tired. My head hurts. And Monkey, stop. Just stop doing that to my glove laces, will you? I’m tied up in knots enough already. I NEED to sleep,” Nong said pointedly, looking at the bed.

“Elephant, would you be so kind?” asked Tiger.

The gentle brown eye with its long eyelashes blinked at the window. “But of course.”

More sounds of vegetation being crushed could be heard as Elephant moved to make way for Tiger.

The silence of Tiger’s leap was broken only by her voice as she bounded over the windowsill.

“Decide what it means to be a hero first,” she commanded before merging into the black night.

“Got a light?” Monkey asked. “Nope? Oh, well then. Best be off. I’ve a hot date tonight in the next village. Hope she’s lively.” Monkey combed his hair with a pinecone, puckering his lips as he admired himself in the reflection of a small rose-pink mirror.

“Monkey!” groaned Nong, pulling his pillow over

his head. Trying to understand the world around him was bad enough without having to cope with macaques.

The cicada chorus heightened in intensity as the sounds and shadows of the forest filled the small bedroom. Within minutes, Nong was asleep, snoring quietly. Purple bruises on his rib cage and upper thigh from Sert's kicks smudged his skin like soot. Above him, Monkey crouched in the rafters, idly scratching his backside as he contemplated dropping the pinecone into Nong's open mouth.

CHAPTER FOUR

THE blue training mats covering the entire indoor area were damp, and a smell of bleach permeated the fresh morning air. Four large rusted grey metal fans turned lazily left and right, creaking as they moved. By 10 a.m. their breeze would make little difference to the heat, as the humidity reached well above eighty per cent during the hot season and even higher after the rainstorms at other times of the year.

Lying on the black shelving running around the two boxing rings lay discarded wraps, worn boxing gloves, black leather belly pads, boxing mitts, kick and shin pads. The gym did not rent kit, as too often items had been slipped into the luggage of guest students. Instead, the trainers directed people to the shop stocked with the merchandise branded with the Dragon's Gym logo next to the reception office to purchase gear.

Dragon's Gym was established in 2005, and since that time, has built a strong brand internationally. The owner, Lucy, worked in marketing before investing in the run-down premises she purchased with her husband. Lucy was a born and bred Londoner. Now older, she had been a boxer herself in her twenties. Lucy had first started training in Muay Thai when she backpacked through Thailand during her college summer vacation. She was fluent in Thai, able to negotiate with boxing promoters and dedicated her time to looking after the young boxers Dragon's Gym sponsored, leaving Joi to manage the training programmes. She would only get involved in the management of the boxers or *krus* if there was an issue Joi asked her to consult on. Her trust in him was absolute. Over the last fifteen years, they had never had a bad word.

On Joi's part, he welcomed the opportunity to manage the camp how he thought best. His respect for Muay Thai traditions meant that he would not have lasted long at any gym, regardless of salary, without strict adherence to those values he held high. With very little involvement in the administrative side of running the training camp, he was happy in what was, for him, the perfect set-up. Dragon's Gym subsidised his housing, paid him a competitive salary and let his son train for free. As at other boxing gyms in Thailand, there was no pension, and if the tourists stopped coming, he would receive no wage. Gan worked part-time in the training camp reception office, and this extra money also came in handy.

Sitting on the concrete wall three feet away from a skipping, sweating Nong was a black-and-white, flea-bitten, battle-scarred tom cat licking its paws. Beside Nong was one of the most promising amateur boxers in the history of the gym, Sert's older sister Natcha. Tall and slim, with mischievous tamarind brown eyes, she stood holding a green nylon rope, inspecting her reflection while adjusting her blue and silver Muay

Thai shorts. She wore a cherry tomato ankle support on her slim right ankle, which clashed with her chipped tangerine orange nail polish.

Natcha, who attended the Saturday coaching sessions, was a better boxer than Sert. Unlike her brother, she always made it to the early morning training sessions on time. Natcha loved the sensation of her muscles working and the strategic thinking behind each strike, when to feint and when to counter. She was disciplined, thoughtful and worked hard no matter how difficult the task in front of her. Sixteen-years-old, she had fought thirty competitive fights, won a regional championship and remained undefeated.

A few months back, she had decided that school was the way forward for her, as she could not see how to earn a living with the sport she loved. Natcha would struggle to realise her wish of fighting at Lumpinee and Rajadamnern in Bangkok, as women were not permitted to fight there and, unfortunately, sexism was rife in the sport, with some media channels insisting that the champion female boxers who did exist wore makeup. Thankfully, at Dragon's Gym it was different, and unlike other gyms, female fighters were not forced to enter the ring by going under the bottom rope, keeping their heads and other body parts low.

Without being able to compete for the big title fights, she would always face difficulties being accepted by commercial sponsors. Similar to many promising female fighters, she had decided to focus on where she had real opportunities in life. Natcha had enrolled to study hotel management and English next year at the local college. Her dream was to be the chief executive officer of a global five-star hotel chain.

In later years, the skills she learned in her Muay Thai training would serve her well in the boardroom She had been taught from a young age to be strong both mentally and physically. Everyone in her family and the wider community strove against difficult odds. They had to. There were no government handouts and parents had little time for children who felt hard done by. In the office, Natcha would have no patience for untrustworthy characters and big-ego types who wanted to dominate every single conversation and would rather stab you in the back than stand up and fight. People who underestimated her would understand what it meant to make an enemy of a fighter.

She defeated her opponents by noting their weaknesses. Like a good writer, she observed her colleagues' expressions and body language to understand what they really meant when they spoke. Be they in a bar after work or in a meeting, Natcha watched and listened, noting if a person struggled to look her in the eye or always glanced at a particular person across the boardroom table. She laughed inwardly when the men stretched their arms out in an attempt to dominate the space around the meeting table to make her feel small. It was at those times that she imagined giving them a jab straight to the nose or maybe a left elbow.

Similar to top-class poker players, boxers learn early to hide their emotions and read the micro-expressions in others. Natcha prized trust, and her colleagues who lied and tried to undermine her would not feel her strike until too late, by which time they were bleeding from being sacked or having to resign. Natcha worked like she fought —to win.

Four other boys lined up next to Nong and Natcha, facing the full-length gym mirror, all of their skipping ropes soon matching, a unified *tut, tut, tut* hitting the floor as they jumped.

"You guys are sooooooo lazy," teased Natcha, addressing all of them, but looking at Somchai. "What kept you?"

"Good morning, Natcha. You're looking lovely today," Somchai replied. "Still talking too much, standing around and not training."

"Nong, how ya feeling?" asked Ram. "You never answered Somchai's text? What did your dad say?"

Ignoring Ram, Nong skipped and deliberated on Tiger's questions. He thought of his football heroes, such as Lionel Messi and Cristiano Ronaldo. Two very different types of personality with very little in common but a lot of money. They drove fast cars, had multimillionaire lifestyles and possessed phenomenal athletic skills. What about the Muay Thai legends? What about them? He thought of his favourite, Chanchai Sor Tamarangsi's impeccable timing front *teep* and his deep knowledge of the art of Muay Thai and Muay Boran or 'ancient boxing' as well as other present-day champions. He thought of his father and the Muay Thai hero of his dreams, Nai Khanom Tom. Both lived the creed that anyone can succeed if they display the attributes of technique, discipline, fearlessness and sacrifice.

But he was not the only one who dreamt of being a champion; his friends skipping beside him did too. On his left were Ram and Somchai, both twenty-one, wearing black and lemon yellow Muay Thai shorts with the club's gold Dragon's Gym logo, and near to them Mongkut and Panit, who were both sixteen. The younger boys wore Ram and Somchai's hand-me-down shorts, rolled over with pieces of rope at the waistband. The four friends had fought over 500 fights. The young men trained two and three times a day, six days a week, dreaming the same dreams as Nong of winning championships and the luxury money could buy.

The older boys had lost their parents in the Tsunami on 26 December 2004, which killed over 4,000 people. Luckily, Somchai and Ram, who were cousins, had been staying at their grandparents when it struck. Mongkut and Panit had arrived with local social workers at the gym, asking to join the programme Lucy ran for impoverished children and orphans. After having successfully adapted to the Dragon's Gym's training programme, they had been allowed to remain.

In groups of twos and threes, the *farangs* began to arrive with serious, tired, or hungover expressions. The trainers came by foot, motorbike or jeep, wearing their

Dragon's Gym branded sleeveless shirts and their own Muay Thai shorts. On entering the gym, the instructors crossed the mats to either sit on the edge of the boxing ring or stand facing the student's practice area. Chatting away, they watched the students dribble in, acknowledging only those who greeted them.

At 7.30 a.m., Joi shouted, "Skipping! Skipping!" The students of all shapes, sizes and nationalities faced the mirror alongside Nong, Natcha and the boys to warm-up. Those students who did not know how to skip stood on dusty black tractor tyres. Feet planted firmly on either side of the rim, they bounced up and down while shadow-boxing. The foreign late arrivals fiddled with their boxing wraps, kidding themselves that slowly jogging on the spot would raise their heart rates. They might just as well have come holding a placard with the words *I can't be bothered* written in bright letters as far as the trainers were concerned.

"Running! RUNNING," commanded Joi, blowing the whistle hanging from his neck several times for emphasis. "RUNNING, RUNNING!" As there were not many students, Joi decided to train Somchai. In the afternoon, he would work on Ram's clinching techniques.

Joi stood with his back to the mirrors, counting each time the lead runner went past: *Neung, Song, Saam*... up to *Sip*. After ten rounds, he called Natcha, indicating with a waved arm that he wanted her to lead the students through the warm-up exercises, which included a series of stretches for the neck, arms, hips, legs and ankles. Feeling in a particularly lively mood, Natcha ended the ten minutes with a three-minute plank instead of sit-ups. By the end of two and a half minutes, only one student remained amongst the collapsed pile of red-faced, complaining pupils.

Joi broke the rising tide of hormones caused by Natcha's stretching session, shouting, "*Lai. Lai.* Come. Come. Line up." Weeeeeeet, weeeeeeet, screeched his whistle. He indicated to the ten trainers that it was time to stand shoulder-to-shoulder in a line. The students arranged themselves so they were opposite the *krus*. Depending on the gender of the speaker, the students said, "*Sawadee kaa or kap*" or 'good morning' and bowed to the instructors. The instructors returned the good morning greeting with a "S*awadee kap*" and a slight bow of their heads.

"Five minutes, shadow-boxing!" called Joi. Soon, he would inform the students which group they would be in. The first group would practice on the punching bags while the others did three rounds of three-minute sparring with the trainers. Then they would switch. Shadow-boxing was important as it gave students the opportunity to warm-up and practice the drills, focusing on technique. The prior week, an Australian man had arrived at the camp, claiming he knew everything about Muay Thai there was to know. The *krus* turned away to smother their laughter when he warmed up. He had worn headgear he had clearly designed himself, a baseball cap with a fishing rod with a cork on the end, which he would try to hit. When he sparred with the *krus,* he kicked with all his might. After two days of his peculiarities and disrespectful attitude, Joi said,

"Somchai, you spar with him."

Somchai didn't go easy. He understood what he was being asked to do: teach respect for the sport, respect for the teachers and respect for the school. The Australian left the gym limping, catching a flight home the following day.

Joi went to where Nong and the others were fooling around. Normally, the hard training sessions took place between 4 p.m. and 6 p.m. Every day, they would focus on different aspects of the art. Sometimes, he would ask the boxers to do an additional weight training session after lunch to improve their core strength. This workout would incorporate kettlebell squats, bench presses, deadlifts, military presses, pull-ups, and push-ups. It was clear to Joi that today, the young boxers were training physically but not mentally, and he had had enough.

"Somchai, you're with me. Mongkut and Panit, you can spar with one another and Nacha go with Ram. Then I want you all back here at noon for strength training. Natcha, that doesn't include you. Nong, you go lift weights. I'll be with you soon. Now, let's get to it!"

Turning to spar with Somchai and smacking his gloves together, Joi challenged, "Okay. What you got today then, boy?"

The cold air blasted into the small weights room. It

was the only space in the training camp that had air-conditioning. Nong tied open the gym door with a skipping rope while pausing to look at the photographs beside the door. Unlike the tourists, he did not need the cold air. In the photographs, faces and images greeted him like old friends. He grinned at the small black-and-white one taken when he was three-years-old. In the image, he sat on Joi's knee during a meal being shared amongst ten of the fighters. Young and old, they crouched or lay in a circle, sharing stories, plates of rice, fish curry, fried chicken legs, green beans and an assortment of smaller dishes. As it was a communal lunch, everyone was sharing plates of food and used chopsticks. Normally, they ate with a spoon and fork. No-one wore a shirt, as it had been a particularly hot day. In the background of the photograph stood a big gas canister beside an upturned fruit crate supporting a small stove. Two large black woks perched precariously on top. Nong peered at the image of himself playing with a bottle of sweet chilli sauce.

Nong checked his phone, frowning. Sert had still not replied to his text. *I'll text my mum*, he thought. Best not to bother Sert's parents. His phone beeped back immediately with the reply from Gan that she had left an SMS last night and this morning, but she had yet to receive a response. Not wanting to disturb his father's class, he asked his mother if he could go and see Sert.

Gan said he could go but that he was to come straight home afterwards and inform his father he was leaving. Nong ran in a zigzag across the mats to avoid the students practising roundhouse kicks. He called to his dad, “I’m off!”

Joi was holding the training pads for one of the clients and shouted in reply.

Nong couldn’t hear over the din and didn’t want to be stopped, so he just waved and smiled in his father’s direction. He sorted through the pile of flip-flops outside the Dragon’s Gym entrance until he found his own amongst the heap, then mounted his bicycle with its dark-green frame covered in stickers from his favourite comics.

The palm, frangipani and papaya trees planted outside the villagers’ houses provided just about enough shade for the stray dogs and cats to while away their days, protected from the sun’s merciless rays. There was no escaping the humidity, however, which had already climbed above 80 per cent.

Nong paused at the roadside to let the equestrian school pass. Two horses and two ponies plodded in single file. The two grey ponies and the chestnut and bay mixed-breed horses sweated under the full glare of the sun, foam clearly visible around their saddles. They swished their tails and jerked their heads in an attempt to remove clouds of flies. The constant fidgeting caused the inexperienced holidaymakers who were riding to feel uneasy. Their knuckles were white as they clasped the cracked, dirty leather reins and fought to keep their feet in the American-style stirrups.

Nong steered his bicycle clear of the large bay

horse's hindquarters and pedalled faster. On reaching Sert's house, he skidded to a stop near the largest coconut palm tree, leaning his bike against the smooth, light greyish-brown trunk beside two dozing black and white *soi* or 'mongrel' dogs. Swollen at the base, the tree was gracefully curved. The tree's fifteen-foot-long, feather-shaped, evergreen leaves would provide just enough shade to prevent the black bike saddle from turning into a burning lump of rubber on his return.

The metal grill of the outermost front door was wide open, but it was difficult to see through the gloom. In the front yard, Sert's mother, Neuy, was hanging washing near the family's sunflower yellow spirit house. These colourful shrines, placed at auspicious places on Thai properties, provided shelter to spirits who might become upset if ignored. Here, there was an assortment of figurines placed around the morning offering of white boiled rice, an open bottle of strawberry Fanta and a plate of orange slices. *Monkey would be pleased with that Fanta*, thought Nong grinning.

"*Sawadee kap,*" called Nong.

"*Sawadee kaa,*" replied Neuy with a warm smile, retrieving a handkerchief from her floral apron front pocket to wipe the sweat from her brow.

"How are you feeling, Boxer?" Neuy asked her son's friend. Although she knew full well how he was feeling, having spent the last twenty minutes talking to Gan.

"Fine. How's Sert? Can I see him?"

"Sert's in his room. Don't let him convince you he can get out of bed. He's been arguing with me about going fishing since first thing this morning."

Nong gave his thanks with a slight bow of his head and entered the house. He called Sert's name before drawing back the faded orange cotton bedroom door curtain and beamed as he saw Sert lying on his bed reading an old Spider-Man comic.

"Hi, Nong. Thanks for the splitting headache and bruises," said Sert without turning away from his comic and clearly stifling a smile.

"Hi. Yeah, sorry about that. I didn't know I could elbow so hard. Budge over."

Sert rolled onto his side to face Nong and make space. Nong perched on the edge of the bed, grabbed a comic from the pile on the floor, and took a good look around the familiar room to see if anything had changed. Apart from the Arsenal football team, boxing champion, and superhero posters, there was no other decoration on the grey walls. The room was furnished with a small pine desk, an old brass reading lamp with a white lampshade, and a rosewood chair with mother-of-pearl inlay. The chair had a heavy look to it. Most likely, it had been inherited from a grandparent.

Sert pointed at his black eye and dressing on his forehead, keeping the deep cut moist to prevent bacteria contamination. "See, I can't box. Mum said she's going to talk to Dad at lunch today to tell him no more. She's afraid it'll be my eye next time. I've never won a single match. Dad needs to stop. That's that."

Nong furrowed his brow. Malicious thoughts of not having won fair and square spat at him like water which had fallen into the oil of his mother's wok. It meant so much to him that he won his first fight. He believed he had fought well, but if he had actually won only because his best friend had given into him, then he was done with boxing. Nong bent down and picked up a manga comic, avoiding having to look at Sert. He took a deep breath and asked, "Did you lose on purpose?"

"No! What do you think? I shoved my forehead at your elbow. No. I'd never throw a fight, especially to you! Did I not tell you I've a headache? I really don't need you in here making it worse," snapped Sert, rolling back on to his stomach and retrieving the discarded comic to let Nong know the conversation was finished.

Silence. Conscious of each other and pretending to read, neither boy spoke for five minutes.

Sert broke the nail-biting stillness.

"I like reading," said Sert with a shrug. "You like boxing. It's no big deal. I prayed last night's match was my last. I promised once I was in the ring, I would try my very best. I didn't want to look like an idiot in front of the whole village. Anyways, who's to say that because I lost one fight, my dad'll stop insisting I fight? I'll tell you who. No-one! He'll be home saying I'm useless before lunch. You'll see. Did you bring me any food on your way up? Any presents for your sick friend?"

"Not a grain of rice," said Nong, pushing Sert

further across the bed. "Not a single thing."

Half an hour later, the big bedroom fan clicked softly, stirring the thick, humid air. Neither boy saw Neuy's warm smile at the sight of them sleeping, heads turned to one side, on top of their comics. It seemed like only a few monsoons ago, they had been babies. Her expression became determined as she vowed not to let her son fight again. She was still undecided as to whether Nong had won or Sert had let himself be beaten. Either way, Sert had been lucky this time.

Some might say coaxing children to fight in the ring is a form of child abuse. Every year, thousands of young boxers in Thailand enter the sport to win prize money for their poor families – almost always fighting without wearing head protection. Sometimes, the child fighters are as young as eight. Tourists at the hotel, where she worked part-time as a waitress, asked Neuy about Muay Thai and her view on young children fighting. But Neuy would only smile and shrug in response. In her view, allowing children to get horrifically overweight was a form of abuse. How did those poor boys and girls ever recover from obesity? Every day at the hotel buffet, she gave sidelong glances, observing the children piling up the cakes, sausages, bacon and fried eggs as if they were never going to eat again. Did these parents not care? Neuy shuddered at the bullying those kids must undergo at school and the health issues they would experience as adults. Neuy worked from early morning to late at night, but she still managed to put healthy, fresh food on the table.

As Neuy looked at the sleeping boys, she sighed and thought that even if Sert had feigned a loss yesterday, then it was just as well. To win, you needed to put your heart and mind into every second of your training and take the experience with you into a fight. Natcha, his older sister, had shown she was prepared to do just that. Glancing at the rusted alarm clock on Sert's rickety study table, she decided that at 11 o'clock, she would wake the boys and send them to the market. The trip would give her plenty of time to tell Warit that Sert wasn't going to fight competitively again. Ever.

CHAPTER FIVE

NONG and Sert rested the woven reed bags on a plastic woven porch chair with rusted legs. They had separated their shopping expedition in two. Nong had left to buy chicken and fish and Sert the fruit, which had come directly from the local small farms dotted around the village. Sert had purchased dark green pineapples that were not yet ripe, jackfruit, silky yellow mangoes with their intense aroma, and sugar apples.

Neuy had asked Sert to get an unripe jackfruit for lunch so she could make a jackfruit curry using coconut milk, water, lemongrass, garlic, red chilli, shallot, salt, galangal, coriander, kaffir lime peel, pepper, cumin, sugar, vinegar. The fruit tasted like a combination of apple, mango, pineapple, and banana. Neuy would freshly ground the herbs and spices, and it was Sert's job to cut through the jackfruit's spiky exterior to get to the flesh found in the pockets surrounding seeds. The exterior was so oily that he had to put on an old pair of gloves to stop it slipping away. Of all the fruit in the market, jackfruit was by far the largest. Nong claimed to have seen one that was over forty kilograms.

"Enjoy your time shopping, boys?" asked Warit, stepping out of the house.

Nong glanced quickly at Sert, who returned his

look, concern apparent in his expression.

"How did training go this morning?" asked Nong. "Sorry I left, but I was very worried about Sert. Everything okay with Somchai? Dad was keen to work with him this morning as his fight's coming up."

"Somchai's fine. He's only appearing in Phuket to keep his muscles warm for his next fight in Bangkok. Don't worry about him. Unlike others, he can handle himself." Warit dropped the edge in his voice, at least temporarily. "What about you two? How are you feeling after yesterday evening? Still talking, I see. Your mother seems set on the idea that you're never going to box again, Prasert. What do you think about that?"

Underneath the banana tree, Sert and Natcha used to kick to toughen up their shins, Nong spied Monkey garrotting himself with Neuy's black bra. The right cup had flipped up over one of his eyes. He looked like a pirate. Monkey's face contorted in several directions simultaneously, as if someone had switched him on fast forward. Unable to explain what he was seeing, Nong blurted, "Yes."

"What are you staring at that old banana tree for, Nong? What does *yes* mean, boy?" demanded Warit with a sigh, thinking *not only is my wife giving me a hard time, but also the kids.*

Nong fixed his eyes firmly on Warit, "I just meant, yes. What you said. Yes." Realising he was making very little sense, he forced his mouth to shut, and stay shut.

But Monkey had a point to make. He reappeared next to Warit, sprinting on the spot. Waving his arms forwards as if directing traffic, gesticulating in the direction of Nong's home and coughing because of his penchant for unfiltered cigarettes, he had transformed the bra into a pair of 1940s pilot goggles, which he wore on his head with the straps tied under this chin.

Time to go. Turning to face Sert, Nong asked, "Do you want to come for lunch today? You haven't eaten at mine for ages. I've got the Arsenal swaps for you." Struggling not to laugh at Monkey, he let out a snort.

Warit eyed him as if he were mad.

"Let me ask Mum."

"Stop. You stay here. You haven't answered my question. Prasert, are you boxing or not?"

Monkey was lying down in the dusty front yard, feigning death just behind Warit, who was oblivious to his presence. Only Nong could see the maddening macaque.

"Dad, I'm tired. Can't I go and lie down? I was only going to ask Mum what she thought."

Warit's expression softened. "Go. Go see your mother and I'll join you. You best run along, Nong."

Nong mumbled his goodbyes, gave Sert a friendly thump on the arm, and collected his bicycle from the shade. Monkey, baring his teeth in a grin, waved at Nong as he wheeled his bicycle across the dusty front yard.

Nong chose the longer route home, along the path through the rubber plantation that had been cleared by the tourist excursion companies trekking towards the beach from the equestrian school. The tall rubber trees stood three metres apart. About two feet from the ground on each tree trunk, half a coconut shell was tied, facing to the sky, to collect the white, sticky milk fluid harvested mainly in the form of latex. Farmers drew the latex by making incisions into the tree bark and collecting the secreted fluid. Nong rarely saw the farmers but sometimes heard them tapping between two and four in the morning. Most days, the farmers would be finished by 10 a.m. In the dry months of March and April, or when there were torrential rains, the farmers could not work. Few families relied on rubber as the sole source of income. He had heard his parents commiserate with the poor rubber plantation farmers whose trees had been damaged by leaf fall disease, a fungal infection that made the leaves drop and production fall by 50 per cent. Life was harsh enough, as it was for the subsistence farmers, without having to contend with plagues.

At the end of the rainy season, Nong never cycled through the rubber plantations surrounding the village as the mulching of rice straw or dried weeds caused a rotten smell to rise up from the ground, which stayed with him for the rest of the day. The mulch covered the soil under the tree canopy and was spread around the circumference of each tree foot. The smell of decay would mingle with the morning mist and humid air as it changed its state from finite to infinite while millions of microbes returned as nutrients to the soil.

Nong was careful not to knock the half-filled coconut shells. He weaved his bike around the bigger stones on the path and across fast-moving spring water rivulets. The trees started to thicken as he reached the back of his house. He saw few animals because the lowland forest had long since been converted to commercial oil palm and rubber plantations. Occasionally, he would spot tiger pugmarks interwoven with the elephant footprints and the upturned scrub caused by wild pigs rooting.

"Mum. Are you home?"

"Yes, love, we're eating in ten minutes. Go shower."

Joi had been in the middle of telling Gan that Somchai was doing well in his usual calm voice. The young boxer appeared to be working hard, and he saw no reason why Somchai would not win in two weeks' time. Carefully, he casually mentioned that one of the boys in the junior's match had fallen ill with pneumonia, and the promoter had asked if Nong could take his place.

Gan gave him a sharp look and pretended not to hear. She needed time to think and busied herself with the sticky rice she was preparing to serve with the mangoes. *How to deal with this now?* she worried, cursing herself for not having prepared an answer to the question of Nong fighting again. As she carefully arranged the mangoes on the white plate, she structured her response. When Nong was back, it would be two against one as soon as this news broke.

"Did you hear what I said, Gan? There's an opportunity for Nong to fight again, and given he's stepping in at the last moment, there's no need to pay the full promoter's fee. The winnings from last night will cover the cost, and it'd be great experience," continued Joi, for once not sensitive to the rising anger in his wife as he was so keen for Nong to compete.

"Great experience for what? And what about the cost to Nong? Is this really the route we want him to take? Once he starts this journey, he won't want it to stop, and it'll be the only life he'll ever have. You know it and I know it. He's filled with dreams of fame and fortune, and what's more, he wants to impress you. No, don't look at me like that. He does. He's a young boy and we can stop this now. We should stop this now. Let him have an education or a job not devoted to hitting and avoiding hits!" snapped Gan as she slapped rice haphazardly on top of the mangoes with a large wooden spoon.

Joi studied his calloused hands. Flexing and unflexing his fingers as if the movement was the most fascinating sight in the world. Surely, Nong could continue boxing without it being a do-or-die situation with his schoolwork. There was no need for such drama. Joi opened his mouth to try a different tact, but then the bead curtain of blond wood rattled as Nong walked through, his black hair still wet from the shower.

"Hello," Nong said cheerfully, squeezing past the kitchen table and heading for the pots on the gas stove.

Curious to know what was for lunch, he lifted the lid on the carbon steel wok that gave his mother's cooking a charred, smoky flavour and released the sweet smell of green pork curry. The heavenly combination of lemongrass, green chillies, garlic, coconut milk, coriander and cumin was comforting.

"Come and sit," said Gan. "Did you see Sert?"

"Yes. He's well, but I don't think he will be fighting again."

"Why's that?" asked Gan, avoiding Joi's gaze.

Nong tried to gauge his parents' moods before answering, sensing the tense atmosphere in the kitchen. His earlier cheerful mood dissipated like the silvery fish in the forest ponds when he reached out to catch one.

"Well, Sert's not really interested in boxing. He likes reading and football."

"And you, Nong. What do you like?" asked Joi softly.

"Err. Food. Food is what I'd like," replied Nong as his stomach rumbled.

"Me too," said Gan. "We've all had enough of boxing for one day." She tipped the green curry from the wok into a blue and white serving basin. Her slim hands grabbed a worn cotton pink and white chequered tea towel to transfer the meal to the table, which she placed alongside a heaped plate of boiled white rice and green cucumber salad garnished with coriander and toasted peanuts.

Outside, the rain had started to fall in heavy drops,

giving the small kitchen a cocooned feeling of safety and comfort. The rain poured down from the roof in a translucent curtain across the kitchen window, causing the light to dim. The family sat and ate in silence, lost in their own thoughts. The quiet was only broken by the occasional request for the chilli sauce. Suddenly, trumpets blared, causing Gan to knock her water glass over into the rice.

"Change that ring tone!" snapped Gan, rising to get a cloth.

The blue luminescent screen told Joi it was the boxing promoter chasing him for an answer. Ignoring the call, he placed the phone face down on the small white shelving unit crammed with kitchen utensils behind.

"Was that the boxing promoter again?" Gan asked.

"Yes. He can wait."

"Can I get some more curry?" asked Nong.

"Ask your mother," responded Joi. " She may want to save some for tonight's dinner."

Joi decided this was the moment to shift the conversation. "Pay attention now, Nong," he said, snatching away the chilli bottle that his son had started to tap with his spoon. "Sert wasn't a tough competitor. What I want to know is, what would you have done if you'd come up against someone better? Do you think you'd have managed?"

"I'd have fought harder," Nong said with a shrug, wishing his father would focus on eating. That way, he could get to his favourite part of the meal.

Gan swore under her breath and decided she had had enough. "Nong, you've another opportunity to compete in two weeks' time. Before you ask, your father can find out who the boy is you'll be fighting against later. But *you don't have to fight.*"

"What!?" Nong gulped down his mouthful of food and punched the air with his fork, causing rice to rain down like confetti.

"No, Nong!" chided Joi. "Listen! You've been going to competitive matches since before you could walk. You've seen people hurt. Bones broken. People blinded. You understand that competitive boxing is tough and the pressure immense. This is not just a match; it's the start of a journey. There's also the reputation of Dragon's Gym to defend. All the fighters and trainers are our family. Should you become successful, there's the honour of your community to protect – many of whom will follow your career's successes and remind you of its failures. Then there are the dangers of corruption. The people giving advice will not always have your best interests at heart. They'll gamble on you or have some hidden agenda. On top of everything, we'll have to ask my bosses to sponsor you sometimes to pay the promoter's fee. Like every other gym, they'll take half of your winnings. Look at me! Muay Thai boxers don't make a lot of money. Do you understand me?"

"Yes," was all Nong could say. All he was hearing was a lot of noise about risk and people he did not yet know or care about. He just wanted to be with his boxing family and not attend school, which was boring.

"What do you understand, Nong?" asked Gan.

"That I want to be a champion," replied Nong. "It's the only thing I want to be."

Nong was not yet even at the precipice of being an adult. But Muay Thai was the lifeblood of his existence. An ancient sport whose heroes he would become when he dreamed each night. He would put food on his family's table and provide a connection to his neighbours, extended family and friends. He could no more say he did not want to follow in his father's footsteps than say he never wanted to see either of his parents again.

Gan hid her face to wipe the liquid pearls on her longan-coloured cheeks. Joi soundlessly took her right hand.

"Mango pudding and sticky rice?"

The matter was decided. Nong would fight and take one step further along the road to becoming a boxer.

CHAPTER SIX

THE thin yellow rope skimmed the floor in a regular *tsh, tsh* as Nong pictured famous fighters. Every great champion had a special name reflecting their courage, attitude or physical appearance. Sports journalists had given Sangmanee Sor Tiempo the name Tharok Nung Laan (Million-Dollar Baby) and Wanchalong Sitsorong Say Anthaphan (The Bad Boy Left). As Nong trained at Dragon's Gym, he would change his birth name to represent the camp and his boxing family. He wanted a lucky name, not a tough name like Iron Knee or AK47. Perhaps something simple would do best, like Dragon? Ram and Somchai would tease him, though. Their request to use the camp's name had been refused, the owners arguing that no single boxer could represent everything the community stood for.

"Nong," called Joi over the training centre wall. "I've spoken to the promoter, and we're all set. The boy is from Phuket. He's about your age and has fought ten times. Good to go?"

Eagerly, Nong nodded his assent. Joi dispassionately appraised his son, leaning his head to one side as he watched the boy skip. His unmarked, thin face thoughtful. He was not blind. His boy was skinny.

Joi had lived and breathed Muay Thai all his life, and as he looked for flaws in his son, he surgically cut through each of the boy's movements. He had dissected every nanosecond of his victory over Sert before concluding that Nong had deserved to triumph. Not because Sert failed to cover his head but because Nong was faster, stronger and more determined. But he wondered if Nong had true courage and was hungry to win enough to never to want to lose? Fighters needed to be as relentless as the red ants that kept marching across the kitchen floor regardless of what was thrown at them. Boxers had to land another punch, fight another round, win another competition, and train another day no matter what. It was the relentless daily training and passion that made a boxer great. The desire to win day-in-day out, to hone one's intuition so no-one knew how you would counter. Such knowledge did not come overnight in a flash but crept quietly into a person's psyche like a gecko creeping undetected through a house at midnight. There were too many unknowns about the boy his son would be fighting next week and only one way to find out if Nong was truly committed. That way was intensive training.

"Ok, then. From today onwards, I want you to start running in the morning on the beach. The sand will improve your footwork and make your legs stronger. Also, you need to begin shadow-boxing with weights. Don't go mad. Use the lighter ones. We've got to work more on your clinching, so start doing chin-ups, as they will build your upper body strength. You can't get the neck hold right to steer your opponent into the corner to use your knee strikes otherwise. Mongkut and Panit will take it in turns to spar with you. You're going to need to train before school and again in the early evening. The best technique for this and every competition you'll face depends on your opponent. And this boy's bigger than you. Nong, think about the opponent. We're going to kick first and then elbow. Finish skipping in ten minutes, sit in with the class as they do their core stretches, and then let's go! Somchai, come."

Nong wondered how he was ever going to find time to eat and sleep. Let alone study. He could say goodbye to his Sundays, that was for sure. The stretching session finished with the line up with the camp *farang* students and *krus*. Nong stood at the end of the row next to a slim blonde Dutch woman of around twenty-five. She was already perspiring and had dark sweat patches on her sky-blue Puma t-shirt. She spoke to him. But Nong ignored her, not speaking English.

Nong went to the broken locker in which he kept his red training shin pads and gloves. His locker was wide open as he never locked it. There was no fear of anyone wanting to steal his battered gear.

Somchai, Mongkut and Panit were talking to Joi, who waited for him at boxing ring Number Two. When the boxers and *krus* held pads or sparred with one another, they did not do four times three-minute rounds as they did with the non-amateur and professional boxers, but they kept going until the trainee could do no more. Pulling himself to his full height of 135 centimetres, Nong greeted everyone. Then he sat on the side of the boxing ring to put on his training shin pads. The faded blue wrap on his left hand had become slack. Pulling the Velcro apart, he readjusted the material, winding it tighter around his wrist, before putting on his gloves.

"Son, remove the pads. We need to toughen up those shins."

"Come on, kid," Somchai said, banging his red and white boxing mitts together before proffering a hand for Nong to grab as he climbed into the ring.

Somchai was relentless. "Jab, cross. Jab, cross, uppercut. Jab, cross, uppercut, right hook. Jab, cross uppercut, left hook, right knee." *Thwack* sounded the pad as Somchai hit Nong. "Keep your hands up. Give me ten right side kicks. Low. High." *Thwack.* "Keep your hands up. Ten left side. Low. High." *Thwack.* You're not listening, Nong. FOCUS! We're only in five minutes. That head of yours is going to be sore. KEEP YOUR HANDS UP!" *Thwack.*

Somchai received a nod from Joi, who stood leaning on the top rope with Natcha beside him. "I bet you he doesn't last another five minutes."

"Oh, he'll last. Nong won't have a problem with the pressure. He's a brave boy. My question is whether his defence will ever accelerate. A lotus flower could move faster. Come on, Nong, BLOCK those slaps. You're fighting soon!" yelled Joi.

Natcha evaluated Nong's courageous efforts to

counter Somchai's onslaught to the left and right sides of his body. She wondered what had prompted Joi to start training Nong so hard. Six years ago, she had undergone the same intensification of her coaching. As had all the fighters representing the gym at around Nong's age. It was necessary and a kindness to teach this way. Better to go through a hard session than receive a blow from an elbow in the ring. But still.

"Joi. Why now?" asked Natcha, her finely arched eyebrows raised.

"We've agreed he's fighting," replied Joi before explaining to Natcha the task ahead. "Nong is in the ring again next week. I've not seen any videos, but an old friend from Phuket said Nong's opponent is tough. He's faster, and his dad's an ex-boxer too. We're all going to have to work with Nong to get him ready, and we don't have much time."

"Got it," said Natcha. "Do you need me to come by after school tomorrow and spar?"

"Thank you," replied Joi. He knew how important Natcha's studies were to her and appreciated the support. She was the best of his students. Not only did she always train hard, but she was intelligent and able to read her opponent's moves well. Naturally light-footed, she also moved faster than most.

"Come on, Nong! Thirty more kicks either side. Get some water and let's spar. Then you can go and do some bag drills. *Neung, Song, Saam…*"

Forty minutes later, Nong pleaded no more. He could not force another sit-up from his shattered body.

Somchai kept pushing, but the continued hits to his stomach muscles with the flat side of the boxing pad while he did crunches finished him.

Drenched, Nong left his bicycle at the camp and climbed onto the back of his father's motorbike, clutching his sweat-soaked boxing wraps. The sun was setting over the treetops. Bats flitted, darting overhead as they hunted, dispersing the black mosquito clouds. The incessant buzzing of the cicadas was like twenty steam trains signalling continuously. Nong did not even register the sounds as his father steered the motorbike past the multiple potholes in the road. He had school tomorrow, and all he wanted was to eat then sleep.

Gan told Nong to put his wraps in the washing basket and kissed her husband hello. Joi returned her kiss, giving her arm a squeeze. Gan cast her eyes over her son. The short black hair, which normally stuck up, was plastered down with perspiration, and his head hung down in exhaustion.

Gan went outside to light the mosquito burner. Next, she wiped down the small wooden table that wobbled on the uneven concrete surface. Tonight, they would eat a simple meal of Tom Yum soup on the porch with a green mango salad. Bending down, she put the wood block back under the leg of the table and watched the rapidly darkening sunset dance with its painterly strokes of scarlet, crimson and vivid oranges and pinks still visible over the heavenly canvas.

The family meal was hurried, with the food being

served and consumed in near silence. Gan only spoke to gently reprimand Nong for resting his head in his hands while eating. As soon as he finished, Joi told him to shower and go to bed. Nong kissed his parents goodnight. His body welcomed the crisp bed sheet as he lay down on one side. But the day's events chirped like a lizard. Turning onto his back he stared up at the ceiling, arms folded behind his head.

As his eyes began to close, he felt the brush of whiskers on his left thigh. The ceiling changed from a charcoal grey to a flame orange. The source of the light was Tiger. The antithesis of darkness, she caused shadows to flit around the room. So brightly did she glow he could not believe that his parents could not see her aura through the curtain door of his bedroom. Her intense amber eyes connected with his chocolate brown ones. As she licked her right front paw, he saw the slash of black scar tissue.

"Ahh," said Tiger, lowering her paw. "I see you have noticed one of my scars. When I was a cub, Vietnamese poachers, paid to capture tigers, would conceal metal snares throughout the jungle. The government was bribed, and we were all hunted. I was fortunate. A group of villagers set me free and placed me back in the undergrowth by the Bo tree, where they knew my mother would find me. My brother was not so lucky and later died from poisoning. My mother mourned his death for weeks. She stood over his body for days, crying into the forest before accepting his passing. And for what? The medicine they think the animals give is useless. Our livers, hearts, bile and paws can't heal what aliments afflict humans. But I did not come to talk about what these corrupt men do. We hurt. We move on. But we don't forget.

"Cub do not fear the path you've chosen. There will be vicious, underhand traps, but that is the way of your species. To stand up and confront challenges is noble, but it is important to make your opponent believe they cannot win. Show them courage and the pride of a tiger. Let your opponent know who you are by the confidence you display before even beginning a fight. At times, this will enable you to win before even having to attack. Tigers leave their mothers to find their own way and choose a path that only they can tread. Alone. Your parents are preparing you for that journey in the way they know best."

Intuitively, Nong resisted the temptation to touch Tiger's horrific scar. "Tiger," he said, "I'm truly sorry for what happened to your family."

"No matter. It's done."

"It's…" said Nong, thinking of his own family. "I'm sorry."

"Remember this. There is no reason for you to fail as long as you stay true to who you are." Tiger's ears twitched, revealing the white circle on the black fur covering behind. Stretching her front legs, she raised her haunches, spreading her front paws. Her claws shone like scimitars in the moonlight. The muscles rippled down her spine as she stood. Lifting her majestic head, she yawned, showing huge, impressive teeth. Nature had designed her jaws for grabbing moving prey, snapping necks, crunching through bone and sinew and grinding flesh into soft mouthfuls. As she yawned, Nong was reminded of her power. Tiger tested the scents of the forest, lifting her chin while her fur transformed into the darkest amber, the black strips barely discernible. In silence, and without looking back at Nong, she disappeared.

Chapter Seven

Joi increased the intensity of Nong's daily Muay Thai programme. Nong practised, went to school, trained, ate and trained again. At night, he prayed that the people who were putting so much effort into his instruction would be pleased with his progress before sleeping without a stir.

During the day, at the gym, he would occasionally spy Monkey, helping himself to cigarettes from people's rucksacks, running along the wall or consuming the food left at the emerald green and gold-painted spirit house near the reception. But he never saw or sensed Tiger and Elephant, not once in the whole two weeks he was preparing for his second tournament fight. At night, he whispered their names, pinching himself to stay awake, listening to the forest moving in the night as it breathed. Once, he thought he heard Tiger outside, but it turned out to be an enormous soi dog trotting past his window. The dog had a long square muzzle with strong jaws and a black nose. Its ears were pulled back as it moved along the path on some nocturnal foray.

Two days before the fight, he noticed a man in his mid-thirties, of medium build, with his hair shaved short, watching him intently while he trained. Dressed in a Guns N' Roses t-shirt, ripped jeans and a big gold watch and chain, he had parked his black Toyota C-HR with tinted windows in the gravel area reserved for the Dragon's Gym owners, where the thick foliage of the trees provided shade. In the front passenger seat, there was a young woman wearing wide black designer sunglasses with gold frames. Normally, when the gym had local visitors, one of the *krus*, students or reception staff would greet them. Nong decided to ignore the man and continued practising his knee strikes against the bag.

The man started filming Nong on his camera phone. Behind him, Monkey sat on his car roof, unscrewing the Toyota's aerial. "*Sawadee kap*, how can I help?" called Joi, excusing himself from his student before walking towards the gym's side exit. The trainers paused to look at the stranger. Joi rarely swore or raised his voice. And the tone of the question was not so much a query but a, *Who the hell are you?*

"I've seen that guy before in Phuket," said Somchai to Ram. "He's involved in the gambling circuit there, and he goes by the name of Ray. He must've come to check Nong out. It's gonna get really interesting if he doesn't put that phone away."

"Yeah, just look at the prick playing at gangster. He's gotta have some balls to walk into our space," sneered Ram in derision.

Somchai and Ram went to the gym side nearest the road to better hear the conversation, but the machine being used to spray anti-mosquito poison made listening to Joi and the visitor's exchange impossible.

The two men smiled and nodded as they spoke. But their eyes were black as diamond chips, the corners as wrinkle-free as mango skin. The visitor fiddled with his phone and showed the screen to Joi. Joi made a gesture as if to say that his eyes were not so good and he needed his glasses. He held out his hand to take the phone, gesticulating he would be just a moment to visit the locker room. Five minutes later, he reappeared. Fine smile lines fanned out from his eyes.

Joi returned the phone to the visitor, who slipped it into his back jeans pocket. Next, he moved to shake Joi's hand. But Joi kept his arms folded across his chest. So he awkwardly patted Joi on the back instead. Joi shrugged at this insincere show of affection and opened the driver's side of the car. The man seemed to want to continue their conversation, but Joi's granite expression caused him to refrain, and he slunk into the car. Joi slowly closed the car door, taking the time to scrutinise the man for a final time. Only when the car had turned back down the dirt road and out of sight did he re-enter the gym.

Somchai and Ram returned to their waiting clients. Joi climbed into the boxing ring nearest the mirrored wall where a *kru* was doing pad work with a tall African American student. The young woman, in her early twenties, was being taught footwork principles and low kicks. "Rocking, rocking," intoned the teacher as he demonstrated how to balance and transfer weight from the front left foot to the back right. All the *krus* focused on this basic skill before progressing to teach other elements of Muay Thai.

To one side of the ring, Mongkut lay face down, resting his head in his arms. Panit stood on his back, kneading the trapezius and latissimus dorsi muscles using his heels and toes, stretching and pushing out the knots. Mongkut's expression was as calm as a dozing cat purring on its owner's lap, apart from when Panit jabbed his big toe in a particularly resistant knot that would cause Mongkut to wince and swear. Leaning over the rope, Nong stood chatting with them about Friday's match.

"You three!" snapped Joi. "What's this, Orchid Spa or Dragon's Gym? Mani-pedi anyone? Panit, go and double up with Ralph. He needs someone to hold the bag. Mongkut, you can help the guy next to him. Nong, I need a word."

Ralph was a tall blond German. An amateur boxer, he was in his second training month at Dragon's Gym. In Muay Thai, a fighting style becomes more distinct each time someone spars with a different opponent. Learning is a never-ending process that flourishes with technical abilities, strength, and stamina. Over time, a boxer's preferred style can change. Ralph's hard work had earned Joi's respect. Unlike Thai fighters, who typically follow a strategy, foreign fighters tend to use their techniques haphazardly and respond to a given situation in the ring rather than follow through with a plan. This adaptability can work in their favour, as it makes them harder for the Thais to fight. When Thais fight Thais, they know when a certain technique is going to be used by the movement in musculature, which is why boxers tend to look at each other's chest. However, to be a champion, you need to think about strategy as well. Champions cannot just rely on spontaneity and must consider the style their opponent is using and how to defend against it.

Joi always explained that there was no right or wrong to the style a boxer prefers. There are two main styles: *Muay Mat* and *Muay Femur. Muay Mat* fighters rely on heavy punches to the face and body and crushing low kicks. They are like enraged Asian buffalos in the ring charging forward to beat their opponent, absorbing body shocks and point losses as they do so. All their energy is focused on achieving a knockout. *Muay Femur* is the style preferred by the technicians of the Muay Thai world. Boxers trained in this school of Muay Thai are graceful and a joy to witness in the ring. Unsurprisingly, they attract the biggest crowd to Muay Thai competitions. One of Joi's favourite boxers, Namkabuan Nongkeepayayuth, used the *Muay Femur* style and was nicknamed *The Ring Genius.* Namkabuan skilfully demonstrated the art of eight limbs and, like a world-class chess player, knew when to advance, defend and adapt, keeping his distance from his opponent, using long-range jabs, kicks and *teeps* to do so. Not many boxers can fight in the *Muay Femur* style, as it requires superb skill, timing, and natural ability. Joi had privately told Warit that as long as Nong trains hard and thinks, he could be one of the best.

"Nong, you saw that man? He'll be at your fight. Sit up and listen to me. He's going to be putting out the feelers to build a relationship. These gamblers watch kids like you and younger when they have ex-professionals as coaches. More of his type will come along. You're listening, aren't you? They're demons and a curse."

"Yes. Yes," Nong replied, not understanding why his father was so irritated. Numerous times, he had overheard adults talk about the erosion of Muay Thai standards because of the gambling and corruption. His ears were numb to the same old complaints and the *when-I-was-young* tone.

Being humble, Joi omitted to say that the gamblers targeted young fighters whose trainers had been successful, winning major titles in particular. The punters believed like father like son. Even if the boy was young, it was still worth betting if they could attract enough risk-takers with deep pockets.

The vitriol his father spat was shared by others within the boxing community. The money corrupting the boxing did not extend to just illegal gambling. Bribes were paid to judges, referees and even the fighters to secure an outcome. Judges had been known to adjust point cards, referees to announce a decision early, and fighters feigning falls or injuries. The temptation to fix a fight was immense. There were cases where the boxers themselves were targeted by criminal syndicates, often with Chinese connections.

Boxers needed to ringfence themselves with trusted

aides and supporters. Nong had heard the story several times now relating to the famous fighter Kem Sitsongpeenong, whose water was poisoned with a sedative. During the pre-fight warm-up, he was offered a cup of water by a family member of the Sor Ploenchit Gym for whom he was contracted to fight. Later, his muscles weakened, and his opponent won the fight. Hospital tests proved he had been poisoned. In keeping with the industry's self-regulation attempts, when Kem complained to the owner of the gym, he was told to leave the crime to the gym management to deal with. Nothing further was said, and it was the last anyone heard about the matter.

"Nong, I need to finish up here with Somchai and Ram. You run ahead," said Joi gently as he pushed his son in the direction of the locker room.

Joi hoped that putting the man's phone in bleach for five minutes had worked. He had asked him to delete the video of Nong, but he couldn't be sure. Joi was thankful that the community at Dragon's Gym was tight-knit. Corruption had become so bad now that individuals were working outside of the criminal gangs and on their own initiative. There had even been an incident when a cab driver had poisoned a transgender boxer on the way to the fight she was expected to win. Muay Thai had become internationally popular since 1993, when the International Federation of Muay Thai Amateur boxing was established. The World Muay Thai Federation was created, and the sport was recognised by the Olympic Council of Asia. But still, there remained strong resistance to further controls. Local communities and networks took it upon themselves to punish perpetrators targeting boxers.

The appearance of the flash guy concerned Joi, and he wished he had asked his full name. Ray was clearly not his first name –too foreign-sounding. In Thailand, most people do not go by their birth certificate names. Joi wouldn't be surprised, given how ostentatious the guy was, if even that gold watch of his was fake.

With the fight only two days away, Joi would ease the intensity of the training. Yesterday, Gan had asked his opinion on Nong becoming a novice at the *wat* (temple) for a few months. Joi was not opposed to the boy helping out at a local *wat.* Why not? He had done so as a teenager, and it had worked out well for him. There was no need to make that decision now, though. Still, he would ask around for recommendations of a suitable *wat*. It never hurt to have a chat about these things in good time.

While watching Ram and Somchai spar, he recalled when they had arrived to live at the gym. They had been as skinny as stray dogs and just as hungry. They had come to the gym from the Khao Lak orphanage in 2006, which was struggling at the time to feed and clothe the children. Dragon's Gym had agreed to provide accommodation and sponsor their upbringing by covering schooling expenses, housing, meals, medical, travel and training. It was not easy growing up at the gym, and some children had not been able to cope. Those who stayed worked hard, learning the importance of discipline, dedication and sacrifice. Ram and Somchai were success stories, having won major belts and title fights in Thailand and abroad. Mongkut and Panit looked likely to follow in their footsteps. The four boys were like brothers and had known Nong since he was born.

Sweat poured off Ram and Somchai as they practised clinching, snaking their arms around each other's shoulders, arms and neck. Joi watched them attempting to throw each other to the ground. Somchai kneed Ram in the ribs, applying just enough pressure to be felt but not hurt. They trained without mouthguards or protective headgear. Because they were practising, they did not use uppercuts or side elbows. The boxers struggled to maintain the physical dominance needed in a match, which would enable a fighter to slam his or her opponent on the boxing ring floor and win major points.

"Ram, Somchai: a word," Joi announced. "Did you know that guy?"

"Yes," replied Somchai, reaching for the flask of cold sweetened tea, which lay just outside the ropes near the back-corner post. "I've seen him at Patong Stadium. His name's Ray. I've heard he scouts out the young kids and persuades them to sign up for the bigger camps in Bangkok. It's a sure way to get a ready supply of talented kids with some training under their belt. What'd he say about Nong?"

"Yeah, I'm guessing he's not here for Sert. What!" exclaimed Ram, weaving to dodge Somchai's swing.

"Respect," Somchai chided. "The boy got in the ring!"

"If you see that man talking to Nong or even looking in his direction, get rid of him," Joi instructed. "I don't want to see his types polluting the kids, peddling their fool's gold about connections to the big time. The reason clients come to train in this quiet town is because our gym is clean. No drugs, no gambling, and, as you know, we don't go in for any other nonsense."

"Got it," said Somchai, his face expressionless.

"Sure, *Kru*. Will do," said Ram with a sharp nod.

CHAPTER EIGHT

THE stadium was as hot as a packed tourist bus with broken air-conditioning and just as stuffy. The majority of the VIP seats had been sold, and people were filtering in through the entrance early to reserve spaces on the top wooden benches. Tourists had travelled out to the stadium north of Bang Naing beach by excursion buses, *tuk-tuks*, and hotel taxis.

The organisers had doubled the number of vans used to drive up and down the main street in Khao Lak town centre with advertising billboards to sell tickets. Thais dressed in black t-shirts with the address of the stadium and a white stencilled image of a Muay Boran fighter had stood on street corners distributing leaflets, friendly words and smiles. From the roadside restaurants and bars on the main strip, down the side roads with their numerous stalls selling beach paraphernalia, the persistent loudspeaker cry of "Tonight, tonight at Khao Lak Boxing Stadium," rang, piercing through the constant drone of traffic, dance music tracks, and the calls of the Indian tailors selling bespoke suits, which were really made in factories and then top-stitched locally. In the late afternoon, a head-on collision between a tanker and a lorry carrying steel pipes on the other side of town prevented people from alternative night excursions to traditional Thai dance performances. So more tourists than usual had purchased tickets for the 400-seat stadium.

The early evening air was thick with diesel fumes and cheap cooking oil. Anyone who had arrived early and could sit in a car with the air-conditioning on freeze did so. The ticket prices were 1,000 baht for grandstand seats, 1,300 baht for ringside and 1,500 baht for VIP ringside with a free drink. Small open-backed vans with wooden benches were dropping off tourists at the edge of the car park when Nong arrived with his father.

Monkey scampered along Nong's side, chattering:

"Be strong and fast like me,
Nimble enough to climb a tree.
Away from danger at the sight of a stranger …

Nong gave a quick glance to his father to check that he had not noticed and hissed at Monkey to shut up. His poetry was irritating enough without the annoying repetition and habit of half-finishing a line.

"Wait here," said Joi. "I'll just go and check your paperwork with the administrator. I'll be back in a second."

Nong signalled okay with a nod and sauntered over to a nearby tree to read a fight card. Plastered on the Anisoptera evergreen trees fringing the carpark with their short buttresses and dark grey-brown thick bark were A3 sized multi-coloured fight card posters announcing "*Muay Thai Real Fight!!*" The posters displayed three-quarter body-length photographs of eight boxers with their national flag below. Tonight, all the competitors were Thai. On occasions, *farang* boxers from Dragon's Gym or boxing schools based in Phuket fought.

Nong was first on the billing and faced his opponent at 9 p.m. There would be six fights before the main headline bout and the fourth match would be fought between two girls.

Nong waved at Sert, trotting towards him. His face was healed, but there was a small scar on his forehead, which stood out against his tanned skin. Sert was eating a *moo ping*. The thin slices of fatty pork had been bunched tightly on a skewer and cooked over a grilling rig on a nearby street food kiosk. The savoury fish sauce and unsweetened coconut smelt divine. Nong could almost taste the moist and creamy richness of the meat.

"Sert, give me a bite of that. One small bite."

"Don't you dare give Nong anything," reprimanded Joi, who had returned from the boxing stadium administrator's office, "He'll be sick."

Sert happily gobbled down more of the pork as Nong looked on forlornly.

"Nong! Forget the food! I've seen your opponent," blurted Sert between mouthfuls. "He's taller than you. Got a ratty face and sticky-out ears. His father's inside talking to the judges. The referee's the same man we had. Somchai and the others have already grabbed seats in the red corner."

"OK, Sert, OK," said Joi in a calm tone. "Now, please stop waving that skewer about before you take someone's eye out and come along!"

As Sert gabbled at Nong in front, Joi asked Buddha to bless his boy and dispel any negative emotions from his mind so he would respond to his opponent impassively and not in anger. As emotional aggression would most likely end in Nong losing. Joi taught all his students to fight in a Thai style with a calm mind and detachment. The judges rewarded fighters who demonstrated control of temperament and skill. Joi often reminded the *farang* students that boxers did not win points if they were perceived to have a rude attitude, which is why Western fighters often lost fights in Thailand, never earning the respect of the boxing aficionados.

Once inside, Sert went to find Natcha. Joi took Nong by the upper arm and led him to the bar, where friends and family waited.

The moment they arrived at the bar, a torrent of advice rained down on Nong, who was frowning with concern. The muscles between his eyes bunched together and his mouth tightened. It was one thing fighting Sert, whom he had known all his life, but quite another fighting a complete stranger. What would the boy do? Was he much better than him, or worse?

"Confidence, son. Confidence," said Joi, aware of how Nong felt. After all, he had been down that path. Joi was unconcerned because he knew that, unlike an amateur fight with older contenders or a professional match, the referee would step in to stop this fight at the first sight of blood. While there were many unknowns this evening, Joi trusted the referee, who was local and a good friend.

"*Lai,* Somchai," said Joi, tapping him on the back of the shoulder.

Somchai flinched slightly, whipping his head around to see who it was. The din from the shouts, music, and loudspeaker announcements drowned out Joi's quiet voice.

"Sure. Let's go." Somchai smiled, giving Joi a slight nod of his head. "Catch you later, guys." He clapped his hands together before attacking Nong with a flurry of mock punches. "Come on, champion, we need to get you warmed up so you can win and buy us all dinner. What d'ya reckon? What do you say? Aren't you ticklish?"

"Stoooppp it." Nong giggled and did his best to wriggle away from Somchai's bear hug. Joi and Somchai exchanged a wink over Nong's head. Nerves were understandable, but dangerous if allowed to intensify. Like a strangler fig they would ultimately smother Nong's ability to grow. Adrenaline would keep him sharp, but panic and tension were nightmarish to control. Somchai's cajoling and light teasing kept Nong calm. The trick was to find a mutualistic balance between negative and positive emotions, as overconfidence was not useful either. Joi was not given much to banter, so Somchai was the perfect good cop to his bad cop.

"Thanks, everyone," said Joi, acknowledging the well wishes alternating between handshakes, back slaps and a raising of his hand. "Follow me: Nong,

Somchai."

Somchai rested his right arm around Nong's shoulders and chatted to Joi about his own upcoming fight as they walked past the bench seats in the direction of the red corner warm-up area, with its single black sandbag, six sky blue square training mats, skipping ropes and a small wooden stool. Diametrically opposite, on the far side of the stadium, the blue corner had the same configuration. As Nong fought first, he did not have to wait for another boxer to leave the area. Never one to miss an opportunity, Somchai asked Joi if he would coach him during clinching practice next week.

"So, how about Monday and Wednesday?"

"Somchai, I can't believe that you're asking me this now?" Secretly, Joi welcomed his student's dedication to practice. "You can see, Nong, why Somchai does well, can't you? He never gives up!" said Joi, clapping Somchai on the back. "Yep, sure. We can train on both days."

"I haven't seen the other boy. Have you?" asked Nong, biting his lower lip in concern.

"No. But it doesn't matter. We'll see him soon enough. What we need to focus on now is getting you sorted and warmed up."

Nong removed his lucky orange and black t-shirt with its tiger motif and held out his hands so his father could wind the hand wraps and tie the gloves. Then he stretched out his arms while Joi applied oil to his rib cage, massaging his legs, back, shoulders and arms until only the soles of his feet and hands were dry. Somchai gossiped to Nong as if they were passing the time of day waiting for a street vendor to finish wok-frying lunch. He told him funny stories about the antics of guests at the gym while his father strenuously rubbed his muscles to warm them. Nong tried to catch a glimpse of his opponent's face, moving his head to see through the crowds in the murky surrounds of the boxing arena. He recognised some of the faces peering through the fence and smiled at his school friends. They responded by pushing their noses up in a pig snout impression, sticking out tongues, giving thumbs up and waving. Oil and gloves on, it was time to start mentally preparing for the fight ahead. Alone.

Nong sipped water, shadow-boxed and stretched, preparing his muscles, going through the same warm-up drills he had practiced since the age of eight. Later in life, Nong's boxing combinations would consist of defensive and offensive strategies utilising any number of techniques: elbows (slash, horizontal, uppercut, forward, reverse, double chop, spinning and mid-air); kicks (straight, roundhouse, diagonal, half-shin, reverse roundhouse, down roundhouse, axe heel, jump kick and step up); knees (straight strike, diagonal strike, curving strike, horizontal strike, slap, bomb, flying knee and step-up knee); and foot jab (straight foot, sideways foot, reverse foot, slapping foot, and jumping). His defences would include blocking with his shin, parries, avoidance by moving his body out of the range of a strike while still remaining in the correct position for a counter strike, evasion by jumping back from an attacker's kicks, disruption by pre-empting an attack with a jab or low roundhouse kick. And lastly, a strong sense of anticipation, such as catching a strike or roundhouse kick to the body.

Now, Nong's arsenal of skills reflected his age. It took years to perfect all the techniques necessary to become a world-class boxer, and even then, many a boxer never learned half of what his father knew. By using the warm-up time to settle his mind, Nong eventually found a calm place from which to speed up his practice and go through the set pieces he had learnt with Somchai and the *krus*. His breathing slowed until it matched the tempo of his movements, and he was in tune with himself. Only then did he start to work with the sandbag to warm-up.

"Somchai, who's judging tonight's matches? Any idea?" asked Joi, keeping a critical eye on his son's progress.

"It's the same two as always. No changes there."

"That's good. You haven't seen that flash guy Ray, have you?"

"Excuse me," snapped Joi, waving away a tourist holding out her camera phone for a photo. "Nong, go and practice on the other side of the bag. Yep. That's right. There." The tourist was the fourth person in three minutes to have approached him for a photo. "Somchai, this is pissing me off."

Somchai WhatsApp'd Ram, who was out of earshot on the far side of the gym. Ram was not wearing his usual uniform of Muay Thai shorts and singlet but was dressed in ripped jeans, a red-and-white Dragon's Gym t-shirt and flip-flops. Ram looked up from his phone and over to where Somchai was standing, one hand raised, beckoning. He gave him a thumbs-up sign, indicating that he would be a few moments.

"What's up?" asked Ram, vape in hand as he trailed over with Mongkut and Panit ambling along behind him, heads down, tapping at their phones.

"Just stand along the mat edges, will you?" Somchai instructed. "Nong needs a bit of peace and quiet."

"Can't stand the attention of the girls, can he? Bit young to be worried about... ouch. Mongkut, what! Ahh, *Kru* Joi. *Sawadee krap.*"

Joi sat on a small wooden stool, mouth set in a straight line, his eyes as focused on Nong. His bony hands – with as much flesh as an eagle's feet and sinewy fingers like claws – were carefully rewinding a boxing wrap that had come loose, straightening each minuscule crease as he did so. It was ten-to-nine. Now was not the time for distractions.

Nong had visualised the fight in his head: from climbing over the ropes to his first line of attack all the way to being announced the winner. He had practised the game plan with his father, who knew his skills and qualities best. Sparring and clinching sessions with Somchai and boys his own age had helped him memorise the sequence of attacks. Nong had been watching the red numbers of the large digital clock above the exit sign while shadow-boxing. Moving his head from either side, releasing the tension in his neck muscles, he was itching to start.

His father helped him with some quick final stretches for his legs. Catching each foot in the crook of his arm, he raised Nong's right leg and then left to loosen the four muscles of his quadriceps. Next, bending down to look into his son's eyes, Joi asked, "You ready, Nong?" Satisfied that he was, Joi tied the small red cape Gan had embroidered in gold letters with Nong's name around his son's neck. Next, he gave Nong some rare words of praise to help his nerves. "You'll fight well. I know it."

Nong beamed up at his father. The boxing gloves prevented him from putting his small, soft hand in his father's powerful fist. With a nod of his head in the direction of the blue corner, Joi indicated they needed to go. Placing himself to the right of Nong while Somchai moved to the left, they walked to the red corner. Ram and the others followed close behind. Nong checked the strip of his mother's sari was still on his bicep for the eighth time, paying no attention to the shouts of encouragement or concerned and disapproving looks of parents in the audience who had never witnessed a Muay Thai fight before; a number of them deliberating how they would feel if their own child was being led into a boxing ring.

The stadium owners had suspended from the ceiling a square wooden frame of four metres by four metres above the ring. Decorating the frame were at least forty national flags, the majority of them tattered and yellowed by nicotine. Having been in the building so many times, Nong did not even notice the decorative attempt and nod to international friendship. But a voice inside compelled him to do so now. That's when he caught sight of Tiger casually lying on the wooden frame, nonchalantly swaying her tail amongst the pennants. Her round amber eyes locked onto his brown ones just long enough for him to feel a rush of electricity followed by a serene coolness and clarity of mind. Nong gave an obeisance, recognising the importance of the gift. It was solely up to him now not to fail.

"Come on, Nong!" urged his father with a hint of concern. "Look at your opponent! Now's not the time to stand around daydreaming."

Asnee, the ratty-faced Thai boy, was taller than Nong but only by a couple of inches. With his hunched shoulders and downcast eyes, he had the appearance of someone going to their doom. Asnee wore rolled-up shorts that had belonged to someone else, and his birdlike rib cage shone with oil like a small quail ready for the roasting tin. *Perhaps*, thought Nong, *he has been made to fight or accepted money to get into the ring.* Unlike other kids, money was not always on Nong's mind. How to get it? What would he do with it? How to spend it? While his parents were not poor like rice farmers, they were a long way from being wealthy. Nong knew that should he win this evening, the money would come in useful. But he had never been pressurised to fight for cash.

There was a man standing nearby with gelled-back hair, gold jewellery and watch, waving red 100 baht notes. It was Ray, clearly looking to attract gamblers. He was gesticulating with aggressive chopping hand movements. The lit cigarette in his left hand glowed red in the night. As he waited for the fight to get underway, Nong thought Ray can't have *jai yen*, a composed heart, as I've been taught. *He's going to attract unlucky attention from a phi, or ghost, with his loud, aggressive behaviour.*

"Nong! Sit down and face me. Here, drink this," instructed Joi, giving Nong an isotonic drink to sip. Nong's calm eyes followed the children cavorting before him, playing tag amongst the drinking adults standing near the bar and along the narrow pathways between the benches. He sensed rather than heard the words of encouragement the crowd shouted as the speakers were blasting the rock band Queen's, "We are the Champions", at such a high volume he could barely understand his father and Somchai.

Nong's chest, no wider than an iPad, rose and fell as he pushed air deep into his lungs. "Fight with heart, Nong. Fight hard," urged his father, giving yet another set of instructions while applying Vaseline to his lips, nose, cheekbones, jawbone and beneath his eyebrows to protect his face from punches. Joi made sure not to leave Nong's face dry to prevent the opponent's leather gloves from abrading his skin. With Vaseline, the punches were more likely to slide off his face, not land square, and limited the chances of Nong sustaining a cut.

The bell sounded and the mystical notes of the *Samara* began. Somchai, Joi and Nong climbed over the top rope into the ring. Joi put the yellow *Mongkhon* on Nong's head with both hands, saying a short prayer before untying his cape.

The rotund promoter Matt wore ripped jeans, scuffed black leather shoes and a dark grey shirt that used to be black. He was an ex-boxer. Not being very good, he had made the wise decision to change his career whilst in his mid-twenties. Not being much of a businessman either, he had never organised a single bout in Bangkok with the major league fighters. Locally, he was respected because he was fair. What's more, the rulings of tonight's judges were largely not contested or criticised. Matt greeted Nong with a hug, took his hand, and led him into the centre of the ring, where he introduced him to the waiting referee. Then he positioned Nong to stand alongside his opponent and the stadium's owner to pose for photos. A *Phuang Malai*, the floral arrangement placed round a fighter's neck to bring good luck, was hung around Nong's neck. The boxers stood hands up in a fighting stance for the camera and were introduced. Next, Asnee and Nong banged gloves, both imagining their victory as they gave one another a curt nod of respect. Asnee prayed he would win so his parents would not berate him for losing money. His mother had made it clear that he had to win tonight at all costs, as she had bet her month's wage. After having completed the *Ram Muay* homage to their teachers, parents and buddha, Asnee returned to the blue corner and Nong the red. Joi gave him a sip of water, then dabbed more water on his face and head and put in his mouthguard.

"Keep your hands up. Fight well. Keep your hands up," Joi repeated while placing his palms on the *Mongkhon*. In silence, he said a short prayer before removing the sacred yellow *Mongkhon* and placing it on the corner post with the *Phuang Malai.* Nong turned and walked to the ring centre, where he stopped to stand face-to-face with the slightly taller Asnee. The bell rang, the referee raised his hand and made a downward slicing movement. Showtime.

BOOM. Asnee *teeped* Nong in the stomach, sending him shooting backwards. Barely recovering from falling, Nong advanced with a left kick followed by a cross and went for a clinch to batter Asnee's rib cage with a knee. However, he received as many sharp knees as he gave.

The crowd whistled and shouted. "Yaaaahy, yaaaahy, yaaahy," swinging their arms together in an upward motion as they counted each blow and counterblow over the *Samara*. "Oi, oi, oi," they shouted, encouraging the boxers on. In Nong's corner, Somchai and Joi banged on the boxing ring floor with their fists, dispensing advice faster than an automatic table tennis robot does ping-pong balls.

Asnee tried to knee back, but Nong pulled him aside with a jerk, bringing in his weight and stepping slightly back with his inner leg. Then Nong attacked him with a knee before shifting his weight again from his waist and throwing Asnee to the floor. The rat-faced boy looked up at him, eyes widened in surprise. *He's overconfident*, thought Nong. I'm going to slow this fight down and move in for an elbow strike.

They hurled punches and jabs, high and low kicks at each other. The referee separated them when they hung on to each other's necks, wavering from side to side as tiredness crept in. Any attempt at maintaining their fight strategy was long gone. The bell rang. Nong raised his hands in the air as he walked back to his corner to signal confidence to the crowd. As soon as Nong sat on the small once-white plastic chair, Joi passed him the water cup and vigorously rubbed each limb.

"Slow it down! Kick hard and fast. I don't want to see any whirling punches that aren't straight!" instructed Joi. Somchai poured water on Nong's head, twittering like a sparrow, while Mongkut and Panit also chirped their advice.

Hell, Nong thought, *I wanna be back in the ring*! The bell rang and he immediately jumped up. Left foot in front with his right food behind, he advanced.

Asnee had clearly received the same advice as he too slowed down his movements. They circled each other, looking for an opening. Nong blocked a right kick with an inner left leg block, placed his foot forward, shifted his weight to his left foot, spun round, and with a perfect technique, aimed a high roundhouse kick at Asnee's head, catching him just below the eye with enough power to knock him sideways onto the mat.

"Stop. STOP!" shouted the referee, pushing Nong with a hand on his chest.

Ray removed his cigarette, throwing it down on the floor. "What the fuck?" he roared.

A sea of arms stretched up to congratulate Nong through the ropes, and he clambered onto the mid rope to raise his arms in victory. "Yeeesss!" he screamed to the applause from the crowd. Behind Nong, an aggrieved Asnee, his left eye badly swollen and cheek cut, stood arguing that he could still fight. But unlike some referees, the old uncle was not going to let the youngest kids compete once blood was drawn.

Joi cupped his hands around his mouth, "Nong, get down!" Hearing his father, Nong descended the ropes. Then he ran a small circuit of the ring, shaking his clasped hands together above his head. The referee grabbed Nong's left arm and raised it in the air, pronouncing him the winner, and then instructed the two boys to hug, which they did without animosity. Asnee congratulated Nong, who, taking Asnee's head in both hands, moved it to the left to take a better look at his eye.

"You've given me a nice one," smiled Asnee ruefully as Nong tested the swelling by gently pressing the hen's-egg bump.

"My thigh's going to have bruises, too. Just can't see them yet," countered Nong, wincing as he prodded his thigh muscle. Suddenly, he felt eyes on the back of his head. The sense of someone commanding him to turn and look was so strong that Nong forgot about the pain in his leg, and he spun round, glaring in the direction of where the sensation emanated from. His gaze locked onto Tiger's steady stare. She was crouching next to the oblivious judges as if indicating that she was also evaluating his performance.

To one side of the ring, the promoter's wife, mutton dressed as lamb, was trying to climb through the low ropes in a mini skirt and low-cut cerise pink halter neck top. A permanently cheerful character, she worked as a waitress during the week and official stadium photographer at weekends. Joi, his normally dour expression bright with delight, climbed over the top rope to join his son. A few people dashed into the ring to put wads of baht notes in Nong's hand. Somchai stood on hand to guide the boy as to the proper protocol.

"Nope, not from you," snapped Joi, slapping away Ray's hand. "I don't want any extra pressure on my boy or your types shouting at him to win you money! Just look at Asnee's mother crying. I bet you persuaded her to gamble on her son, when she most likely doesn't have much in the first place."

"Now, no need for that, is there. On such a happy night!" said Ray, his uneven bleached teeth showing through his ingratiating smile. "Let's have a drink sometime. How about next week?"

"Joi," interrupted Somchai. "Come on, we're waiting. Nong is wanted in the photo area by the door

Please excuse us, Ray. The fans await!"

"Hi, Somchai. How are you doing?" Ray said. "Joi, catch you some other time. Hope you don't mind, but I got some really good images of your boy fighting."

"Great, great," Somchai said. "Joi?"

"Yep. I'm with you," said Joi, deciding to let the whole conversation go. Tonight was not about his personal animosity to Ray's type. And he wasn't going to be provoked into losing his temper. Nong had run off somewhere, and Gan would be fretting at home. Despite having grown up with boxing, she wasn't finding Nong's fighting easy. As he left the ring, he squeezed Somchai's upper arm in thanks. "Let's go and find Nong."

CHAPTER NINE

THE crash of the waterfall tumbling into the emerald-green rock pool roared above Nong and Sert's shouts as they propelled themselves from the largest boulder into the freezing water. Red dragonflies skimmed the water surface, and a male, blue-banded kingfisher with a broad blue-green band across its chest rested on a branch and watched the boys, its head tilted to one side.

Somchai, Mongkut and Panit posed for photographs, their arms flexed to display strong biceps and bodies dripping wet. Nong, uninterested in building an Instagram following, alternated between swimming after the small fish darting between rocks and attempting to dunk Sert by grabbing his ankles. They boys passed the time by splashing, wrestling, and lazing as they refreshed themselves in the transparent water away from the glare of the midday sun.

They had earned this midday respite. Earlier that morning, they had essentially been construction conscripts back at the Dragon's Gym. Since 7 a.m., the group had been shovelling earth and sand, dragging wooden beams, raking cement, and wiping sweat from their eyes. Beneath their domed cages of woven bamboo, two fighting cockerels had monitored their progress with beady eyes. Joi had overseen the boys' work, never missing the first sight of someone slowing in their pace. When necessary, he would shout commands, not unlike his Muay Thai coaching, to encourage the team to get the construction job completed faster.

The sun roasted the sand. Barefooted and wearing only shorts, the boxers-turned-construction-crew moved the building supplies to a square grid that marked out the bungalow's foundations with old white twine twisted around a branch firmly planted in the ground. The dwelling would eventually have three rooms: an open-plan kitchen, one bedroom big enough for two twin beds and a bathroom, the interior whitewashed in the same paint as the exterior. To access the structure, there would be three steps leading up to a small veranda that could accommodate two garden chairs and a round table just wide enough for two dinner plates.

Like the other accommodations at Dragon's Gym, this bungalow was raised from the ground primarily as protection against flooding and to keep out reptiles, insects and mammals. The monsoon rains brought torrential flooding to the region, and the local people knew it made sense to work with mother nature rather than against her. The bungalow would be plainly furnished but adequate for Dragon's gym guests. Air-conditioning units would be installed. The furniture would be functional and kept clean. The shady space under the larger bungalows could also be used for storage. The buildings were functional dwellings that adequately provided for the needs of the gym's guests.

At 11 a.m., Joi said they could stop, promising to join them later for a barbeque. Waving goodbye, he left for a much-needed shower and change of clothing. The vacuum cleaner sound of his motorbike engine faded rapidly. As he neared home, Joi thought, *I want to spend some time with Gan. Otherwise, the whole day is going to disappear. The boys are just going to have to wait a while.* Waving at his wife, who was chatting to her cousin in the front yard as he approached, he parked his bike before he gave her a kiss on the cheek.

"Whaa! Look at the state of you!" said Gan, holding up her hands to push him away.

"Yeah, I know," grumbled Joi as he greeted his neighbour while removing his shoes. "I'm off to shower."

The sandy, grimy boys trailed past the double glass office doors facing the entrance to the training area. The sound of their voices disturbed the owner, Lucy, who was using the reception computer to work on the accounts, air-conditioning on full blast. One of the receptionists had called in sick, so she had stepped in to cover the staffing shortfall. Lucy pushed back the leatherette office chair and grabbed the Ford Ranger keys from the top of a plastic desk edged with particleboard.

"Hey, wait up! *Sawadee ka.* How did this morning go?" she asked. "Can I offer you a lift back home?"

"*Sawadee kap,*" came back the response six times.

"Thanks, but we're going for a swim," replied

Somchai, smiling warmly as he stepped in to lead the conversation. Being the oldest in the group, he believed it was his place to be the spokesperson, a role he also liked. Somchai knew that no-one was keen to return home. Sitting down in a sparse bungalow on bunkbeds with Ram, Panit and Mongkut was not appealing at the best of times, and Nong and Sert were eager to be off. Out of earshot from Lucy, he could hear the two younger boys muttering about wasting time.

Lucy noted the tired smiles, stiff body language and sweat-stained shorts. "Great. Where can I drop you guys?" The beach, lake or rock pools? Oh, and by the way," she added, "how did the work go this morning? All good?" Lucy never stopped thinking about work. It was her life. She and her husband worked all day every day and could not understand people who didn't. The Tsunami had razed their home to the ground, and it was only by borrowing money from friends and family that they had been able to purchase enough land to build and develop Dragon's Gym. Being fundamentally good people, they gave back to the local community as and when they could. No-one who worked at the gym thought in a nine-to-five way. The boys and their parents depended on its success, so they didn't grumble too much about having to spend their one day off working to build more guest accommodations.

"All good. Joi was there. He's gone off to get some food, and we're meeting him at the rock pools," said Ram, fidgeting and eager to leave.

"Yes. All done," chipped in Mongkut, wondering to

himself how much longer they would have to hang around and make small talk.

Lucy did love the sound of her own voice and could really talk once she got going. The worst was when the tone switched to lecture mode. It was enough to make Mongkut fall asleep.

"Yes, all good, all good," he insisted with a note of finality.

"Rock pools, please. Thanks," said Nong.

Somchai flashed Nong a sideways look, not happy that Nong had spoken up. Somchai asked Lucy if she would drive them to the waterfall, which lay behind the village to the north.

"I hope she does take us there," said Mongkut under his breath, kicking the dirt. It was his favourite place to swim and free from tourists. Since he was a young boy, he had felt the enchantment of swimming in the magical rock pool.

The waterfall had five levels and a year-round water-flow, which weaved its way down through the forest to the seashore, where eventually it would become one with the sea. As the fast-paced river flowed down the mountain side, tributaries branched off to form smaller rivers and streams as well as ponds. In one of the larger ponds, nearest to the Andaman Sea, there was an elephant 'eco-lodge'. Tourists paid to bathe, wash and feed elephants, and their expenditure provided a vital source of revenue for the elephants' survival in an area undergoing rapid industrialisation and illegal logging. On Sunday afternoons, the boxing friends would occasionally spy on the tourists in their swimming costumes, gingerly entering the murky pond water to bathe alongside the adult elephants and, occasionally, the babies. Ram and Somchai placed bets on whether the elephants were likely to defecate and if certain tourists would be able to avoid the large floating lumps of faeces. Given the slipperiness of pond banks, climbing from the water was no easy task.

"Come on, then," said Lucy with a grin. Locking the door to the reception and turning the air-conditioning and lights off. Nong and the others clambered into the back of the four-wheel-drive pickup truck. She drove them through the dusty track, passing into the lush tropical evergreen forest covering the undulating mountains of Khao Lak, Khao Saeng Thong, Khao Mai Kaeo, and Khao Plai Bang To.

The ancient forest had an incredible variety of tree species with leaves of deep green jade to turquoise and perfumed flowers. Palms, bamboo, magnolia champaca and epiphytes such as white orchids and ferns were common sights. As they neared the most ancient part of the forest, the trees became enormous. The noon tropical sun had already caused the majority of animals to rest in the shaded undergrowth. The only animals they saw were monkeys and the occasional bird, even though Malayan tapirs, weasels, colugos, binturongs, tigers, Sumatran serows, langurs, deer, barking deer, great argus pheasants, woodpeckers, eagles, emerald doves, scarlet minivets, hornbills, and various reptile species all called the forest home.

Near the rock pool there was a 40-metre *ta-khian* tree with a trunk diameter of five metres. According to local folklore, the tree was at least 600 years old. The forest monks who lived in a *wat* less than one kilometre to the north of the top rock pool had tied lengths of mustard yellow, tangerine silk, duck-shell blue, lavender and malachite green around its trunk. There was a red lacquered low table nestled in the tree's roots and carefully folded women's silk dresses in earth tones.

For in this tree lived *Lady Ta-khian,* a tree deity who in Thai folklore was also known as *Nang Mai*, or 'Lady of the Tree'. Often, she appeared as a beautiful young woman wearing traditional ochre-coloured Thai clothing. It was said that *Lady Ta-khian* haunted the area around the tree where she resided.

No villager would ever fell the tree for lumber as they believed she would haunt their house and curse their lives. It was only in the Buddhist monastery that the wood could be used, given its spirituality. In order to protect venerable old trees from loggers, Buddhist monks wrapped lengths of satin around the *ta-khian*'s trunk. Should the villagers need to chop down a tree, a special ceremony had to be performed to ask for permission from the spirit within. However, at times, some of these very ancient trees were felled regardless.

"Thanks for the lift, Lucy," they chorused, jumping from the back of the pickup truck and into the long grass at the forest perimeter. Waving goodbye, Lucy turned the vehicle around and sped off in the direction of Dragon's Gym.

The short red earth path leading up to the pond was overhung with vines and falling branches. At times the boys had to stoop down to avoid hitting their heads. The recent storms had uprooted several trees. The thick mud rendered walking in flip-flops impossible, so they went barefoot. Before clambering over fallen tree trunks, they checked for insects, especially Asian forest centipedes, fearsome predators that could grow up to 38 centimetres and deliver an incredibly painful and venomous bite. The cool breeze caressing their sweat-streaked faces and the sun dappling the forest foliage signalled their arrival at the waterfall.

* * *

Later that afternoon, shattered after a morning of hard labour and rowdy swimming, Nong lay on the largest boulder by the pool, watching the lazy flight of a small white butterfly amongst the pale pink dendrobium orchids drooping from the lichen-covered branches of a champaca tree. Sunbeams danced on the surface of the pond, daubing the flora and stones below with dashes of gold. Somchai and Ram were wrestling one another, splashing water in each other's faces instead of gathering dried branches to make a fire, while Panit and Mongkut brushed leaves and twigs from the largest boulders to create space for eating and sitting.

Where the cascading waterfall entered the pond, the surface bubbled and burbled, creating a white foam.

The sound lulled Nong into a satisfying daydream. An ant bit his left arm, and he slapped it without bothering to open his eyes. Again came the bite. *Hell. I might be lying on a red ant's nest,* he thought, and opened his eyes to take a look. But there was no insect. What had been irritating him was the sharp end of a long-pointed stick. Nong expected to see one of his friends as he looked over his shoulder for the perpetrator. Instead, kneeling down, feet pointing behind, her black hair cascading to one side and over her shoulder, was a beautiful young woman. The leaves upon which she knelt had not bent or cracked. Nong gulped in fear as his hands started to tremble. In desperation, Nong glanced over at his friends, who were all still larking around in the water, judging the distance between them and him to see how quickly they could come to his aid.

"Nong, your companions can neither see nor hear me. Don't fret. I've been the guardian of this forest for a long time, and I'm not going to harm you. When I was a young girl, my father would take me hunting here and would kill many animals. Animals such as forest lions, which you've never seen. Many of the animals that lived here no longer exist. May I tell you a story of when I was your age many, many years ago?" She asked, looking at him gently with magnetic dark brown eyes.

Her face was open and kind, but Nong felt as naked as when he had been skinny dipping only ten minutes ago. It was as if he could feel her mind walking through his brain, searching and probing for areas of weakness like an art critic in front of a painting. Nong hurriedly said, "Yes, please." *At least*, he thought, *her story will take the focus off me!* His mother had once told him that you needed to be very careful with tree spirits as they had a dark side to them and could change their tune as quickly as a *Samara* musician. It was always best to be humble, not offer an opinion and NEVER, EVER be impolite.

"Wonderful," replied Lady Ta-khian, moving slightly to better straighten and smoothen her ankle-length skirt of bright jade and russet silk. She took hold of both his hands, smiled and said, "Listen carefully, as in the end, I have a question."

"One day, when my father was out hunting, he came across two tiger cubs. He shot both those cubs for their fur. For many nights after, I'd hear the mother crying and calling outside the village. The sorrow she felt, I, too, felt deep in my heart and cried with her. A week later, my father went to hunt for fun with his friends and came across a troop of crab-eating macaque monkeys. There was one female that couldn't escape as fast as the others. This was because the baby clinging around her waist was causing her to move slowly. I tugged and pulled at my father's sleeve, asking him not to shoot the monkey, but he did. I rushed forwards and plucked the young monkey from the fur of its dead mother, and it screamed. My father skinned the mother and hung her fur outside on a nail next to the tiger cub skins he was hoping to sell."

"The baby macaque cried and cried and would not

eat. My mother was breastfeeding at the time, and I persuaded her to give me some milk for the baby. But it was still no use. Two days after my father had shot its mother, the little monkey escaped from my arms and through the open window of our house, straight to the drying skin of its mother and screamed, clinging on to the dead fur with tiny paws, doing its best to wake its mother. From that moment on, I knew that animals are no different from us. They think and feel. They love and suffer just like we do. I have dedicated my life to protecting the forests and trying to teach people to respect our animal brothers and sisters. You know the mother of those tiger cubs. She comes to you at night and guides you and your thoughts. Monkey, who both irritates and amuses you, is the baby monkey I saved. Elephant's parents were used by the illegal loggers that have decimated much of this ancient forest, and she came to this pond as an orphan. I cared for her until several years ago when she passed."

"Now, Nong. Stop it!" she said at the sight of his tearing up. "There is no need for that nonsense. Listen to what I have to say. Tiger reports that you are strong and courageous. Is Tiger wrong?"

"No," sniffed Nong. "I'm fine." In truth, he was not fine at all but felt rather foolish and selfish for being so concerned about his life and cars and the riches of football players. He glanced back to the others and wondered how it was possible for them not to see him sitting here talking. *Maybe they can see, and they just think I'm mad*, he thought. Her dark eyes had started to flash with flecks of green and the brightest gold. The hands resting on his were beginning to make his own feel uncomfortably hot. "Sorry, sorry," Nong spluttered, concerned she could read his thoughts.

Raising her left eyebrow in acknowledgement of the apology, Lady Ta-khian continued, "Nong, I want you to learn more about the forest and the importance of having respect for all living creatures. There is a *wat* not far from here where the forest monks live. It was those monks who ordained this tree. When your mother asks you to stay at the *wat* and learn the ways of the forest, will you go? *Tham lai pa khue ahm lai chat* – to destroy the forest is to destroy life. If you agree, then drink the blessed water at this tree's roots to seal your oath." Without another word, Lady Ta-Khian released his hands and disappeared.

Nong sucked the forest air into his lungs, pushing the air right down into his stomach and slowly exhaled. He repeated the exercise to calm his mind while looking at the green canopy and the birds flitting from branch to branch overhead, struggling to absorb the conversation. His eyes drifted across the pond to where his friends had been playing earlier. Panic struck. There was not a soul in sight.

"Let me go!" protested Nong, shrieking as wet hands scooped him up under his shoulders while another two sets grabbed his ankles.

"Time for you to get back in, daydreamer," laughed Somchai, dripping all over him like a wet dog. Somchai stood at his head while Mongkut and Panit held an ankle each. They carried him to the pond's banks, swung him to and fro counting to ten, before pitching him into the water sideways. The freezing mountain water numbed his brain. He flipped himself around underwater and swam between the large rocks tossed down by the waterfall above and to the other side of the pool, where the longest of the ta-khian dark brownish-grey roots reached down into the water. Nong put his hands around the thick, deeply fissured outer bark, pulling himself from the water.

Small, fragrant, yellowish-white flowers floated downwards from the top of the tree. Nong picked one flower up to inspect its triangular petals and long ruffled tips. As he bent down, he spotted that between the buttress of the tree and the formation of rocks rainwater had collected just as Lady Ta-khian had said. He felt a tug on the hem of his dripping, tattered Muay Thai shorts. Monkey, his octogenarian wrinkled face solemn and his intelligent hazel eyes steadfast, held out his left paw. Nong let the monkey climb up onto his chest and wrap his arms around him. Heart to heart, Nong made a vow to protect the forest and do as Lady Ta-khian had asked. He cupped his hands, drew from the water, and drank.

"Nong! Food!" shouted Ram.

"Be right there!" responded Nong, taking a deep breath.

Monkey scarpered, the tender moment forgotten in a second. Nong was left by himself, wondering if the macaque had tricked him into taking the oath that he knew couldn't be broken. Diving back into the pool, he swam across to the other bank, where his father and the others were eating overcooked chicken pieces from a skewer and drinking soft drinks. He was so wrapped up in his own thoughts he had not even noticed Joi arrive, let alone start the fire and cook the food. His father was tearing a piece of meat from a skewer and held a can of beer in one hand. Nong tried to give him a hug, but being soaking wet, his father avoided his embrace with a laugh. Over the fire, balanced a metal grill on which was an assortment of meats. Everyone was responsible for turning the skewers, which meant that no-one did, and the food burnt.

Large drops of rain started to fall, causing the fire to splutter and spark. There was a panic as everyone rushed to gather belongings and salvage lunch, grabbing large palm leaves to use as umbrellas. The torrential rain extinguished the fire. The rain poured and the whole forest rang with the tapping and splashing of huge raindrops. Nong attempted to retrieve at least one of the skewers before it was all cleared away, but everything had fallen into what had once been their fire and was now covered with sodden black ash.

"Come, Nong. Come, Sert," ordered his father. "Let's leave this lot and get back home."

The others waved them off as they sheltered under the trees, not bothered in the slightest by the tropical storm. Lightning crackled overhead, electrifying the air. Thunderclaps shook and roared. This time, the path back to the roadside was beginning to flood. Joi and his two charges picked their way along the path, looking out for sharp stones. It took the trio twice the time to make the return journey, and when they reached Joi's motorbike, which he had thoughtfully sheltered under the roof of an abandoned rubber plantation hut, they were as wet as when they had clambered from the forest pond.

The sun shone brightly again and the leaves of the forest glittered with water gems. Soon the humidity would start to climb. They dried themselves with the towels Joi always kept in the storage area beneath the motorbike seat. Joi mounted the bike first and steered it into the direction of home. Then Nong straddled the bike in front while Sert clung on behind Joi, arms wrapped around his waist.

"Sert," said Joi, once he had got the bike underway, "I'll drop you off first, then Nong, as I need to stop by Dragon's for a bit."

"Thanks," came Sert's muffled reply over Joi's left shoulder. Sert rested his cheek there so he didn't keep banging his head on the bumpy ride over stones the rainwaters had unearthed on the dirt road.

They rode in silence, the water evaporating and the wind drying their clothes. Nong thought about food. It seemed an age since he had eaten. When he got home, he planned to inspect the fridge as well as the cooking pots and then go straight to sleep.

"Look at the state of you!" exclaimed his mother when he entered the kitchen covered in mud again from the splashes from the drenched road. Cross, she grabbed the mop with its grey string head taped into place. “Go on, clean up that dirt. You should’ve washed yourself down outside with the hose pipe before coming in here. What do you think you’re doing?” Gan paused and looked at the sorry state of Nong. His shoulders were hunched as he mopped the floor, the usually smiling mouth down at the corners and the eyes flat brown like the surface of a glass of cola left for too long. “Have you eaten?”

“No,” was Nong’s grumpy reply. Taking a good look at the floor to check that he had caught all the mud, he handed the mop back to his mother. Gan followed her son as he walked, trailing dirt to the bathroom and wiping the floor as she went. Looking at his narrow back and torn shorts, her brow creased in concern. It had been her hope that he would have had a day of fun after Friday’s fight. She was worried that he was experiencing too many emotional highs and lows. *I know what I’m going to do. Nong is going to live with the forest monks for a few weeks,* she thought as she recalled her dream from the previous night. *It’ll give him time to learn skills and have some peace away from the boxing camp. School breaks up next week, so I’ve got time to talk to his father again.*

The forest *wat* was old, small and humble, with only five monks living there permanently. The monks were well regarded in the local community for their good works: helping to protect the forests from the Bangkok registered logging companies, providing education for the children of poorer families who could not afford school, and educating farmers in conservation practices.

Gan had heard that some of the very determined and intelligent children who were ordained at the temple were able to complete secondary school as a novice or monk, graduate from a monastic college, and go on to attain a bachelor's degree or even higher university education in Thailand or abroad. Her mother had told her that decades ago, the majority of Thai boys were ordained at the age of puberty. Being a monk offered the young boys an opportunity to raise their economic and social status and lead a secure life. Nowadays, with state education, the link with the Buddhist monastic order, or *Sangha*, has weakened.

Nong is suffering, fretted Gan as she sat at the small kitchen table with the breeze from the old metal upright fan cranking behind her, her head in her hands. *He needs an education in addition to the same lessons' day-in-day-out at school and has to get away from learning only Muay Thai during the summer. Those boys talk about Muay Thai, dream about Muay Thai and very little else. How can he dedicate himself to such a life?* she thought.

"Well," she said aloud. "Whatever Nong decides to do in life, a stay at the *wat* can only benefit him. What could possibly go wrong?"

CHAPTER TEN

NONG and Klapet focused their thoughts on winning the fight in the second round. The Chiang Mai audience welcomed the ringing of the bell with whistles, claps and cheers. The squat, broad-shouldered referee, his bald patch glistening with sweat, gave the signal to engage.

Straight away, Klapet jabbed Nong twice in the face. Nong responded with lightning reactions *teeping* Klapet hard in the stomach and knocking him back three paces. Moving forwards, right foot first, he lifted his left leg, the bone of his shin turned outwards to block Klapet's retaliatory kick to the kidneys.

Frantically, the gamblers signalled to one another as the fighters duelled, indicating with their hands to show if they were accepting bets for the blue or the red corner. At times, the punters hedged their bets by betting both ways. Gamblers could bet anything between 1,000 baht to 100,000 baht on each match. Highly superstitious, many gamesters wore amulets as well as prayer beads and made donations at the temples to ask for good luck.

Limbs attacking in a blur, Klapet attempted to catch Nong's right leg by the ankle, but Nong twisted away. He came back with a swift kick to Klapet's inner right thigh. They jabbed at each other and circled, maintaining a striking distance. Nong moved in for a clinch, and they wrestled one another, exchanging knee blows until the referee stepped in to separate the pair.

Momentarily pushed apart, they soon recommenced their dance. Nong flinched as Klapet kicked him in the side and followed an iron bar strength move with a cross to his head, which Nong barely managed to avoid. Again, Klapet attacked, moving his left leg with such a speed that Nong, unable to block the move, decided to grab Klapet's leg while stepping to his left to lessen the impact of the blow. Klapet twisted his leg, pushing and pulling to escape. But Nong held his leg up higher and jabbed him in the face, forcing him down on the mat once again by kicking Klapet's right leg from the inside, sending him off balance. Klapet jumped back up, stumbling as if dazed. The sweating referee gave the signal for them to continue. They exchanged a number of middle-high kicks and head punches before the end of the three-minute round bell sounded. Both fighters returned to their corners, arms raised high, roaring in triumph and claiming victory.

Somchai rushed towards Nong, wiping the sweat from his face with a towel. Nong noticed that Dang was shouting he was to put all his strength into the third round. Now was the time to start closing down the fight and give it everything he had.

CHAPTER ELEVEN

GAN stood in the temple courtyard holding her son's hand. A warm, westerly breeze melded the perfume of a moringa tree's cream flowers with the heavenly scent of the frangipani trees. From beneath the shaded trees on the far side of the sandy clearing, a pack of fifteen soi dogs approached, barking in warning.

There were brown dogs with black square muzzles, tan-coloured sides and strong paws. A small dog, no bigger than a Yorkshire Terrier, hopped behind the others on three legs. A large black and white bitch with swollen teats trotted out from underneath the stilts of the *Wat Trees of Life* temple, followed by gambolling puppies. Some of the whelps were pure black, and the other pups were carbon copies of the mother. Sitting on the perimeter of the forest clearing, still more dogs with crusty red mange patches scratched themselves.

The braver dogs came right up to them with lowered heads and tails wagging, asking to be petted. Nong scratched a particularly friendly-looking black puppy behind the ears, checking first to make sure his mother was not looking. Gan ignored the dogs, focusing on rehearsing her speech to the abbot. Determined to improve Nong's future, she half-dragged him through the circling dogs, barging past the larger ones.

Suddenly, she felt a strong tug as Nong pulled her backwards, the temptation to tickle the fattest of the puppies' belly irresistible.

"Can I have one?" pleaded Nong. "I'll take good care of it."

"Be a good boy and you can have a puppy," said Gan. Happy to have something to barter with him and thinking it was a small price to pay for his acquiescence.

Over the past two weeks, she had argued her case against Joi. Over mealtimes, she had broached the subject in a light-hearted way, extolling the benefits of learning to be at peace and the importance that the forest had in their lives. When the conversation became terse with her husband, they would go outside, not wishing to argue in front of the boy. Joi's reluctance to engage in conversation was harder to deal with than the strong words. But Gan persisted in the belief that Nong would benefit from staying a short while at the monastery, helping the monks with their work.

Joi relented. Not because he agreed, but because life at home was becoming difficult with the food he was eating as sour as the expression on his wife's face. His favourite lime juice drink for three consecutive days had been so sharp his teeth were in agony after just one sip. Years of poor dentistry didn't help protect him from the acid. Eventually, Joi realised he was being selfish. He would miss the boy if he disappeared for a few weeks. From a coach's point of view, he was concerned that Nong's training would suffer. Joi had already arranged for several follow-up fights. Even going to the extreme of visiting a different training camp an hour's drive away with Nong to suggest to the head trainer that his boy should fight with one of their juniors. Nong needed to get experience, and a fight arranged during one of the local fairs would give him valuable practice.

"Isn't he cute?" said Nong as he slipped his hand from Gan's grasp to pet the largest of the litter. The white puppy with one black ear wriggled and squirmed, waving its chubby legs in the air. Its mother stood watching. Her paws were firmly planted, ears raised and forward, with a stiff tail. Two hazel eyes warily observed Nong, following his hand as he rubbed the puppy's milk-swollen tummy.

"No," said Gan, never taking her eyes off the mother. "Leave it alone. Here, wipe your hands. Come on. Leave the dog, I said."

"But …"

"No. Give me the tissues. We're expected."

The dogs ambled back to the shade, flopping on the ground beneath the giant teak tree that had been ordained a few years before by a Buddhist monk in a ceremony attended by the local community who witnessed him blessing the tree. The monk had tied an old saffron robe without any fanfare and uttered a quiet incantation, not loud enough for the audience to hear. After the tree had been ordained, the villagers took a white thread used in Buddhist ceremonies and tied it from tree to tree to create a holy space. Over time, the community donated land to the monks who had declared the grove a holy sanctuary. More trees had been marked throughout the forest as worthy of preservation and, therefore, valuable. Gan had participated in a tree ordination ceremony and tied the faded Buddhist robe to the *ta-khian* tree near the waterfall pond. She had walked further than the villagers, tracking through the densely packed foliage to do so. When tying the robe, she had not only asked for the tree to be preserved but also for her son to be watched over and to relieve his suffering.

They were a humble family with little or no power, and she was concerned for the natural environment and the impact of its destruction on all forms of life. When she was a child, her parents grew what the family ate. The only things they needed to buy were spices and salt. Like their neighbours, they had given land to the monks who taught that the forest was the root of everything in the natural world, the dharma and natural law. Forests were the font of life and comprehension, the location where Buddha first had a revelation.

The *Trees of Life Wat* was not painted in bright reds and golds with impressive serpent-like protectors of Buddha and the guardians against bad or evil spirits that typically flanked the walls of temples or the staircases that led up to them. Nor were ferocious *Garuda* half-man, half-bird creatures present. Gilded half-women and half-lion *Apsonsi* were also not to be found on the upper terraces with *Hongsa* swan-like figures. Whereas many temple compounds featured the

Yaksha, a grimacing giant statue which often has a brightly painted face, at the entrance to the *Wat Trees of Life* there were only ordained trees. The roof was also plain and unadorned by the *Makara,* which is an aquatic monster symbolising rain that is part crocodile, part elephant and part serpent.

The temple entrance had neither an *Erewan,* which is a three-headed elephant of tremendous size, nor a *Singha,* which is a lion-like figure from Chinese mythology. This temple was plain and nestled amidst the thick, tangled trees as quietly as a mushroom. No glitz, no glamour, just a place of solace away from contemporary life. But at the same time, linked to it via the monks' use of technology and engagement with local communities through teaching programmes they run both for locals and foreigners in need of a retreat from the world. The monks only accepted a limited number of visitors from abroad, preferring to focus their energies on relieving the suffering of local people inflicted by land grabbing from corrupt middlemen and local officials.

The *wat* consisted of a number of straw-thatched small buildings with similar architecture but different functions and importance. There was an *ubosot(h) or bot,* an ordination hall, an open-sided pavilion known as a *Sala,* and the *Kute* of the monks' quarters. In some temples, the *ubosot* was only open to the monks and did not serve as a sermon hall. Inside the hall, there was a small altar with a stone-carved Buddha.

Waiting at the entrance stood Abbot Anurak in his

saffron robes. Being a monk who had maintained his monastic precepts unbroken for a period of ten years, he was typically addressed as *Ajahn* or 'teacher' Anurak. His bare right shoulder and arms revealed a thin, wiry physique. His eyebrows, as well as his head, were shaved. Like the other monks in the *wat,* he depended on the villagers for his sustenance. Gan had told Nong she was taking him there for a three-week stay, but ultimately the decision was his. His work there would be no more than simple cleaning and supporting the monks in their daily activities, attending scripture and meditation classes. The time in the forest would provide him a welcome counterbalance to his boxing training. Gan coped with her son both studying and training at his young age, but during the holidays, just boxing and being around the gym did not provide enough of an education. During his stay, he would attend meditation from six to nine at night and again in the morning from 3 to 6 a.m. After that, he would go out with the other guests and monks to check on the trees and undertake manual jobs such as sweeping, tending the gardens and helping prepare meals.

"*Sawadee kap Ajahn,* Anurak," said Nong, his hands held together, palms facing together in a prayer pose at the centre of his forehead before bending the upper half of his body at a slight angle, bowing his head.

"*Sawadee kha Ajahn,* Anurak," said Gan, repeating the same gesture as her son but also moving a foot behind her body and bending her leg slightly to create an even lower bow.

As was customary, Abbot Anurak did not return the bows as he stood barefoot on the lowest of the immaculate three wooden steps ascending to the *Sala*. Still, he gave them a warm smile and said, "Welcome, *Khun* Gan, Sirichai. Please come in, and let's sit."

Nong trailed slightly behind his mother, struggling to recall the points of protocol Gan said he must follow during his stay. He was only there for three weeks, so little was expected of him. Still, he did need to ensure that he mastered his behaviour and learned to follow simple rules. In contrast, the novice forest monks studied the 227 precepts, which taught what you can do, cannot do, and should do before studying meditation and, lastly, attaining wisdom. This latter study stage involved teaching, reflection and experiencing intuition, which comes from the stillness of the mind.

Nong and Gan sat on the grass mat floor facing the abbot with their feet pointing to the entrance. It was considered rude in Thai society to point the soles of your feet at monks or Buddha statues. The abbot sat cross-legged on a badly scratched wooden dais. Stretched out underneath him lay an enormous ginger tom cat with a torn ear and moss-green eyes, licking its fur and feigning to notice their presence. Nong shuffled forwards on his knees to stroke its luxuriant marmalade coat.

"I wouldn't do that if I were you," said the abbot in his mellifluous voice. "Haven't you noticed how he's decorated my little seat here! From that little action you just made, we can learn a lot. The cat is not paying you attention. Why disturb it? If you do, what do you think its reaction will be? Look at its eyes. Are they friendly? Your desire to approach the cat is not what your mind should be listening to. You must wait for it to come to you, and even then, you must think, why should he pay any attention to me? What does the cat want? Humans are no different. You must look and learn, and then your intuition will tell you what you should do. Even in the childish yet very human desire to stroke a cat, there are many lessons to be learnt from our need to dominate."

Reprimanded, Nong looked at the abbot as warily as the cat was looking at him. He had only been there a few moments and already felt as if he had committed a heinous crime. Looking up under his long eyelashes, he muttered, "Sorry." Nong thought to himself, *just keep quiet. Don't move*! Resting on the highly polished floor in front of him was a bright green praying mantis. Relieved to have something to distract him, he watched it rotate its triangular head a full 180 degrees, hunting. The mantis turned its slender body slowly to listen with its only ear, which was located in front of its hind legs for echolocation. "You should keep away from girls too, Mr Mantis, just like the monks," sniggered Nong.

Deep creases fanned out from the corners of the abbot's laughing brown eyes as he purposefully lowered the tone of his voice, adopting a gravelly serious pitch, "So, Sirichai, do you have something to tell me?"

Gan had seen the praying mantis and knew that her son was itching to grab it. Before Nong earned himself another lecture and decided that the whole idea of his staying at the *wat* was terrible, she interjected. "Abbot? Thank you for seeing us today and considering my family's request. My husband and I are very, very grateful, and I'm sorry he couldn't be here today. Am I right that Sirichai must confirm he wants to be here?"

Abbot Anurak observed Nong as he sulked and fidgeted in irritation at having to sit still. Nong was very young and impressionable. A short spell at the *wat* would take him away from the macho Muay Thai world and teach him another different perspective and life skills. Many boxers habitually lived from one competition to the next without considering alternatives. Having learnt Muay Thai himself as a child, the abbot knew it was a difficult life. Having Nong stay at the monastery would not be a problem for them, as there was always work to do. But not wanting to spend the next three weeks reprimanding the lad, it was important he agreed to submit to the monks' lifestyle and programme of activities. The abbot frowned and said, "Well, Sirichai? What do you have to say?"

Nong already knew his answer, as he had made a commitment to Lady Ta-Khian. Unfortunately, at this crucial moment, shock rendered him speechless. Monkey cavorted on the altar located to the left of the abbot. In his left paw, he held a Buddha's hand, a big, yellow, lumpy five-fingered citron fruit, and was making inappropriate gestures. Jumping up and down, baring his incisors, and brandishing the Buddha's hand, most likely stolen from the offering plate, he gesticulated and turned cartwheels. His face beamed with immense satisfaction as he gibbered with delight at having swiped his bounty in broad daylight.

"Boy! What ARE you looking at?" snapped the abbot. "Apart from the altar, which I sincerely hope you're not beholding with what appears to be shock. I can't see anything outside but tree trunks and chickens scratching in the dirt." The abbot was beginning to wonder if the boy was a bit slow. Although a kind man, he did have a strong sense of self-importance and did not like being ignored – especially by a ten-year-old boy. Gan prayed. Now really was not the time for Nong to dream. The abbot was a dreadful gossip. She did not want the whole village to hear the abbot refused to accept Nong because he was incapable of answering a simple question. All he needed to say was yes and that he was grateful. Surely this wasn't beyond her son? Gan pinched Nong's thigh hard enough to make him wince.

Nong had opened his mouth, but no sound came out. His brain had short-circuited. He could hardly say that there was a monkey giving him the finger with a citrus fruit, could he? His mother's pinch jump-started his mind, and he partially admitted the truth of what he saw. To tell a lie to the abbot was unthinkable, but he couldn't mention the misuse of the fruit.

"There was a monkey..."

The abbot leaned in closer to take a good look at Nong's face. "Really, a lone monkey? That's very odd. Monkeys do pass by here, but only in troops. We hear them crashing amongst the foliage, just in time for us to remove the daily offering behind me. But I didn't even see any monkey just now. Did you *Khun* Gan?"

"*Luang Por*, 'venerable father', I wasn't looking in the same direction as Nong, but rather forward, listening to your teachings. There might have been a monkey," replied Gan. She suspected that her son was off with the spirits again, but some conversations were best kept in the family. Like Nong, she would not lie to the abbot, but there was no need to raise suspicions either. Also, a little flattery, never hurt.

"Well?" asked the abbot irritably, his mouth set in a straight line. "I do have other things I need to be getting on with, you know. While I may not find it entirely unpleasant to sit here waiting for your response, there are people who need my time and work that has to be done," he huffed, readjusting his robes and staring down at Nong.

"Please, Abbot," replied Nong.

"Yes, please. Sirichai. You have to say why you're pleased," encouraged Gan with gritted teeth, her eyes rolling in exasperation as she turned away from the abbot so he couldn't see how frustrated she was!

"Yes, please, may I come here to the *wat*."

Abbot Anurak and Gan caught each other's irked

expressions and burst into laughter. The abbot with relief at having concluded the conversation, and Nong's mother at the affirmation of his stay.

"Well, let's hope that's the least convoluted meeting I have to go through today," chuckled the abbot, smiling as Gan thanked him with a bow whilst surreptitiously slapping Nong on the back, to remind him that he also need to do the same.

The abbot watched Gan and Nong walk across the compound, some of the dogs trailing behind until they reached the forest trail. Then he went to inspect the offerings set amidst the pink and white frangipani and orchid flowers in a woven bamboo basket. "That's strange. I'm sure there was a Buddha's hand there earlier," he pondered. "Perhaps there was a monkey, after all."

Chapter Twelve

Nong crammed his faded t-shirts and shorts, toothbrush, soap, two tubes of toothpaste and his mathematics schoolbook in his blue and red Spider-Man rucksack, sighing as he did so. His father was drinking coffee on the porch, waiting to take him to the *wat*. Nong could not close the zip, so he hitched the packed bag onto his left shoulder, leaving it open. Then he went to the kitchen to see if there was any food to be had. At the *wat*, the last meal was at noon, and the monks only ate vegetarian fare. His mother had had to go to the market early and left a breakfast of rice and chicken drumsticks wrapped up in a banana leaf for him. Picking up his meal, he went outside to join his father. He pulled up the small blue stool, sat down and unfolded the bright green leaves.

"You'll be back before you know it," said Joi between sips of his coffee sweetened with condensed milk. "Don't look so concerned. Three weeks are nothing."

Nong chewed his food as slowly as possible, dragging out the time before they had to leave. "Can't I stay here?" he asked. Though he had made a commitment, both at the waterfall and the temple, Nong was still just a boy nervous about being away from his parents and his home.

"Your mother and I are not sending you to the *wat* because we want to get rid of you – we'll miss you! Just think how much better you'll be at boxing thanks to the new skills you'll learn," said Joi, taking another sip, determined to be supportive of what was really Gan's decree.

"Yes," sighed Nong, a resigned expression on his face. There's no point in arguing, he thought, masticating slowly and keeping one eye on where his father was looking while flicking the cucumber slices to the hens scratching beneath the mango tree.

"How are Somchai and the others doing?"

"Great. Somchai won his fight and the others are improving," said Joi, smiling. "But Ram needs to practice his clinching techniques more and improve his upper body strength. He's a long bean and doesn't have enough muscle on him."

"Really, Dad, but he's HUGE," said Nong in disbelief that Ram could possibly train harder.

"Yep. Really," said Joi, thinking of changing the subject. "Sert says hi, by the way. Yesterday he visited the gym looking for you. I let him know you'd be away for a few weeks, and he wished you well. Then I went to meet Abbot Anurak last night to give a donation to the *wat*."

Nong gulped. He knew his parents had very little money and was unsurprised when his father said, "Don't let me hear we've wasted our money. I want you to pay attention to what they say. You know your mother will test you when you get back."

"Test!?"

"Yes, and if you don't do well enough, she's quite capable of sending you back, so listen and remember everything you're told."

"Can you bring me some food?" wheedled Nong, who hated the thought of living off vegetables and donated meals. "Or can I come back and eat here some evenings?"

"I don't want to hear that question again," snapped Joi, looking at his son sternly. Nong's continual attempts to chip away at the rules of the *wat* were beginning to grate on his nerves. "You posed that same question to your mother last night."

"Yes, but the meals are…"

"I know. Now you've finally finished, put the leaf in the bin and take my cup back to the kitchen. Don't forget to wash it and clean your hands and face."

With a shrug of his shoulders, Nong did as he was told, leaving his bag behind while his father went to start the bike. When he returned, his father had already balanced his Spider-Man rucksack on the handlebars and started the engine.

Being the high season, his dad worked extra-long hours and tried to fit in as many private classes as his body could take. The one-on-one classes were where Joi made money. Most of his clients were *farangs* wishing to hone their skills or beginners who needed to learn basic skills. The majority of his individual students were fine, but some were late or turned up smelling of alcohol or unclean. Ram, Somchai,

Mongkut and Panit hated witnessing people disrespect their teacher and put the behaviour down to ignorance. Some of the trainers thought, *just take the money and move on*. The owners had put notices in the reception area to remind people to shower and not drink alcohol before class. Joi, at the end of the morning group sessions, reminded the class that Dragon's Gym put a strong emphasis on family values as well as respect and asked everyone to obey the rules regarding no drugs, cleanliness, obedience and hard work.

"Got everything?" asked Joi, embracing his son. "Come on, it's going to be okay." He cupped Nong's face in his hands, kissing his cheek. He could tell his son was fighting back tears. This was going to be tough for him, but he would pull through. The monks were stern but well-meaning. Last night, he had told Gan he was worried Nong would get bored at the *wat*. But she had stood firm, saying it was too late now, the abbot's permission had been sought and received. The boy was going.

"How about I fix you another few fights for the coming months, and we can see how you get along?" asked Joi. "Let's really make a boxer out of you. Just think of Nai Kanom Tom. He was in jail in Burma for a few years. A few weeks lazing in the forest with some friendly monks is nothing."

Nong straightened his back, pushed out his thin chest to demonstrate to his father how strong he was and managed not to cry by blinking several times.

"Here," Joi added, "you can carry your bag. You're

a strong man. They'll be eager to welcome you at the *wat.*" He walked towards the motorbike with an air of finality.

A pack of dogs greeted their 10 a.m. arrival. The monks would have only just finished meditation practice.

"Let's give it ten minutes," said Joi.

Nong ran to the puppies rolling in the dust, tussling over a twig. "Hello, boy," he said to the large black dog that trotted over to sit at his feet, holding his palms upwards so the dog could see and smell that he had no food.

Joi kicked the dirt as he waited for the monks. Suddenly, he heard a slight tread and a rustle of cloth.

"S*awadee kap,*" said Joi, turning to see who was behind him.

"S*awadee kap,*" said the novice with a broad smile. In his late teens, he was taller than Joi at 1.8 metres and thin. "My name's Bhan. The abbot thought it best I met Nong today. I'll show him around and explain the daily routine of basic reading, writing and memorisation of Buddhist prayers and scriptures."

Bhan had a privileged air. He seemed a bit too rich, a bit too arrogant and a bit too laid back. Noting Bhan's soft-looking hands and overconfident manner, Joi took an instant dislike to him. "How long have you been here?" Joi asked with a calculating look.

"I arrived a month ago. I'll be studying architecture at Chulalongkorn University in a couple of months, and my parents thought it'd be good for me to come.

They're the owners of the five-star Ocean Breezes Hotel chain. You know it, don't you?"

"So sorry, but I don't," replied Joi, although he did. He could picture Bhan driving around Bangkok in fast cars, getting into trouble and being bailed out by his rich parents. "I'm just a boxer. We don't get to stay in many hotels."

"Err. Really? Oh. Is that your boy over there playing with the dogs?" replied Bhan, stepping back a pace. He didn't feel comfortable being assessed by Joi. There was something about the man's piercing gaze he found unnerving.

"Yes, that's Nong. He's on his school holidays and will be staying for a few weeks. My wife and I want him to learn Buddhist teachings and the importance of caring for the forest. Did you know, the monks set up the first school programme to help villagers learn to read and write? His mum attended classes here when she was a child. Over the years, the monks have helped improve the roads and electricity and built a temple and pathway to it. But I guess you wouldn't know that. Why did your family send you to this *wat* when there are so many famous ones you could've gone to in Bangkok?"

"Well, I'm keen to understand how the monks integrate the sense of religion with their environmental work," blurted Bhan. "Also, I thought I could learn something that'll help me in my studies. Eco-architecture is all the rage, and we should all be learning to live with nature rather than work against it.

Don't you agree it makes sense? Think of the flooding in Bangkok and beyond because of what has happened with deforestation."

"Yeah, I get it," replied Joi not just referring to the importance of looking after the forest, but also the lack of truth he perceived in Bhan's body language and heard in the faltering tone of his voice. He decided to give the young man a break. After all, he was supposed to be guiding his son, and he needed to have a positive conversation with the teen. Lightening the mood of their exchange and ending the interview, he shouted, "Nong, come over here and say hello to Bhan. He's going to show you the ropes. No, leave the puppy there. You can see him later." Shaking his head, he smiled at Bhan, saying, "He's a good kid, Bhan. Just can't seem to leave any animal alone!"

Nong put the puppy down and patted its head before walking towards his father. *Why's there a rich kid disguised as a monk next to Dad?* he wondered as he weaved his way through the chickens scratching in the dirt.

"Nong, meet Bhan; Bhan, meet Nong," said Joi. "Now, I've got to go and teach. Nong, here's your rucksack, be good and listen. Do as you're told and remember to focus!" Joi knew he was going to miss his boy and wanted to give him lots of advice, but it wasn't appropriate to do so in front of a stranger. He bit his tongue and opted to give Nong a hug, say goodbye and set off for Dragon's Gym. Waving one last time before turning his bike around, he drove down the red earth road, steering to the left and right to avoid the overhanging vegetation and fallen branches which had been brought down in last night's storm before he finally disappeared in the forest gloom.

"You like Spider-Man, then?" asked Bhan, observing Nong's sad face, still staring in the direction his father had gone.

Nong's shoulders were hunched, and one hand clutched the strap of his rucksack. Its bottom was covered in dust from where he had let it rest on the earth. Bhan felt sorry for the boy. He was just a kid, after all, and it can't be easy being dumped in the forest for a few weeks with monks. Bhan would never have admitted it to the *wat*, but he was glad that Nong had arrived. The boy would help break up the monotonous days. The abbot had said that he was to befriend him and help.

"Come on. Let me show you the penthouse suite where you'll be staying. It's definitely minimalist in style, and there's no maid service. We have to spend a lot of time cleaning not only our rooms but sweeping leaves from the paths. I never get that: we're in the middle of a forest! Our exciting duties include polishing the temple wood and dusting too. But I guess there's something to repeating the same task and staying in the forest. When I arrived, I couldn't sit still for five minutes, and now my meditation practice has really come along. I don't feel the need to constantly talk and fill in the gaps in conversations. I can control my thoughts a lot better too. Saying that, just now, I lost it. Your dad's a bit intense, isn't he?"

"He's my father," replied Nong with a shrug as they trudged uphill along the narrow track through the tall bamboo. His dad was not a big talker. Nong hadn't understood half of what Bhan had said. His words were just hammering his head like an Asian koel, a large, long-tailed cuckoo with distinctive red eyes. "How old are you?" asked Nong, thinking that perhaps Bhan was much younger than he appeared.

"Nineteen," laughed Bhan. "Well, aren't you like your dad? Nice and chatty. What sort of question is that? Don't you want to know what you're going to be doing over the next few weeks?"

Bhan remembered when he had arrived. One of the hotel company's black limousines had driven him. Not ever having been to the forest before, his parents had no idea that the driver would only have to leave him two kilometres from the *wat*. Bhan had had to trudge up the steep forest path, following the hand-carved signposts, which seemed to be pointing forever upwards as he made his own way. Right from the start, he felt he had received a lesson in humility. His father had been too busy in a meeting to see him off. *Bit different to Nong's father*, he reflected.

Nong smiled at the older boy to signal his interest in learning more. But really, he wasn't curious at all. As far as he was concerned, he was here to follow orders, and there wasn't a lot he could say about staying at the *wat*. He was interested in whether they had Wi-Fi, but that was about it, and food. He cared a lot about the food.

"OK, great. First of all, let me explain what we get up to every day. This is seven days a week, mind you. No hanging out at the beach on our day off because we don't get one. The idea is that we're humble and think about how we can relieve the suffering of our fellow human beings. Got it? Every day, we walk through villages to collect donations for the temple. We eat our first meal at 8 a.m. and a second at 11, as we cannot eat after midday. After the three weeks, Nong, you can tell the head monk you've completed your time and pray for the temple to remember you before returning to the laity. Basically, three weeks of work for a lifetime of blessings!" said Bhan, laughing. "What do you think of that?"

"Boxing's harder," replied Nong as he struggled to believe how dense the bamboo was on either side of the path. It reminded him of the bamboo he saw martial artists swing on in action movies. The wooded ring stems were straight with a brownish-green smooth surface. The largest reached up to 30 metres in height and 35 centimetres in diameter. The younger shoots were a blackish purple, and the blades seven to 10 centimetres long. The upper surface of the sheaths was covered with stiff, gold and brownish hairs, while the under-surface was glossy. Nong loved eating young bamboo when it was soft and green. Gan would peel off the black leaves covered in tiny hairs until the white meat was visible. She would cut the small ones into finger-sized pieces, and the family would eat them as a vegetable with sauces. The larger pieces would be used as an ingredient in a main course dish like *pad ped moo sai naw mai* (sliced pork with bamboo shoots in red chilli sauce) with fresh hot rice. Nong's belly rumbled as he thought about his mum's cooking.

Bhan continued chatting, pointing out individual trees and sharing snippets about life at the *wat*. Nong thought he sounded a bit like a cricket chirping. Not really annoying like the chainsaw squeal of cicadas, but a persistent noise, nevertheless.

It took less than ten minutes to arrive at the accommodation area. There were seven wooden boxed rooms on stilts dotted around the small forest clearing. Each room had a six-stepped wooden ladder leading up to a small veranda on which was a simple bench. Nong would discover that each room was furnished with a futon, bedsheets, a simple chair and desk for writing, a small electric fan, torch and textbooks about the life and teachings of Buddha. Hanging on a hand-carved wooden peg to the left of the hut entrance door was a padlock and key. The monks always had to secure their rooms from curious monkeys who would steal anything they could get their paws on.

Situated at the perimeter of the clearing opposite to the end of the path they had just travelled up was a white-painted and tiled outhouse with two lavatories and two showers. Outside the outhouse was a large metal sink and draining board, next to which was a two-metre by two-metre cupboard made from bamboo that housed the monks' cleaning materials: twig brooms, washing and cleaning cloths, buckets, soap and mops. The outhouse was swept, scrubbed and mopped by the monks in rotation, and it was spotless. Everyone was expected to clean their rooms daily.

Bhan led Nong to the smallest of the rooms. Copying the older boy, he slipped off his flip-flops, leaving them underneath the lowest rung of the hand-hewn steps, and ascended barefoot, looking around and trying to catch a glimpse of his neighbours. Bhan took down the key from the peg and opened the door, shoving it gently with his shoulder as he did so. Nong peered around his waist to see inside.

The room had no decoration apart from a framed photograph of an elderly monk. There were small windows that opened outwards on each side of the room and faded brown curtains that barely reached the windowsills. Each aperture let in a beam of light and had a mosquito grill that slid back. The walls of the hut were made with reeds from the local lakes, ponds and rivers. On constructing the *wat*, the monks had insisted on the use of natural building materials with minimal environmental impact and were biodegradable.

Bhan explained to Nong that in Thailand, this traditional building craft had been common for millennia and was still the predominant building technique in certain regions. The monks were teaching him how to use reeds as a low-carbon contemporary building material. "Here, Nong," he said. "Take a look out the window, and you can see the hut I'm building over there."

Nong's eyes followed where Bhan pointed. On the other side of the clearing, he could see a wooden box resembling a four-poster bed leaning to one side. Similar in size and the exact shape of his own, it was built on wooden stilts. The framework for the veranda had yet to be built, let alone the walls made.

"Do you think you'll finish it before you leave?" Nong asked.

"I will with your help," Bhan replied, grinning at Nong in the knowledge that he could hardly refuse to lend a hand.

Nong decided to ignore him. Exhaling loudly, he let out a deep sigh. "How long do I have to stay in this room every day? Can I get Wi-Fi?"

"Hey, Nong. It's not so bad," said Bhan. "We're not in the dark ages, you know, but there's no Wi-Fi. The point is contemplation, not contacting friends the whole time. Look, I've got a lot more reasons to be on the phone than you. I've a great girlfriend who is smart and good-looking. What are the chances of her still being around when I get out? Don't suppose you've a girlfriend, eh Nong?"

"No!" said Nong fiercely. "I'm going to be a famous boxer. I don't have time for a girlfriend. Not until I've won several Lumpinee belts, anyway. Then maybe my dad will let me."

"Whoa! Probably for the best. I've had a few girlfriends. All of them left me," said Bhan, nudging Nong with a wink.

Nong decided it was best to ignore Bhan's last

remark. More important matters weighed on his mind. Nong had seen the monks in the early mornings collecting alms for the day. His mother would always be up at first light with her donation of boiled rice and vegetables on behalf of the family. He imagined that he was going to have to trudge through the village in a robe with bare feet, rain or shine, like the monks. "Do you get enough food every day?"

"Sure. It's easy! I get more than enough food, so will you, shorty. People do put some really weird shit in the alms bowls, such as paper money and cans of Coke, so there may be some bad food days. But the monks are not sanctimonious. They've genuinely done a lot of good for the people around here. I can promise you that no-one'll look down on you when you collect the daily offerings. Who knows, by the end of your stay, you'll have learnt something? Now leave your bag, you can sort that out later. Let's go eat. It's coming close to noon."

Unlike at many monasteries, the monks ate together in an open-sided pavilion or *sala.* At times, people from the village would join if they wished to petition the monks or natter about a matter. Today, the *wat* had no visitors, and as the boys ascended the steps, they saw six monks sitting quietly eating their meals with their hands directly from each of their alms bowls. Abbot Anurak returned Bhan and Nong's bows with a smile and waved his right hand at the space by his side, indicating that they were to sit near him. The other monks gave barely perceptible nods. In a hushed tone,

Bhan, who had stopped off to pick up his alms bowl on the way to the *sala,* removed the saffron cloth covering to reveal what was inside. It was a hotchpotch of boiled rice, sweets, a purple plastic frog, cooked vegetables, roasted nuts and fruits. Bhan took the frog and hid it inside his robe. "A gift from my kid brother," he muttered. As it was Nong's first day, a meal had been organised for him of rice, vegetables and pulses.

"This afternoon, Nong, I want you to clean your room and think about what it means to stay here. Then we can discuss your thoughts later," said the abbot. Turning to address Bhan, he asked, "Have you told Nong about his duties?"

"Yes, of course," said Bhan, "and I've explained what we do during the day."

"Well, that is not really the same now is it?" responded the abbot. "What I or the brothers do is very different to what we expect Nong to achieve. I don't think that Nong is going to spend his days completing your hut for you. As that is not why he is here."

Nong sniggered. "Got your number," he said under his breath.

Putting the handmade flat-based steel *hua sua* (tiger head) alms bowl to one side, the abbot considered Nong for a moment before speaking. "Nong, each day you'll attend study classes and aid us in our work in support of the local communities. What is involved in the classes will become clear over time. For now, I'd like you to return to your room, clean it, shower and be back within an hour. We need to hold a short ceremony so you can be dressed appropriately in a robe. The robe has three parts. Given his interest in fashion, Bhan knows that we have not updated our look for twenty-five centuries," he said with a gentle smile to a blushing Bhan before continuing. "You'll be pleased to hear that the robes are all purchased by the local people and donated. Like many forest temples we use the heartwood of the jackfruit tree as dye. In the time of Buddha, the robes were made from discarded pieces of cloth that may have been chewed by rats or stray dogs and were typically covered in filth. The monks would wash them, cutting away the frayed sections and make patched robes from them. This afternoon we will first wrap the *sabong*, or inner cloth, around your waist. This cloth will reach down to your knees and is held up by a fold, a tuck or a cord belt. Next comes the *ungsa*, the upper cloth, which goes around your torso and shoulders and is like a one-shouldered waistcoat that has two pockets and is joined on the left side by tying tags. The outer robe is called a *civara* or *jivorn*. The *jivorn* is the biggest piece of cloth and is passed around the body with the two ends rolled together. The roll is taken over the left shoulder and beneath the left arm so that the end can be held in the left hand or held between the arm and the body. Lastly, there is the *sanghati,* the outer cloth, which is folded in a particular way in a long rectangle and hung over the left shoulder. This cloth is only for ordained monks. Outside the monastery, both our shoulders and arms are covered, but inside, the robe is worn so the right arm is exposed. Any questions?"

Nong had many questions but decided the best course of action was to cut the conversation short. “Not now, abbot. No, I don’t,” he replied with a slight bow of his head.

“Good. Brothers,” said the abbot in a louder voice, “may I introduce you to Sirichai, who is happy for us to call him by his nickname of Nong. He’s a local boy. For those of you who appreciate Muay Thai and sometimes take a VERY slow walk past the training grounds when the sparring sessions are on, you should know Nong already. He’s the head trainer Joi’s son. Most of you have met his mother, Gan, as she’s an active member of the community. His parents have asked us to ordain Nong, and this afternoon, the ceremony will take place. Nong, you need to change and rest assured that you follow in a long line of famous Lumpinee champions. National champions and even world champions were once novices, such as Pairojnoi Sor Siamchia! Ahh, I see our visitors have arrived. Welcome.”

Nong turned around to see the visitors. Standing in the doorway were Somchai, Ram, Mongkut, Panit, Sert and his mother. Nong stared in disbelief, his mouth hanging open. He started to get up but sat back down, feeling the eyes of the abbot on the back of his head.

“Your first lesson is we do not turn our backs on the Buddha, my child. Now, off with you. I’ll see you later,” said the abbot, his mouth twitching as he struggled to be stern.

Gan opened out her arms to Nong, who grabbed her

around the waist, breathing in the clean scent of lemongrass soap. Gan asked, “You didn’t really believe we would just leave you here and go, did you? Today is a day of celebration, and you get to dress up as a prince. Come on, let’s get you changed. I’ve brought your lunch with me.”

They headed back to Nong’s room, which he could tell was his by the rucksack on the veranda. *Lucky the monkeys didn’t take it,* he thought. His boxing brothers waited outside as his mother laid out a white t-shirt and trousers for him while he ate the unexpected lunch, grateful his parents had decided to bring him something after all. When he finished eating, his mother handed him a towel and a bar of soap, instructing him to take a quick shower and come straight back.

“Run, Nong. Run!” shouted Somchai, who was lying in the shade of a coconut palm. “We need to get this over and done with so we can go and have a nap before training.”

Still damp from the rudimentary shower that consisted of a hose with a shower head fixed to it, he trotted back to his room and changed.

With heads bowed, Nong and the boxers prayed, fidgeted and occasionally stifled yawns as the monks chanted sacred texts. Nong’s newly shaved head felt strange and sensitive to the forest breezes. He resisted the strong urge to stroke his scalp as he could feel his mother’s falcon eyes observing him. Finally, the ceremony finished, and he was handed his new monks’ robes. The entire ceremony, the shaved head, and the orange robes signified that he had left behind the petty concerns of his daily life. When in the monastery, he would be able to wear his robe in a more informal way, leaving the right shoulder bare and tucking the upper cloth under his armpit. It was cool in the forest at night, and there was no heating in his room. Gan said she had been told by the monks that the robes were suitable for any situation and would keep him warm and protect him from winds. Also, she had pointed out they could be spread on the ground or a chair to sit on, and he would not have to think about what to wear for a whole three weeks.

The ceremony lasted just over an hour. Nong was glad to have his friends and family present. He understood that his father could not be there, given the pressures of his work, but he missed the silent force of his strength. During the ceremony, he watched the ginger cat under the altar. Tiger also lay nearby with her huge head resting on her massive paws, regarding him with a softness in her eyes that he had never witnessed before. The sun shone on Tiger's noble face, illuminating the hidden specks of gold in her black-rimmed eyes and timeless, fire-opal depths. In his heart, he knew that she was conveying a sense of pride and support as she oversaw the ceremony and observed the movements of the abbot like a majestic queen, verifying that the members of her court followed the correct protocols.

As the abbot concluded the ceremony by leading the final chant, Tiger gave a twitch of her tail and showed her fangs, wrinkling her nose in the process. Tiger's huntress gaze locked on Bhan. Nong felt the power in her intense stare and wondered how Bhan's skin was not burning. Slowly, she turned her head to Nong, her eyes becoming calm. He gave a barely perceptible nod to show he understood the warning and to express his gratitude. After shooting a final snarl in Bhan's direction, she lay down on one side, stretching to her full length, and started to lick one paw. Her dusky, rose-pink tongue, with its numerous small, sharp, rear-facing papillae, caressed her fur as she faded into a grey shadow and then disappeared.

* * *

The small windup alarm clock startled Nong awake at 3 a.m. Momentarily confused as to where he was, he lay listening to the sounds outside his room, where small mammals crept and wild pigs rooted in the undergrowth. The fresh green scents reminded him that he was not far away from home. Last night, he had forgotten to close the curtains, and from his bed, he could see a collared scops owl perched on the branch of the frangipani tree. Its facial disk, a muted yellow with faint, darker, concentric markings, was lit by the silver moonlight. In the owl's greenish and dusk-yellow beak hung a lifeless mouse. He heard the loud call of a Gould's frogmouth ring across the forest with a "weeow-wah," its cry melding with the sounds of the forest. A binturong, also known as a bearcat, chuckle as it ate a wild fig.

Gan had left the rusted little alarm clock for Nong. Bleary-eyed, he ran his hand over his smooth bald scalp and brow ridge, recalling yesterday's shaving ceremony and Sert's efforts not to laugh. Nightmarish images of the *sabong* falling into a pool of material on the floor had plagued his sleep. He roused himself as he mentally prepared to do battle with his monk's garments. In the dark, he grabbed the torch from the scratched wooden desk and ran down to the shower wrapped in a towel with his shorts on, clutching his toothbrush and toothpaste.

Still damp from the shower, he made his seventh attempt to dress, cursing and swearing at the coarse material's refusal to remain in place. The *sabong* was supposed to stay up by passing a thin woven belt and two long cords around the waist. The cords should be tied in a bow at the front. But somehow, the saffron cloth kept shifting, slipping and sliding around his body. Nong stood still. He breathed in deeply, counted one and then paused. Then two, and then paused until he reached ten. Following the advice that his father had given him on how to calm his mind and fight any rising sense of panic. As he slowed his heart down to relax, he cast his mind back to when he and the other village children visited the monks, curious to know their customs. They would hide behind the trees or sit in the branches amongst the dense foliage. Once, they spied a monk working on moving fallen tree branches who had removed his robe and *ungsa,* thinking he was alone.

Much to their delight, and the monk's horror, his *sabong* fell around his ankles, leaving him totally naked. It was only when their shrieks and howls of laughter echoed around the clearing that the embarrassed monk realised they were even there. Nong recalled the monk making every attempt to preserve his dignity by pretending he had not heard them as he recovered his clothing from the forest floor and walked stiffly back in the direction of the *wat*, leaves and twigs sticking to the cloth. The children followed behind, impersonating his stilted movements and clutching at the waistbands of their shorts.

Within the confines of his small room, he started to perspire, becoming more and more frustrated. The faint sound of chanting could be heard as he continued to struggle. Not wanting to miss the first morning of prayer, he tied his robes as best he could, grabbing the surplus materials in both hands. He managed to keep the robes from falling as he hurried down the path but arrived five minutes before the end of morning prayers, looking like he had been mugged by a set of bed sheets. The monks ignored his dishevelled state as he bowed and knelt down at the back of the room, clutching his robes. Nong stared at the wooden floor while the monks finished their chanting, not raising his gaze even as the monks collected their alms bowls and hung them around their necks. When he did raise his eyes, he saw the abbot had stayed cross-legged on the dais with his palms facing upwards in his lap, radiating authority. He beckoned Nong, his expression stern.

Nong uncrossed his legs and struggled to stand by bending his knees in front of him and pushing himself up onto the soles of his feet. With mouse steps, he scurried to the abbot, bowed and gave a greeting while grasping the ends of the robes in his fists. His face had crumpled by the morning's horrors and the expectation that a lecture was forthcoming.

"Nong, *mai b'pen ria*. If your robe falls off, pick it up and put it back on. How people react to your robe slipping should not move your own sense of balance. Think of this robe as a piece of material that is worn to support our lives, nothing more. It takes a long time to learn how to sit on the floor, stand up, and make a flawless bow to a senior monk in the robes. These rules we will teach you during your stay here. You will also learn how to move modestly, neatly and politely, and you will not be collecting alms until your last week here or until we are satisfied you can conduct yourself in public. You need to walk slowly, keep a neutral expression with your eyes downcast and be careful not to brush up against anyone. Being young and short, you'll have no problem walking at the right speed, unlike Bhan. Here, let me fix that robe for you!" In a matter of seconds, Nong was presentable. "Now," said the abbot, "I have work to do, and breakfast is at 8 a.m. I want you to go back to your room and practice, practice, practice. When you take off the robe, pay attention to how it has been put on. It is no more difficult than walking back down a road you have walked. Do you understand me?" he asked, waving his hand to signal the end of the conversation.

"Yes, Abbot," muttered Nong, annoyed that he had not done better on his first day. *How could such a simple task as putting on three pieces of cloth be SO difficult?*

The first few days at the *wat* were spent learning the rules of interaction with the lay people and other monks. Nong swept and polished the floor of his room until it was spotless and cleaned the shared washroom facilities. He attended prayer sessions and meditation practice. By the end of his second week, he was ready to go on his first alms collection walk in the village. He saw Bhan during the group sessions but hardly at any other time. *So much for his 'I'll guide you,'* thought Nong as he wondered about the older boy and what it was that Tiger had warned him about.

While dressing carefully, he reminded himself *mai b'pen ria* as he tied each section of the robe. On the morning of his first alms collection, in his last week, at 5 a.m., he caught up with Bhan while they walked the twenty minutes downhill to the largest village. As they trudged through the lush forest, birds called to one another, and the occasional sharp cries from a troop of monkeys reverberated in the thick canopy. Dawn would not break for another hour, so they lit their way with torches. Even the insects had yet to make themselves heard at the early hour, unlike the cockerels at the monastery, which sporadically serenaded them. Two black dogs and a large white one with their tails wagging and tongues lolling accompanied the monks as they too hoped to find breakfast in the village. Nong was excited about everyone seeing him in his monk's robes and kept checking to see if everything was as it should be while ensuring that he walked with the correct posture and speed, which caused him to lag behind the group. He was last in line behind Bhan.

"Nong," said Bhan in a low voice as he slowed down his pace to create a distance between him and the monk ahead. "Tell me a bit more about your dad. My relatives have boxing connections, you know. Some of the military guys who run the boxing circuit in Bangkok are family friends. Maybe I could swing it so you can go and train in a camp in the capital where the real champions come from," offered Bhan. "What do you say?"

Nong's eyes shone eagerly. "Bangkok's the dream! But my father's the best coach. He was the southern champion of Thailand and fought at Lumpinee. He trains my boxing brothers, and they've won the big titles. Without understanding why, Nong felt the need to defend his family and friends and boast. The conversation was making him increasingly uncomfortable, and the senior monk in front of Bhan had already turned around to give them a stern warning look. On his first day on the alms procession, Nong was trying hard to remember the rules about comportment, keeping his eyes downcast and trying to move in a measured and considered way.

Bhan's mind, on the other hand, was elsewhere. He was thinking about the money he needed at university.

His parents funded him, but he lived way beyond his allowance. Owning a percentage of Nong's fighting purse could help in the future. Bhan softened the tone of his voice, adding a more conciliatory note and changing tack. "Nong. I'm sure your dad was a huge champion in his time, and I'd love to hear more. But tell me, does he have the connections to get the big deals, the sponsorship opportunities? Can he make it happen? Get the big brands like Nike, the TV deals? I mean, who sponsors your so-called brothers? What major firms? I bet they still live on the camp. I have the right connections to make it happen. Don't you want to make real money?"

"I dunno. You'd have to ask my dad," replied Nong, hitching up his robe to avoid it catching on a gnarled tree root.

Bhan continued blathering on about the possibilities for Nong's future and how he could make a difference. But Nong had fallen as silent as the lichen-covered tree trunks. The wind had dropped as they walked through a grove of the oldest trees, where their branches touched one another, brambles and ferns entwined at their buttresses. The sun was not yet up and moonlight lit the uppermost leaves, filtering through the canopy, silvering the forest floor and stream. The still puddles, which the hot rays of the sun would dry by mid-morning, resembled mirrored stepping stones.

Bhan broke the silence. "Well, I suppose you're just a kid right now, at eleven. But in four years' time, you could have your first fight at Lumpinee Stadium.

Fifteen is old enough. Don't you think you need sponsors?"

"Shhhhh!" said the Phra Richard, the *farang* monk who was considered the most devoted of the forest monks. "Stop talking or go home!" His normally serene and earnest expression was stern and his forehead furrowed.

"But it wasn't….!" replied Nong.

"No more! Enough!" hissed Phra Richard, turning around 180 degrees to face them while holding on to his robe to ensure the abrupt movement did not alter their place. "This is the last time. As it is, I'm going to report you to the abbot."

Normally, his face was as smooth as a pebble, but in the fading dark, Nong saw Phra Richard's face had folded up into creases as deep as the cracks on a tembusu tree trunk. Nong reorganised his expression into what he considered to be his best representation of humility.

Crestfallen, ashamed and determined not to give Phra Richard any further reasons to castigate him, he took a few steps back from Bhan and kept his eyes fixed on the trail until they reached the outskirts of the village. There, they would proceed in single file, holding out their steel bowls to the lay people kneeling outside shops, homes, bars and hotels, ready with their offerings of food, drinks and occasional envelopes with money.

The days passed with meditation practice, alms collection and cleaning. As he lay in bed, he dreamt about fighting in front of an enormous crowd and the trappings of success. *Bhan is right,* he thought. *Somchai and the others have won major fights, but they still share a room, and all they do is work. For what?* As he replayed Bhan's words they burrowed into his beliefs, causing doubt. But his confidence came to the fore, and he pushed the negative thoughts about his father aside and replayed the monks' teachings about the forest and relief from suffering.

One night, in his room, his phone glowed. Picking it up, he saw a message from Sert. The boys had texted infrequently as Joi had told them to let Nong focus on his studies. In his wider circle of friends, the same message had been spread in the community. Tomorrow morning, he would leave the monastery. Sert was asking if they could meet in the early evening. Over the weeks, he had begun to think of the forest as a good friend, and he thought back to the rock pool and the last time he swam there. It seemed a lifetime ago since the conversation with Lady Ta-khian. The monks' lessons helped him understand what the tree spirit meant by *Tham lai pa khue ahm lai chat* — 'to destroy the forest is to destroy life.' Pulling up the rough cotton bedsheet for comfort, he cocooned himself in a tight ball. "Goodnight, Lady Ta-khian," he whispered, eventually dropping off to sleep.

Still tired from a fitful night's sleep, Nong checked and re-checked every fold and tie in his robe, then brushed it until it was immaculate. Beneath his room, the dogs sheltered in the shade. He could hear the puppies playing tug-of-war over a piece of dirty blue rag near the steps leading up to his room. Resisting the temptation to bring his favourite white and black puppy upstairs had been more difficult than following the behaviour guides set out by the monks. He often called to the spirit animals during the night but always slept alone. After that first pre-dawn alms walk down to the villages, he had begged Tiger to come, but she did not show a whisker. His eyes had searched the temple eaves and vegetation for glimpses of a tail or paw, and he fretted.

"What have I done?" he worried. Confused by their absence, he went over and over every detail of his last sighting of her, questioning if he had been disrespectful in any way but finding no reasons for her silence. Finally satisfied with his robe, he made a wish that Tiger would appear before the afternoon ceremony.

A woman's voice called up the stairs, "Nong, come on down, let us see you."

He looked out of the window and saw his parents smiling up at him.

"Coming," Nong cried. Picking up the folds of his robe, he charged down the wooden steps, almost slipping on the humid wood that had not yet been dried by the sun. He hugged his parents simultaneously, luxuriating in their warmth and presence.

"How's my little monk?" Joi asked, stepping back to better look at his boy.

"Good. Good," said Nong. He really was. Good and ready to leave. He had completed his time at the *wat* without any real mishaps, and it had been lonely at times. He desperately wanted to be at home. "Don't cry, Mother," pleaded Nong in anguish, seeing the tears rolling down his mother's cheeks. "What's wrong?"

"Nothing. Quite the opposite," Gan replied, regaining her composure, wiping her face with the back of her hand. "My love. Why are you wearing your robes? Come. Your father will help you remove them. You have to dress in your white shirt and trousers!"

Joi lifted Nong's chin so he could better look into his eyes. "How have you been?" Satisfied with what he saw, he patted Nong on the back, pushing him gently in the direction of the steps. "Let's get you sorted."

Gan hung the handles of her large handmade grass-woven bag, containing a spare white T-shirt and trousers, over the stair pillar and walked to where the puppies rolled and nipped one another. Each play-fighting puppy tried to gain possession of the rag. "Let's take a look at you," she said, not forgetting to check where the mother was and spotting her sleeping in the distance. Gan guessed by their size they were around three months old—a good time to start learning to interact with humans. Looking around the clearing, she counted how many offspring the worn-out-looking mother had. There were eight in total and they were starting to look thin. The pups had stopped drinking their mother's milk, and while the monks provided food, they also needed to fend for themselves and take trips out in the forest to trot off to the villages to seek scraps.

She went to retrieve a towel from her bag, then wrapped it around the squirming black and white pup. She held the warm furry bundle in both her hands to get a good look at its round face. The puppy tried to lick her, so she held it further away, remarking, “Well, you look healthy enough. You’re coming home with us.” Gan remembered the promise she had made, and while they could do without a dog, her son deserved a reward. *It’ll be good for Nong to care for something other than himself, too,* she thought. Removing Nong’s extra clothes, she put the towel in the bottom of the bag and carefully placed the puppy inside. As he tried to clamber out, she stroked and petted him. Eventually, he settled down and lay on one side to chew on the cloth. *He’ll be asleep in a minute, just like Nong*, thought Gan, smiling secretively and wondering what on earth was keeping her husband and Nong. “Hurry up,” she called up the steps. “We’re going to be late for the ceremony!”

Abbot Anurak had instructed Nong on the protocol for his formal departure from the monastery and the receiving of a blessing from the monks. He needed to bow down in front of the monks, saying: “I am now a layman.” Also, he had to return his saffron robe and recite passages from the scripture. Once the ceremony had been completed to the satisfaction of the abbot, he would be permitted to join his family and friends in the pavilion, where they waited near a table of offerings.

A bald, jubilant Nong joined his family and friends in the pavilion, which, despite the breeze entering from the open side and the whirring of electric fans, still managed to be stifling with the humidity. His boxing brothers, after commenting on his lack of eyebrows and hair, pummelled him on the back and joked that he would only be capable of skipping for a few minutes tomorrow. His parents chatted with the monks and the extended family members, as did the trainers who had come from the gym on this special day. Impatient to leave, Nong went to retrieve the handwoven bag he had seen his mother carrying earlier. She had left it under a white cotton-covered chair she sat on near the offering table. He lifted the bag, which was surprisingly heavy. Putting his hand inside without looking, he felt around to see if perhaps there was a food box. He had eaten only rice, vegetables, crisps and chocolate for the last few weeks, and he was desperate for his mother's hearty cooking. "Ouch," he shouted, letting the bag fall to the floor. "Something bit me." Silence fell like a stone, crushing all conversations. The bag had tipped onto its side, and everyone apart from Gan watched in horror as it shook and jerked about. Trying to structure a sound reason in her head as to why she had brought the puppy into the pavilion and not wanting to shout, Gan did not say a word. A yelp from the bag was followed by the appearance of a small pink nose and a puppy's face.

Abbot Anurak glanced at Gan, raising his voice above the shrieks of laughter. "It seems that Nong has been blessed with a memory from the *wat*. Normally, we humble monks repeat the teachings of Buddha. But it appears MOTHER nature has decided something more needed to be given!" he said, grinning in a very obvious way at a shamefaced Gan.

"Ahh, a mother's love. It knows no bounds. Does it, Nong?" said Somchai teasingly. "Go on, pick up the puppy. It's yours."

Nong blushed as he gathered the puppy into his arms and looked at its cute face and bright eyes. Murmuring into his fur, he held onto it with one arm and bent down to pick up the bag and the contents, which had spilt out. Then he went to his mother, who stood red-faced and embarrassed, talking to the abbot. Nong whispered into the warm bundle that he was going to call him Sam.

"Nong," said the abbot, his wise eyes twinkling. "I was just sharing your *wat* report. You've been a good pupil, although I hear from some of the others that you have difficulty concentrating, and Bhan tells me you got him into trouble with some of the senior monks by talking! But it takes two to talk now, doesn't it? Go now and get back home before your canine charge has a mishap!"

Everyone gave their bows and thanks, leaving donations on the side commensurate with what they could afford to give. The monks took their leave and wished the group well.

"Follow me, family," said Joi, pointing to a nearby frangipani tree, "I've parked over there."

Nong, Joi and his mother squashed up onto the motorbike like seeds in a custard apple. Nong sat in front of his father, who drove with Gan sitting behind him, her arms wrapped around his waist. His son held onto the puppy with one arm while it rested its oversized front paws on the handlebars, mouth open and small ears flapping in the wind.

Chapter Thirteen

EXHAUSTION. Swosh, swosh, swosh. The monotonous sound of the skipping ropes hitting the mats echoed in the early morning. Over the last few years, Nong had grown in stature and skill, but the training sessions never got any easier. To win, he had to push himself. Every. Single. Time. Now fifteen, he had over fifty fights under his belt and had not lost for twenty matches. He was also popular with audiences. In his amateur career, he had lost three fights, fought with courage, was clever as well as skilful and, thanks to his long legs, strength and speed, had an exceptional double left kick. That same left kick had even bested Somchai whilst they sparred, though his friend was ten years older.

One mistake could leave him injured and unable to continue in this life he had fought so hard for. In the ring, he was courageous and smart, always wanting to win, was never lazy and never missed a day off school, even after a fight. His days of making kites with Sert from plastic bags, twigs and odd ends of rope tied together were behind him.

Unlike the children at school, he had little time for leisure. The closest he had come to a fair was the celebration of Children's Day, *Wan Deck*, at the school on the second Saturday of January every year. Before the fun activities, such as shooting ranges where you could win soft toys, dancing competitions and musical performances, they all sang the school song and were reminded that "Children are the future of the nation. If the children are intelligent, the country will be prosperous." Many non-profit and cultural institutions as well as the military, organised special events and let children in for half price or even for free on this day. The children loved the free treats, trips and sweets. It was the only chance that Nong had of visiting a zoo or an amusement park. He would spend ages at the big cat enclosures, marvelling at their athletic beauty, until one of the teachers hurried him along to join the rest of the class.

His favourite ways of relaxing were still swimming in the rock pools, fishing and beach football. Increasingly, he had nothing in common with his school friends and saw little of Sert. As his profile grew, so did the pressure to move to a Bangkok gym. Money. It was always there. The gamblers shouted their advice while his boxing gym brothers sought to protect him from their insults and barrage of comments by blocking off their approaches with their bodies and engaging them in banter to distract them. Joi believed two fights had gone against Nong on points because of the influence of the local gambling circuit at one of the stadiums where he fought. Joi had been furious, shouting at the judges, who refused to acknowledge him, as they gathered up their belongings, rushing to exit the stadium before the protests of the crowd at the judges' decision escalated.

All his opponents were from poor backgrounds. No-one was on a diet packed with beef. Rich meat diets were for rich kids. Unlike other gyms, where curious young boxers started experimenting with cannabis and alcohol and harder drugs, Dragon's Gym was clean. Joi kept a watchful eye on both *farangs* and locals alike, questioning any out-of-character behaviour or mood swings.

Nong focused on his boxing, while his mother was supportive but concerned. She had no illusions about the hard life a boxer led and reminded him it was not too late to change his mind. However wise Gan's words, Nong still dreamt of being a champion and could not be dissuaded from following the path his heart was set on. The hardest part of training was always making his weight class.

Nong was ready for his first regional title at the Chiang Mai Boxing Stadium in the Santitham area, about one kilometre to the north of the Old City's Chiang Phueak Gate. The stadium was one of the largest outside Bangkok and purpose-built. It staged professional Muay Thai fights three evenings per week and had hosted famous boxers such as Gussakon Noi, Mahamonkon and Tanapet. Seats at this venue came with higher price tags than the other boxing stadiums in Chiang Mai.

The serious pose on the billing post had taken Nong ages to perfect and involved much ridicule from Somchai and Ram, who teased him mercilessly about his champion face pose. They said he looked more constipated than fierce. Nong spent hours practising in front of the mirror at home until satisfied, he had managed to pull his features into some semblance of a confident expression that resembled the visages of his heroes. Even his father, on viewing the photo on Somchai's phone, said it wasn't bad. Gan had asked the Dragon's Gym receptionist to print the image. To Nong's embarrassment, it now hung on the kitchen wall in a bamboo frame. Thankfully, his friends rarely entered their kitchen.

Lucy had packed the saline drip for after the weigh-in to rehydrate Nong and booked the flights to Chiang Mai, for which the promoter would reimburse her. The promoter would get all the ticket sales, any filming rights, and sponsorship, plus profits from the bar. Even if he became a professional, Nong would earn a pittance compared to two-fist boxers or MMA fighters. Not only was the purse smaller, but the prize money was also often divided amongst many people—the trainers, the gym, the fighter's family, the promoters—the list continued. The fighter received a very small portion of the prize money. In Nong's case, the money would be divided between his gym, which covered his costs, and his family. For some fighters, the temptation to accept money from gamblers was real, as the tips they gave could be more than the actual fight purse.

Somchai and Ram would accompany Nong but not Joi because he could not afford to miss his private classes. Two days before the fight, they would catch an early flight to Chiang Mai, as it was more than a twenty-hour drive by car. On arrival, they would make sure that Nong could do any necessary running for water loss and not miss the weigh-in. Like all fighters, Nong would try to get to the lowest possible weight at which he could still perform at an optimum level. Nong packed his sweat suit not because it helped him burn fat but because it caused him to sweat profusely. As he was already whippet lean, he would not lose up to four kilos in a thirty-minute run like some of the bigger boxers.

The sun had not risen when his father woke him with a shake. The forest was still a squid-ink black, the moon a silver half-coffee mug stain in the sky, and the nocturnal animals had not yet gone to bed. Nong rubbed his eyes and rolled onto his side, hauling himself into an upright position to look at his father perched on the side of his bed. "What time is it?" he asked, stretching and yawning.

"4 a.m.," replied Joi, the naked light bulb giving him a ghostly appearance.

"Five minutes more," Nong pleaded, moving to lie back down again.

"Come on, Nong. Your flight from Phuket leaves at eight. Lucy will be here in half an hour. Get up, Champ!" said his father, shaking him gently. "You need to get moving."

"Are you still staying here?" asked Nong grumpily, uncomfortable that for the first time, he would not have his father in his corner, Joi shielding him like a rock from the crowd. Along with the audience, he applauded and gave encouragement, cheering every strike Nong made by raising his hands and leading the shouts. It was always his father's cries of support that he heard above all others, and he dreaded his absence.

"You're going to do great without me. Better, in fact, with Ram and Somchai. There's very little they don't know about boxing," said Joi. He dearly wished he could go with his boy, but there was nothing he could do. "Somchai is one of my best coaches. You've trained with him for years now, and he will be by your side. Chin up, Champ. Here, I've got a present for you," he said, handing Nong a package almost gruffly.

Nong looked at the square lump of crumpled old newspapers held together with gardening twine. "I can see you tied the present," grinned Nong, leaning back to duck a swipe from his father and laughing. "What is it, two pebbles?"

"Dodge like that on the night, and your opponent will never get near you! Go on, open it."

He squeezed the present and shook it next to his ear, then made several attempts to undo the knot. But Joi had tied the string too tightly, and in the dimly-lit room, it was impossible to see where the ends of the twine were. Cautiously, Nong slid the fastening over one end, savouring the moment. It was rare that he received gifts from his father.

"Just open it, will you? I can always take it back, you know. And hurry. The boss arrives early. You know she does and she hates waiting. Setting off with tempers won't be auspicious. Go on. Open it."

Not wanting to ruin Joi's good mood, Nong tore the black and white printed sheets. "Wow, headphones," he exclaimed, putting them on and moving his head up and down to get a feel for their fit.

"Don't wear them now! They're noise cancelling. Somewhere in the paper, you'll also find extra batteries. Thought you could use them before the fight. You can hand them to Somchai before he puts on the *Mongkol.* Although I'm not there, my gift will help you focus before the match." Joi hugged Nong, and the two of them sat for a brief moment in the dark.

Three nights ago, Joi had argued again with Lucy. She refused to let him accompany his son. Nong's fight purse was worth more than the five private classes he had to teach. He was not comfortable stepping down from being in his son's corner on the occasion of such an important fight. But she had argued they needed to think long-term. The students were good customers who paid decent money to train privately. Competition was tough for the steady income provided by locally living *farangs* who regularly took individual classes. Within a twenty-minute drive from Dragon, there were at least three other gyms offering one-to-one training with former champion boxers. Joi was by far the best teacher and most experienced. Lucy received complaints when he was not available to teach the students their regular lessons, and a number had already threatened to leave.

Lucy thought Nong was old enough now to not need

his father permanently in the corner. Joi had remained silent with a grim expression. He knew the temptations out there for Nong. He had heard the reports from Somchai and the boys that Ray sometimes slowed down for a chat in his flash car and spoke to Nong when they were out running. Somchai had overheard Ray talking to Nong, praising the Bangkok gyms. Somchai had squared up to Ray when he became too persistent about giving Nong a lift back to the gym and would always cut their conversation short if he started criticising Dragon's Gym and their lack of connections with the big money.

In a nutshell, Ray wanted to break the father-and-son relationship. Joi was not a man given to worrying, but with his boy, it was different. He knew what they saw in him was a rare talent. Because he could see it too. He never argued with Lucy, but this time, she was wrong about his boy's safety. Too proud to voice his concerns, he would not show weakness. He acquiesced to Lucy's instructions and turned on his heel, angry at himself but preferring to keep face and not lose dignity by pleading.

The following day, Joi gave Somchai and Ram strict instructions not to leave Nong's side in Chiang Mai, then shot off home to break the news to Gan. She had tried to send him back to plead with Lucy, but he told her it was too late. The decision had been made. It was the first fight he had backed down from as far as he could remember. However, he knew they needed the money, and while Dragon's Gym was not perfect, it was a much better option than the family upping sticks and moving to a boxing camp in some horror of a place like Pattaya, where drugs and sex tourism were rife and the cost of living twice as expensive. Above all, Lucy was honest.

Nong walked into the muted dawn kitchen wearing his headphones, dressed in ripped jeans and a branded Dragon's Gym t-shirt with a black kit bag slung over his shoulder. Behind him trotted Sam.

"Good morning!" he shouted, drumbeats blasting in his ears and all concern about the fight ahead fading with the morning gloom.

Gan sat at the kitchen table, her face an ashen grey. "Milo?" she asked, leaving her half-drunk coffee and hiding her worried expression. Gan made a show of making herself a new cup of coffee and Nong's drink. She stared at the grey concrete kitchen wall, reassembling her features, reminding herself to stay positive. Talking over her shoulder, she forced a bright note into her voice, "You've got your present, then! Hope you like them. They're top-of-the-line, you know, not some cheap imitation. Real Sony's, not fakes!"

Gan did not see Nong bouncing around the kitchen, waving his arms in the air and practising dance steps. But the scraping of the furniture on the concrete floor as he pranced about the small kitchen, moving it out of his way, caused her to turn around sharply.

"I can see you like them!!" she said. "Are they a good fit?"

Receiving no reply and irritated at being ignored, Gan raised her voice, repeating the question as she returned to sit alone at the kitchen table. Still she did not elicit a response, and the sight of him dancing when she felt such concern annoyed her even more.

"Nong!" WILL YOU REMOVE THOSE HEADPHONES?" she snapped, reaching out to grab one of the ear coverings, letting it slap back down on his ear.

"What?" he protested, frowning at Gan. Removing the headphones and hanging them around his neck.

"I was talking to you!" she retorted, angry at herself for getting upset before he was about to leave.

His mum was normally as calm as the surface of a forest pond. But this morning, her voice was as sharp as a monkey's scream. Giving his mum a chance to calm down, he made a show of unzipping his rucksack and picking up the packet of wafers and two bananas from the table. With the weigh-in being only two days away, he was only permitted a small amount of food. Unable to fit the fruit into his bag without crushing them, he stuck one in either side of his front jean pockets giving him the appearance of young boy playing at cowboys. Trying to assure Gan, he said, "I'm going to win, you know, and I'll be fine. Somchai and Ram are coming."

The sense of frustration at being unable to prevent him from leaving stabbed at Gan's conscience. She moved towards Nong and embraced him. "I'm fine," she sighed over the top of his head. "You don't have to go if you don't want to, Nong. There's always a different road as long as you decide to travel down it for the right reasons. No-one will think bad of you if you don't go," she said, telling a white lie. Nong had committed to competing, and it would upset people if he backed out now, as money had been paid and promises made. "Well?"

Nong withdrew, putting the headphones back on his head without turning on his music. What he needed was people to be supportive, not to question what he was doing. "Why wouldn't I want to go? I'm a boxer. What do you think I've been working so hard for? All you ever do is question and tell me how to get out of winning. What's your problem?" snapped Nong.

"That's not what I'm saying at all, Nong. What I'm trying to say is you have choices. You're young and smart. You can decide and—"

"Stop! I've heard it all before," groaned Nong as he threaded his arms through the straps of his rucksack and hoisted it on his back. "Gotta go."

An engine roared outside.

Sam raised his hindquarters up, stretching out his front paws. Wagging his tail and barking, he rushed to inspect the newcomer. Then the sound of Lucy and Joi exchanging pleasantries echoed in the morning air. Unaware of the hurt he had caused his mother, Nong ran after Sam. He was a young man, thinking he knew all the answers but was unable to ask the right questions.

Not trusting her self-control, Gan stayed in the

kitchen, contemplating the future and re-living the past. Outside the window, the world was waking as the rising sun turned the sky to a dark sapphire blue, streaks of gold and red visible over the canopy. Birds tweeted, trilled and celebrated the new day. Gan sat down back at the kitchen table and put her head in her hands together as if in mourning. She felt a wet nose brush against her left knee. Sam rested his white head on her lap and whined. Stroking the dog's silky big black ear, she remembered when he too had been a rebellious youngster.

CHAPTER FOURTEEN

GUILT. It nagged at him. Replaying the kitchen conversation with Gan, Nong tugged at the synthetic blue and red checked threads hanging from the economy class middle aisle seat. Shivering, he wore a black sweat suit over his clothes to provide a barrier against the grey threadbare airline blankets that itched and did little to alleviate the jet's Arctic conditions. The sky, which had been a brilliant turquoise above the clouds, now lay hidden below a smoky grey haze. The pollution caused by the slash and burn of crops, as well as forests, also smudged the verdant and stone colours of the surrounding mountains and flat green plains. The region had endured a haze problem since 2007, which had been traced to the animal feed businesses. In turn, the feed industry tried to scapegoat the hill tribes and their culture for the severe health and economic damage caused by the steadily worsening annual pollution.

At school, Nong had spent time studying the ancient city of Chiang Mai, the largest city in northern Thailand and capital of Chiang Mai Province. A major Thai city, it was located 700 kilometres north of Bangkok, near the highest mountains in the country. The settlement, founded as a royal residence in 1292 and as a town in 1296, served as the capital of the Lan

Na Thai kingdom until 1558, when it fell to the Myanmar. In 1774, the Siamese King Taksin drove out the Burmese. In addition to the famous temples, the city was renowned as a centre of Thai handicrafts. Small villages nearby specialised in crafts such as silverwork, wood carving, and making pottery and lacquerware. Traditional Thai silk was still woven at San Kamphaeng to the east.

“Nong, grab your stuff!” instructed Somchai, yanking his own black sports holdall from the plane’s overhead bins. Keen to get going, Somchai was first to his feet when the seatbelt light pinged. Across the aisle, Ram helped Lucy retrieve her Louis Vuitton holdall. It was mid-morning, and the time Ram and Somchai typically ate post-training breakfast. They were eager to leave the airport and find food.

Whilst waiting for his baggage, Nong suppressed his hunger pangs by studying the Chiang Mai city seal painted on the wall in front of him. It featured design elements representing the Suthep Pagoda mountain, clouds, Great Naga (dragon/snake), rice stalks, and Thai flower design scripture. At the centre of the image was the stupa at *Wat Phra That Doi Suthep*. This *wat* was a sacred site to many Thai people, who travelled from across the country to visit its location 15 kilometres from the city of Chiang Mai at an elevation of 1,703 metres. In a semi-circle below the stupa, blue, stylised clouds represented the moderate climate in the mountains of northern Thailand. In an outer ring surrounding the clouds, the Great Naga, believed to be the source of several rivers, especially the Ping River that supported the Chiang Mai people's life as well as the nearby province, was depicted in gold. The Great Naga had a head on either end of its long serpentine body with gold rice stalks coming from each mouth. Completing this outer ring at the top of the seal was a line of text Nong was unable to decipher.

Clusters of colourfully dressed people stood around the baggage carousel, conversing in Thai dialects. The tunnel leading to the winding rotating rubber belt at long last spat out his scratched, sticker-covered suitcase. Lucy's smart, shiny orange Samsonite followed shortly. The budget airline they had flown with was strict on hand luggage weights, always angling to earn a bit extra, charging fines whenever it could.

"We good to go?" asked Lucy, accepting her case from Somchai with a friendly smile. "The promoter has sent one of his friends to greet us and drive us to our accommodation. Nong, you'll have to eat your food in the car, as you need to be training by 2 p.m." The opening chords of 'The Flower Duet' from the first act of Léo Delibes' opera *Lakmé* delicately floated up from Lucy's phone. Retrieving it, Lucy gave them a signal to follow her as she strode in the direction of the exit, shaking her head and shouting.

"Come on, Champ," grinned Somchai, thumping Nong on the upper arm. "Someone at the camp's getting an earful. We've got to start preparing you to break a guy's balls!" Noting that Nong was staring at

Lucy's back with a worried expression, he added, "Don't be nervous about Lucy. If it weren't for her, none of us would be here. She's the boss and has to be serious. But let me tell you, she's a sucker for a man like me with good looks."

"Fuck off, Somchai! As if your arse face ever got any girls looking at it. Let's leave him to his dreams, Nong," said Ram, his face furious. He always leapt to the defence of Lucy as without her insistence, they would never have had the opportunity to train and live at Dragon's Gym. "Nong, go grab Lucy's case, will you, and pull it for her?"

Nong chased after Lucy, trailing his own luggage with his rucksack bobbing along on his back. Weaving between the crowds, he overtook Lucy and stretched out his hand to indicate that he could help.

She responded with a broad smile. Putting one hand over her phone, she said, "Thanks, but I'm fine. You focus on yourself. Soon you're going to have to skip and run, run and skip until you've lost at least three kay-gee!"

Breezing through the wide glass exit doors and into the heat, she gave thanks for the heat. "It'd have been a nightmare if it'd been raining as the weather forecast predicted! Nong wouldn't meet his weigh-in target until Songkran!" she said. Mentally checking off her to-do list, she groaned. At 7 p.m., they wanted to watch videos on her laptop of Klapet, Nong's opponent. Absently, she wondered how Somchai managed to get the footage of Klapet's last three fights.

Somchai was now twenty-five and showed no signs of settling down. His boxing career had taken him far in his weight class. Crowds loved him, but he was never going to be a world champion. The magic was just not there like it was in Nong, who had an almost instinctive connection with the art of Muay Thai. Similar to Roger Federer, the world-class tennis player whose artistry and style was described with a reverence usually reserved for poetry and classical music, Nong's stamina and spirit set him apart from his peers.

The grace and joy he showed when fighting was a gift that could be witnessed in all art forms and had many different names, most of which were difficult to describe in English. The Balinese use the word *taksu,* which could be translated as 'connection with spiritual powers'. The concept of *taksu* is something that is commonly accepted in the Balinese culture. However, just like the concept of love, it cannot be measured or weighed empirically. A dancer with *taksu* captures the eyes of the audience, a Balinese with *taksu* heals his/her patients with mysterious powers, and a speaker with *taksu* becomes fascinating and inspirational.

Similarly, in Spanish, there exists *duende*, a word that many experts regard as the hardest word in Spanish to convey in other languages. In the dictionary, the word is listed as 'elf' or 'magic'. However, in actual practice, *duende* is rarely in the context of a woodland spirit, although that is where the word's etymology begins. In 1933, Spanish poet and theatre director Federico Garcia Lorca gave a lecture in Buenos Aires titled 'Play and Theory of the Duende', in which he addressed the fiery spirit behind what makes great performance stir emotions:

"The *duende*, then, is a power, not a work. It is a struggle, not a thought. I have heard an old maestro of the guitar say, 'the *duende* is not in the throat; the *duende* climbs up inside you from the soles of the feet.' Meaning this: it is not a question of ability, but of true, living style, of blood, of the most ancient culture, of spontaneous creation … everything that has black sounds in it, has *duende*."

All arts are capable of *duende*, but where it finds greatest range, naturally, is in music, dance, and spoken poetry, for these arts require a living body to interpret them, being forms that are born, die, and open their contours against an exact present.

There is a strong spiritual side to Muay Thai that is not taught in the West. Words like *taksu* or *duende* often represent an emotion or response to a selected piece of art. In the art of Muay Thai, there are rare occasions when boxers fight as if they are dancing to the chords of the universe. Chanchai Sor Tamarangsri, who fought back in the eighties, was an example of such an artist and was famous for his agility and balance. Opponents would find themselves incapacitated by his toe jabs or the kicks to the underside of the chin, rendering them senseless.

Outside the airport, drivers of private taxis and hotel shuttles stood around in groups, speaking the international language of cabbies. The world was terrible, the customers awful and fares they could legally charge too low. Their *duende* was the vitriol that drove up from the clutch they pressed as they steered their way through the increasingly jammed streets of Chiang Mai. Their lives were not peaceful but fraught with fights of their own making, such as refusing to start taxi meters, taking longer routes and on occasions not attempting to understand the tourists, just seeing them as cash dispensers rather than families delighted to be arriving on holiday.

A number of the drivers stood alone, leaning over the green rope running either side of the path leading out from the airport exit. In their hands, they held up placards with names. Local drivers approached luggage-burdened tourists searching for business but ignored the Thais, who would never accept their inflated prices.

"Pay attention and look out for the sign with 'Dragon's Gym' on it, will you?" Lucy pecked like a mother hen. Her charges were jostling, pointing out girls and bantering with one another strategically out of earshot. She was keen to get to the hostel, check in and have some quality time alone. Back home, one of the Dragon's Gym guests had sliced his head open riding a moped he had rented from the gym. She had to deal with the matter personally as the guest only spoke broken English, let alone Thai. The reception staff could not understand a word. She had deciphered he was talking about making a police report for an insurance claim. What's worse, the guest stank of stale alcohol. He probably could not even recall how the accident had happened, and the police would have breathalysed him. Her staff were loyal, diligent and unfailingly polite with the guests and understandably did not feel comfortable dealing with irritated and panicked customers and would escalate the issues to her. It was not the Thai way to shout and scream but rather to smile and attempt to avoid conflict and diffuse angry exchanges.

"Lucy, the guy's over here," called Somchai, interrupting her thoughts.

Lucy turned to where Somchai was pointing and spotted a swarthy, short guy holding up a sign. Unlike the smart framed hotel signs, which had the names of the guests printed in a clear black typeface, their driver held up the torn lid of a cardboard box with the letters of Dragon's Gym hand-scrawled. "Perfect," said Lucy, raising her left eyebrow sardonically.

The Monkey King Gym was located at the foot of *Wat Phra That Doi Suthep,* Chiang Mai's most sacred temple. The *wat* lay at a height of about 1,060 metres on the 1,676-high mountain and boasted stunning views of Chiang Mai. Compared to the dust and heat in which the Dragon's Gym boxers normally trained, the Monkey King complex felt air-conditioned, with its fragrant forest breeze and lush vegetation. Somchai, Ram and Nong introduced themselves to the head trainer, Dang, a close friend of Joi's, and presented him with a gift of Johnnie Walker Red Label. Then, they greeted the other trainers in the gym and Dang's son,

Yut. Introductions over, they ran one kilometre up and down the winding asphalt mountain road to warm-up for the afternoon's training session, which would focus on shadow-boxing.

Somchai had picked a quiet corner of the gym for them to cool down. He helped Nong stretch, alternately lifting first the right and then the left leg in the crook of his arm while Nong lay on his back. The trainers were friendly and left the southern Thai boxers alone, knowing Nong had a fight in just a matter of days. The gym was deserted apart from the three trainers, as it was two in the afternoon and group classes did not start until four. The gym had two boxing rings and, like most Thai boxing gyms, was open to the elements. Outside, feral cats slumbered in the afternoon shade not far from the soi dogs. Nong shadow-boxed, making every movement count, aware that he was being watched. Confident, he communicated to curious eyes his abilities with straight jabs, uppercut elbows, defensive strikes and kicks.

Kru Dang watched Nong's talented display approvingly from the other side of the gym. Joi had asked him to keep an eye out for his son and not to interfere with Somchai's direction unless absolutely necessary. Dang, however, could not resist testing his own son against Nong. It was his gym, after all, and it was too good an opportunity to pass up for his boy's education.

"Hey, Nong, how about you do a sparring session with Yut? Show us what you got when you've finished."

"*Kru* Dang. Nong would love to," interjected Somchai, "but our champ is a bit on the heavy side and needs to work that weight off. Joi'd kill us if he thinks we've been lazy and fooling around when we should be training."

Somchai was shocked Dang has asked. To refuse would make Nong look weak. It was also Dang's gym and to not accept the old champion's invitation would be an insult. Joi had given him strict instructions that the only exercise Nong was supposed to do was skipping and shadow-boxing to cut his weight further. Being so close to Nong's first big fight, there was no way the bout could happen during training.

"Sure, he would. But everyone needs to work extra hard before a weigh-in. Ten minutes of sparring is not going to make any difference, is it? You know what, practising with a stranger will do Nong good. Yut get over here."

Noting a slight tension in the air with the same sixth sense that a person has when someone is staring, the Monkey King trainers swivelled around to observe the exchange between their boss and the southern visitors. The other boxers noted the exchange like writers taking note of a particularly interesting conversation for a book.

Yut sauntered over in a carefree, easy manner. The Dragon's Gym boxers sized him up. A young man, sixteen, he was taller than Nong and as lean. Yut's dark brown eyes flickered between Somchai and Ram before resting on Nong.

"Hi, how did the run go?" asked Yut warmly. "Did you make it up to the top? I run it most days, and even then, it's still a pain."

Somchai was about to make a smart retort, but Nong responded first with a smile and offered his hand out. "No, not today, but there's always tomorrow. Your dad has asked me to spar with you. You okay with that?"

"Sure. Ready when you are."

"Can you give me ten more minutes to finish up and I'll be over to ring one?"

"Yeah, no problem," Yut replied, going to find the gloves and shin pads, which he had left lying around somewhere from the morning session.

Somchai seethed. This was not how their first training session was supposed to go. He was pleased Nong had spoken up, and maybe even a little bit proud of Nong's handling of the situation, but also unsurprised by his easy acceptance of the informal challenge. *Nong wouldn't be cowed by facing a world champion,* he thought.

"So, you feel ready for your big fight, Nong?" teased Dang while making a gap between the bottom two ropes.

"No, thanks, I'm not a girl. I'll go over the ropes if that's okay," said Nong, not wanting to enter the low rope like female Muay Thai boxers had to.

"That's fair enough," replied Dang. "You take right after Joi."

"Ahh, you know how it is," Nong replied, not rising

to the bait. His mind was calm and focused on what he needed to practice the most: defence or offence, patterns of attacks, and the hand combinations he would use to set up his low kicks. His ego was not important, and Joi's teaching about the need to weather storms, regroup and dominate fights was paramount in the lessons he had been repeating to him of late.

Joi taught that sparring should never be a full-on fight but an opportunity to practice, to learn how to stay centred and build more skills once a firm foundation of experience had been achieved. The goal was not to win but to practice technique and boxing strategy. Nong and Yut had known the rules of engagement with sparring since their ages were still in single digits. In principle, sparring partners helped each other improve, and it was important to understand what each sparring partner required and to adjust power accordingly—not tapping as if they were shadow-boxing but not striking as powerfully as in a competition either. Each partner should adjust their speed and power and it was always best to train with people of different strengths and heights as well as techniques. Powerful heavy weights could learn to deal with the speed of a lightweight and vice-versa. The experience gained in sparring was invaluable in the ring. Even if they hurt one another, they would not show it; neither would they take things personally or get frustrated. The goal was not to build one's ego but to learn.

Mouthguards in, they circled one another, slowly and lightly as black eagles on a thermal, maintaining a fighter's stance of one foot in front of the other. Nong had been learning how to fight southpaw over the past year—a reverse stance with the right foot forward and left foot back. Joi wanted him to be proficient in switching stances.

"Hands up, hands up," encouraged Ram as Nong struck out first, kicking Yut in the solar plexus. Somchai frowned. Nong was going in too hard. He should be starting light and testing Yut's reactions, not giving full-force kicks.

Yut staggered back, shaking his head as if saying to himself, *you've got to focus. This may be a warm-up and there aren't supposed to be winners and losers, but still, there's no point in looking like a loser.*

"Whoa, wake up, Yut!" chided Dang. "You're supposed to block, you lazy ox."

Yut advanced, weaving his head like a cobra looking for ins through Nong's defence. He struck out with a left hook, which Nong just managed to dodge by moving backwards swiftly.

I'm gonna have to maintain my distance with a kick before moving in. The guy's got monkey-arm reach, thought Nong, moving up his left elbow to cover the side of his head with his arm from Yut's right hook and then dipping to the same side to block an uppercut to just below his ribs.

Nong stepped forward, placing his right foot parallel to Yut's front left foot. He twisted his torso round and swung his arm back at a 45-degree angle, punching Yut in the face.

"What the fuck!" shouted Dang jumping over the ropes and rushing over to his son, whose nose was bleeding profusely. "What sort of arsehole are you? Get out. NOW!"

"I'm so sorry," said Nong, ashamed. "I was trying to box off my other foot and didn't measure the power properly. I didn't mean to smack him so hard."

"Nong didn't throw a friggin' elbow. That's allowed. You know it is. Yut should've blocked," said Ram, defending Nong while keeping the other trainers from the gym in sight out of the corner of his eye.

"You're going to tell me what's allowed in my gym, are you, lad?" snapped Dang, tipping Yut's head back and holding a rag against his nose. "I don't think so. If Joi wasn't a good friend, you'd get a right hiding. I said go. I'll call Joi to explain why you're kicked out."

Hell, thought Somchai. *This is my fault. I should have told Nong to ease up.* His hand rested lightly on Ram's upper arm in warning, applying pressure with his thumb and fingers when he felt his biceps hardening. *Where are we going to train now for the next two days? Joi's going to kill me.*

"*Kru* Dang, Yut," said Nong, desperately hanging his head. "I'm very, very sorry. It was not right to go so hard so soon."

The whole gym fell silent, tensely waiting for *Kru* Dang's decision. The only sounds were the whirring of the large metal fans and a dog yapping in the distance.

"Somchai, walk with me," said Dang with a beckoning wave and heading straight out of the exit without looking behind him. He only stopped when he was well out of earshot near the huge, dusty, black lorry tyres used by the boxers for muscle training. "You know why I asked the boys to spar, don't you?" asked Dang, lighting a cigarette, his tone calm.

"I know, I know," said Somchai, concerned about the hassle of having to find somewhere else to train at short notice and the call that he would need to make to Joi. The response was not going to be pretty. "That was my fault. As a coach, I'm supposed to keep Nong balanced. We'll be on our way."

"No. You can if you want, but Nong stays," said Dang calmly, staring hard at Somchai in reproach. "Joi asked me to take a look at Nong today, and I can tell you if he doesn't centre himself and maintain his cool, he's going to lose. This is his biggest fight and it's going to be tough. He has to fight with his brain as much as his brawn. Flash moves won't get him anywhere, and he's inexperienced. Tell me, Somchai, how do you think you did?"

A castigated Somchai realised the responsibility on his shoulders. This was Nong's first non-local fight. If he felt that sparring today was not right for Nong, he should have stood up to Dang and said so. Nong was on fire to prove himself, so of course, he would accept any challenge. "I guess," said Somchai, "I could use some help."

Dang looked Somchai up and down and locked hard, ebony eyes on Somchai's indirect gaze. *Joi's a good judge. He wouldn't have let Somchai come so far with his boy if he were not a good kid*, he thought, suppressing an uneasy feeling to the contrary. "How about this? Come join my Chiang Mai boxing family for the next few days. I'll sit in on all the coaching sessions and be at the fight in Nong's corner. Let's work together as a team," smiled Dang, holding out his hand for Somchai to shake, silently committing to calling Joi later. The bee of concern still buzzed.

Exchanging banalities, they returned to the others, walking side by side like two old friends. Yut stood laughing with Nong and Ram, a bloodied rag in one hand. The skin around his eyes already starting to bruise.

"Yut, you're lucky Nong didn't break that beak of yours. Weave out of the way next time," teased Dang. "Come on, Nong. Let's get you up and training. Put your sweat suit on and we'll crush some kilos."

CHAPTER FIFTEEN

"DON'T give him the popcorn, Ram! Nong's got his weigh-in tomorrow morning!" said Somchai, grabbing the yellow and red plastic bag with a deep sigh. "Really, it's like looking after a group of nursery school kids. Can't believe I have to do this when I've got my own training to focus on."

"Yep, sorry. Can you shift over and play the video again?" asked Ram, ripping the popcorn from Somchai's grasp and cramming yet more popcorn in his mouth.

"What! You've watched Klapet fight a million times already," said Lucy wishing they would take the hint and leave. She was getting fed up with the boys occupying her room and lolling about on her now-crumpled bed. Lucy had banned Somchai and Ram from calling room service before popping to the reception to print some documents. On her return, half an hour later, they had already ordered three pizzas between them, as well as Cokes and ice cream. The young fighters preferred her room as it was bigger, had a minibar, and they had discovered that via a cable, they could hook up their phone to the TV. To support Nong, everyone had decided to keep away from the temptations of the night market, bars and cafes and stay in the hotel.

"OHHH! Nong. Look at the strength in his low kick," said Ram, pointing at the TV with one hand and grabbing yet another fistful of popcorn with the other. "Come on, give that back, please Ma'am," whined Ram as Lucy snatched the box of popcorn and threw it in the rubbish bin with a glare.

Nong groaned. He was bored with analysing the video shots and the griping of the team. What was more, his stomach kept rumbling. Making his weight also put him on edge. "I'm going for a walk."

"Right. See you later," replied Lucy with a sigh of relief. Using the opportunity to regain some space, she added, "Ram, Somchai, you two can go back to your room."

Eyes fixed on the TV, they said, "Sure," in unison without budging from the middle of the bed, where they lay flat on their stomachs.

"NOW!" shouted Lucy. "Leave now." The last two days had been intense for Nong, and she could only imagine how hungry and thirsty he felt. Ram and Somchai were not helping the situation one bit. So much for staying in to support him.

Nong turned left out of the hotel and wandered in the direction of the old city wall, relishing the thought of spending time alone and feeling the spring of adventure lighten his step. Chiang Mai looked much older than he imagined. There seemed to be a temple on every street. He watched where he walked on the uneven paving stones, moving aside for the tourists from all corners of the globe. To avoid one Chinese group following a guide with a loud hailer and a flagpole, he had to cross the road, dodging the multitude of mopeds and cars. He barely avoided a *Frozen*-themed *tuk-tuk* decked out in silver, pale blues and a frosting of plastic snow on its roof as it shot out from one of the hotel entrances. Between the streetlamps, thick bands of electric cables hung down in large black loops. In the dark, he could see sparks spit and splatter off a number of the poles, and occasionally, he heard the crackle and pop of fuse boxes. The smell of chilli and recooked oil from the street vendors was tempting. No food or water was allowed to pass his lips, so he resolutely ignored them. The smell of raw sewage periodically caused him to cover his mouth with his hand.

He followed the road as it weaved through the narrow streets, taking care in his open-toed flip-flops to avoid the discarded fast-food boxes, dog mess and cracked paving stones that could stub his toes. As he walked, he mulled over tomorrow night's fight. Klapet fought in the Muay Mat style and was sure to come at him like a bull. Klapet's plan would be to engage him in a close exchange and try to break him down by battering his defensive walls like heavy artillery against a city wall. Nong was not intimidated by this style of fighter, but it would be the first boxer he had met with such a full-frontal attack.

As he meandered down the small streets, he did not notice the slick bar with its neon lights and small terrace with three-foot-high plastic lipstick palms in peeling gold painted buckets plonked at staggered intervals around the fake green grass perimeter. Three slender girls sat near the entrance on crimson plastic-coated bar stools wearing tiny red shorts and white low-cut tops, entreating tourists to enter with suggestive smiles and beckoning hand gestures, the pumping beats of the dance music drowning out their voices.

"Hey, Nong, wait up!" called a familiar voice. "Nong, over here."

Nong turned to his right with a puzzled expression as he was a stranger in Chiang Mai. He scanned the street and nearby terrace, then spotted Bhan sitting at a small, brushed steel round table with two girls around eighteen years of age and an older man in his mid-thirties with slicked back hair, a big paunch and long scar slashing across his right cheek. Two small paws materialised, gripping Nong's left shoulder and two more were suddenly resting in his hair. Chattering softly, Monkey wrapped his tail gently around Nong's neck. Keeping his expression blank, Nong managed to hide the stumble in his step at the shock of the appearance of his old friend. It had been a few years since he had felt the presence of or seen a whisker or tail of the spirit animals.

"Hi, Bhan! Good to see you," called Nong, forcing himself to push his shoulders back and hold his head high despite Monkey's prehensile tail gripping him around his neck. No longer the shy boy Bhan had met in the forest *wat*, Nong held his former friend's gaze.

"Come, sit down and join us," invited Bhan,

stretching to grab one of the chairs from the empty table behind him. "It's been ages. Let's have a drink! This is Daw and Anong and my good friend Aye."

"Hi, everyone," said Nong, barely managing to mask the cautious tone in his voice. "Good to meet you and to see you again, Bhan. I was just on my way back to the hotel. I'm competing tomorrow and have my weigh-in first thing."

"Nong. Come now, there's no need to be shy in front of these stunning girls. One drink's not going to make a difference, is it?" said Aye.

Nong sucked his lower lip. He did not want to be rude and just walk away, but his instincts were screaming WALK. "Sure. I'll sit down for a moment," he said, plonking himself down in the chair next to Bhan and smiling at the group.

"Get this famous young boxer a drink," instructed Bhan to the lurking waitress with a piranha smile.

Suddenly he felt Monkey give him a sharp tug on his left ear, as if warning him to take care. Nong flinched and pretended to drop his wallet to hide his face. "Lay off, will you?" he hissed at Monkey while picking it up.

"What are you drinking? Vodka, gin, whisky?" asked Bhan. "Come on now, don't give me that look. One drink is not going to make any difference. So good to see you. I can't believe you've stuck with the boxing. My friend Aye here's a great guy, knows all about the business side of things."

"Diet Coke, thanks," replied Nong with finality.

Warily observing Aye, he felt unimpressed by the man. There was something about his style that reminded him of Ray. He had the same shark smile, flashy air and penchant for obvious displays of wealth. *His gold Rolex is most likely as fake as he appears to be*, Nong thought, straightening his back as he moved his head from side to side to give himself a stretch.

"Now, Bhan, don't pressurise the boy," Aye chided, smiling in Nong's direction. "I'm guessing you're not much older than fifteen, are you? Tell me about tomorrow, Nong. Do you think you're worth a punt?"

"What do you mean?" asked Nong, wishing his father was with him. There was something furtive and cold in Aye's expression that turned his stomach.

"Well, you know, if I put money down on you to win tomorrow, would I make some easy cash? What do you reckon?"

Nong sipped his drink to give himself time to think of a response. Bhan smiled encouragingly at him while waiting for an answer. The girls talked between themselves, showing no interest in the newcomer, who was clearly a poor boy from the provinces.

"We going dancing, honey?" wheedled Daw.

"Yeah, soon, babe, soon," soothed Bhan, his hand on her thigh while keeping his eyes fixed on Nong. "So, yes or no, friend?"

Near his left ear, Monkey chattered, "Tell him you don't know. Speak to Mr Joi. Nong, Nong, we go. Come, come, come." Monkey tugged at the hair on the back of his head in time to his words for emphasis.

Luckily, Nong had sat in the seat with its back against the wall, so the rise and fall of his hair could not be seen.

Keeping his voice light and taking in a huge gulp of his drink to finish it, Nong attempted to airily reply, “My dad deals with that stuff. Speak to him. Thanks for the Coke. I’d best be off.”

“So soon, stay a while longer. How about coming dancing with us? We’d all like that, wouldn’t we, girls?” asked Aye.

Daw and Anong were sitting with their arms crossed, expressions as sour as tamarind.

Not finding much support there, Aye tried patting Nong on the back and another tactic. “You ever been asked to pull a few punches in the past?”

SMASH. Aye’s glass shattered into a thousand pieces. Monkey bounced back up from the tablecloth to re-perch on Nong’s shoulder. The table was covered in a mix of glistening ice cubes and tiny shards. The girls jumped up from their chairs, clutching their small Fendi bags to their chests. The dark rum and Coke streamed down from the table into Aye’s lap, covering the crotch of his white trousers.

“What the hell?” he screamed. “You, girl, get me a fucking cloth.”

Spying an unlit cigar that had rolled onto the cement floor, Monkey bounced down again quickly to grab it and disappeared from view. Then paws grabbed Nong’s shirt from behind as he felt Monkey shove the cigar in his back pocket.

"Err, best be going," said Nong, standing, his eyes averted from the chaos. "Thanks for the drink."

"Yeah, right," replied Bhan, brushing down his trousers and glaring at the servers standing nervously by. "Which stadium are you fighting at?"

"The new one."

"We'll be there. Look out for me, as I'll be looking for you," said Aye, snatching the towel from the waitress's hand with a growl. "We'll have a proper little chat, and none of this 'speak to my father shit'. You're your own man, aren't you?"

Nong nodded his head at Aye, the girls and Bhan with a frozen smile and left. Outside the bar, he turned back in the direction he had come from and gave a huge sigh of relief.

The night air was muggy, and the cacophony caused by the traffic and bars blasting music made him wish for home. As he walked, Monkey sat on his shoulder, chattering and inspecting Nong's hair.

"Where have you and the others been, Monkey?" asked Nong under his breath. Over the last few years, he had convinced himself that the tales of spirit animals only appearing for children were true.

"Always here," was Monkey's reply, "Always." With this unsatisfactory reply, he jumped up onto the roof of a parked Scooby-Doo-themed *tuk-tuk* before disappearing off into the night market with its throngs of tourists, street food, Chinese goods being passed off as locally made handicrafts and genuine products made by the local hill tribes.

CHAPTER SIXTEEN

THE following morning, Nong stood in his underpants on the scales, his back to a mixed bag of boxing promoters, local media and cronies of the fighters. Nong thanked his stars that he had reached his target weight of forty-seven kilos. Klapet's weight matched his. Height-wise, Nong was one centimetre taller than Klapet, at 163 centimetres. Both the boys had fought over fifty fights, had a few losses and a draw. Nong had the better fight record by one win.

Ten hours later, he sat with his arm stretched out as Somchai wrapped his right hand, stopping every now and then to check that the folded padding sat properly on his knuckles. Nervous, he focused on the fight due to start in fifteen minutes as he pushed the negative thoughts from his mind, slowing his breathing as the monks had taught him in what now seemed to be a lifetime ago. Ram rubbed Tiger Balm into his shoulders, boasting about how he could beat one of the fighters billed in the main event.

Klapet had powerful punches and knee kicks with a very strong physique. Clearly, he had done a lot of running to strengthen his leg muscles. Dang had commented that he must have focused on making his punches and kicks as hard as possible, but his speed could be an issue. Nong, in contrast, was more balanced overall in his style and used several traditional Muay Boran techniques. His training had focused on improving his techniques and feeling for distance so he could use his flying kicks. Like him, Klapet would have undergone two days of very hard training before the intensity was reduced in the last few days to no more than shadow-boxing to focus on fighting tactics, reducing weight and massages. While in Chiang Mai, Nong had shadow-boxed for relatively long periods. Each training session contained three or four rounds of five minutes each.

Klapet would approach him fast and aggressively, so he needed to have an iron-clad defence, paying particular attention to his guard. Somchai had called Joi to discuss what he thought would be the best approach, and they had agreed that Klapet would become slower and weaker during the course of the fight, most likely by the third round. Nong would then be able to take control of the fight and start applying his own pressure. The challenge was to maintain the defence. They agreed the best strategy for Nong would be to fight southpaw as Klapet had never fought a boxer with a southpaw stance before. Above all, Nong had to act full of confidence, not get upset by any provocation and impress the audience and judges with the consistent assertion of his own fighting style.

Nong and his team stood in the hallway where boxers and their entourage waited to be called into the arena. Behind Somchai stood Dang, smartly dressed in his only pair of suit trousers and a long-sleeved white shirt. Outside, in the arena, Lucy was in the audience, ready with her phone to video the match. Nong half-listened to the last pieces of advice as he replayed his fight plan against Klapet. As Somchai tied on his gloves, he bent his neck sideward, first right and then left, to ease the tension in his neck. At last, he had managed to get a firm grip on his nerves. Gloves on, he gave Somchai a quick bow of his head and stood.

With his corner team by his side, Nong started to shadow-box. Nearby were groups of people involved in the organisation of the boxing tournament as well as members of the gambling syndicates. Their network had facilitated them coming backstage to look at the form of the fighters before the audiences. A particularly swarthy short man took a keen interest in Nong, sizing him up like a bookie would a racehorse. The air was stale with cigarette smoke, but at least it was air-conditioned. Joi had already warned him that tourists made up about eighty per cent of the audience, so he could expect some unfamiliar shouts from the stands and pushy demands for photographs. The song 'Monsters', by the band All Time Low blared out from the loudspeakers. Peeking through the curtain dividing the backstage area from the boxing arena itself, Nong got his first glimpse of the ring. The promoter had told Nong and Klapet to keep the *Ram Wai* short. On entering the ring, they could perform the Wai Khru circle in a counterclockwise direction and pray at each corner. Being Buddhist, both fighters would bow their heads at every corner three times in salutation to

Buddha, Rama, and the Sangha of monks before commencing the *Ram Muay*.

Bouncing on the balls of his feet behind the black curtain with Somchai just to his left side and Ram and Dang on the other, he wanted to get going. But the promoters who earned money from the TV and social media platform distribution agreements insisted all competitors kept to the tight schedule provided. A pretty girl in jeans and a red t-shirt held the curtain rope and let him know he had one minute to go. Nong nodded his head in thanks and gave a deep sigh.

"Let's start," he puffed impatiently as Bhan shoved past Somchai, a drink in his outstretched hand.

"Hey, Nong," he said, trying to slip an arm around his shoulder. Lightning fast, Dang reached around Somchai, knocking the drink to the floor. "What do you think you're doing," growled Dang. "Nong, do you know this guy?"

"Yes, he was at a forest *wat* with me," snapped Nong, irritated at Bhan for breaking his concentration and sensing the tension in his cohorts.

Dang sized up Bhan, slowly raising his gaze from the floor to the level of his eyes. He did not like what he saw and the scar-faced man behind him even less. They stank of gambling. "Nong, one minute," he said, pushing the teen back lightly on his left shoulder as he leant towards Bhan. Whispering in his ear, he warned, "I don't know who you are or what you claim to be, but if I ever catch you around Nong or any of my boxers before a fight, you'll regret it. You can take your isotonic drink offers and fuck off."

"What did you say to them?" asked Nong, unable to catch Dang's words above the blaring rock music.

"Just, you weren't thirsty, that's all. Let's focus, Champion," said Dang, glancing over his shoulder to make sure Bhan and the scar-faced man had retreated.

In response to the tannoy announcement, the ring girl was pulling the curtain chords apart. Beyond the collapsing black curtains, a packed audience roared. As Dang stepped aside for Nong to pass, he threw a questioning look at Somchai, wondering why he had not moved to block Bhan. *What would have happened if I had not been here*? Dang pondered.

Nong jabbed, crosscut, jabbed and uppercut his way along the thirty-metre ramp to the ring. He skipped and jumped, making sure that his black polyester cape with its Dragon's Gym logo flared out like the superhero he felt he was, relishing the attention. He slapped the palms of the outstretched hands and gave thanks for the well wishes with a wave to the audience in the back seats. The match officials pulled down the top ringside rope for him. He paused as he clambered over to stand on the middle rung and lean his hips against the ropes. Raising his arms, he saluted the audience. Standing in the middle of the ring, he looked back at the curtain, waiting for this opponent and then above him, hoping to spot Tiger where she used to perch up in the rafters, but she wasn't there. Tonight, he was on his own.

CHAPTER SEVENTEEN

AFTER two rounds, Nong knew now was the time to throw everything into finishing the fight. Wasting no time, he and Klapet re-engaged. Hard, fast, short-range kicks were exchanged. Strong jabs were thrown and countered before Nong determinedly moved in for a clinch in an attempt to twist Klapet around and hurl him on the floor. Klapet responded by throwing his weight forward and pushing Nong against the ropes. The bruised and battered opponents struggled to dominate one another. The incredible strength in their shoulders that had been built by hours of weight training and pull-ups showed in the rippling muscles of their backs. Too entwined to strike effectively with their knees, they tried to gain the upper hand, twisting and turning their arms around one another's shoulders. As they clinched, Nong made a sudden move to the left, leveraging himself off the ropes. The referee shattered the deadlock embrace and gave the sign for them to restart. Klapet struck out with a hard-left kick just below Nong's ribcage, followed by a jab and right kick to Nong's outer left thigh and a right cross, driving him once more towards the ropes. Nong side-stepped to his right to break away from the fierce onslaught.

They exchanged further punches and Klapet moved

to kick again with his right leg, but this time Nong caught the heel of his foot. Gripping it tightly, he pulled Klapet's leg forward while shifting his own weight onto his back left foot and kicked Klapet in the side of his head with his right. Nong took a sharp step back to give himself pause to breathe, but Klapet sprung forward, his left knee striking Nong hard in the stomach, driving him, with a flurry of punches, once more against the ropes. Nong struck Klapet hard in the stomach with a knee and circled away from the ropes to his right, catching Klapet with a strong left hook as he did so. Facing one another again, their chests heaved with the exertion. Klapet struck out with a *teep*, attempting to push Nong back and attack with another series of strikes.

But Nong struck out with his own left leg, connecting hard with Klapet's right thigh. Then, once again, Nong flipped his opponent to the mat, earning himself additional points from the judges and a huge roar of appreciation for his technique from the crowd.

Back on his feet, Klapet breathed in deeply and re-engaged, narrowly missing a toe jab to his stomach by moving back to his right. Nong advanced and struck out for a clinch to throw Klapet to the mat again to show his dominance and wear down his confidence. They exchanged knee blows again and again and again as Nong pushed Klapet against the ropes in a torturous embrace. The crowd whistled and cheered. As the referee wrenched them apart, Nong saluted the crowd, thanking them for their support with a huge grin.

That boy's a boxer and a showman, thought Dang from the sidelines, shaking his head in wonder at the demonstration of skill from the boy he had first met in nappies. *Joi and Gan are going to be proud.*

During the corner break, Somchai rubbed Nong's limbs vigorously, dispensing Tiger Balm but no advice. There was nothing to say apart from, "you're doing great." Dang checked to see that the oil was being applied correctly. The crowd was communicating loud and clearly how well Nong was fighting. He was showing a depth of knowledge beyond most professional boxers, let alone a boy of fifteen. Without a doubt, he was a *Muay Femur* fighter and Lumpinee beckoned.

Fourth round. Loud cheers, hoots and whoops came from the crowd as the two boys again traded punches and kicks, knee thrusts and elbows. Nong stepped back, narrowly avoiding a sharp left elbow from Klapet to the right side of his face, a strike which would have finished him. The audience greeted the incredible speed and determination of the fighters with a roar, egging them on and encouraging them with shouts of "*Ooheey, Oooheey.*"

"Stay on the balls of your feet, Nong," shouted Somchai. "Move faster and get out of the way. This isn't Western boxing. You're going to get thrashed by those kicks!"

Facing one another, the boxers switched stances, faking kicks as they attempted to misdirect each other so they could break through one another's defence.

Again and again, they advanced and retreated, trying to spot the perfect opportunity to commit a full attack. Klapet's roundhouse left kick was too fast for Nong to block, and he gasped as his ribcages took the full strength of the impact. They bounced back apart and advanced to close the gap, barely missing a beat. Punches were struck. The referee struggled to separate them from a clinch as the boxers used all their arm, back, shoulder and leg strength to dominate. With a sudden, sharp twist to the right, Klapet threw Nong to the ground, cartwheeling him over. Nong sprung up and saluted Klapet for the move with a cheeky punch in the air. They re-engaged in a clinch, Nong dipped down to one side, twisting Klapet around as he drove him towards the ropes. Klapet crashed through the middle two ropes, his head hitting the ground on the concrete outside the ring. For a moment, he stayed there, splayed, his feet pointing up to the ceiling.

Nong stepped back, smiling with satisfaction at the sight of a humiliated Klapet pulling himself back through the ropes, the referee having to help him rise to his feet. Within three seconds of Klapet re-entering the ring, they clinched again. The referee only managed to separate them by pulling with all his body weight and wedging his knee between them. The tourists in the crowd, along with the locals, jumped to their feet, applauding and cheering frenziedly. Then the bell sounded. Nong jumped into the air, sensing that victory was his, pushing Somchai away as he tried to wipe the sweat from his face so that he could continue to celebrate. Dang charged into the ring, grabbing Nong's arm, knowing that he should take the opportunity to sit for a minute and take a breath. The fight had not been won yet. Before Nong knew it, he was back up for the fifth round.

Dark purple bruises showed on both fighters' sides. Blood seeped from the cut above Klapet's right eye. They continued grappling and pounding each other in the side and stomach with knee strikes. When the referee separated them, they struck each other with low and high kicks, *teeps* and punches before re-engaging in a clinch. As they twisted and turned against the ropes to gain the upper hand, the blood from Klapet's head cut mingled with Nong's sweat. Nong twisted Klapet around, forcing him back into the ring corner, holding him so he could not move or knee strike effectively while he kneed him repeatedly. The referee grabbed Nong by the throat and around the chest, heaving him back to slow down the onslaught.

In a show of respect, the fighters reached out and tapped one another's gloves before resetting. A sharp, high kick to the head followed by a low right kick sent Klapet reeling, but still he stood. Nong evaluated whether to go for elbow strikes, but he held back. The din from the crowd and a quick glance to his corner told him he had won. There was no need to show disrespect to Klapet by being vicious. He respected his opponent, and the fight had been fair. As they traded punches before the final bell, gamblers could be seen, their backs to the ring, exchanging wads of cash, their faces either scowling or elated. Gambling was supposed to be prohibited at the ringside, but not three metres from the boxing ring, Thais and *farangs* stood either dispensing cash or receiving it. Only two gamblers stood watching the final moments: Bhan and Aye. Both men seething at the amount of money they had lost.

The final bell sounded. Klapet and Nong embraced as they congratulated each other on a match well fought. Exhausted but triumphant, Nong ran to the ropes, jumped up on the bottom rung and raised his arms.

"YESSS," he shouted, springing back down again and running around the ring. Dang, Somchai and Ram rushed over, Dang with a towel to wipe off the sweat. Somchai posed for photographs with the boxing promoter, his corner team standing behind him as the cameras flashed. Nong waved at Lucy whistling and clapping at the ringside. Her face shining with pride. As he accepted the fight purse from the boxing promoter, he leant over and whispered to Somchai,

"Let's get out of here. I want to call my parents."

"You got it," replied Somchai, stepping in front of Nong so that he could escort him from the ring. Acknowledging the congratulations from the crowd, Nong and his team walked back down the ramp and through the black curtain to the changing rooms.

"Your father'll be proud of you," said Dang, almost skipping with joy alongside a bruised and battered Nong, the numerous purple blotches covering his body like so many polka dots.

"That was amazing," agreed Ram with a vigorous nod of his head. "Lumpinee beckons and a few cold beers!"

Tiredness smothered Nong's limbs like a heavy blanket. But the jubilation of a fight well fought eased away the pain. Tomorrow, they had an early flight back home. Now he wanted to get a good meal and relive his win. First, though, he needed to shower and change before meeting Lucy outside the changing rooms and going out for dinner.

"Here, Champ, sit down and let's get those wraps off you," said Somchai. Nong looked around the stark changing room as he sat upright on the edge of the massage table, the elation of winning ebbing away and a feeling of tiredness overwhelming him. Behind a curtain to his right, a boxer was lying face down, a twenty-something man kneading his quadriceps.

"That was fantastic!" said a voice, followed by a slap on his back.

"Thanks?" said Nong for the hundredth time, not bothering to turn round.

"Khun Tanawat, *sawadee kap*," said Dang with a respectful inclination of his head.

Recognising Tanawat, Somchai and Ram also greeted him with deference, asking after this family.

Nong was intrigued and gave Tanawat a sideways inspection. It was the first time he had heard Ram refer to anyone other than his father with such humility. Curiosity piqued, he shifted his weight on the table and turned to properly greet the newcomer. Before him stood a well-shaved man in late middle-age dressed in a dark blue suit, a brilliant white open-neck shirt, and black shoes as shiny as a beetle's shell. On his left index finger, he wore a discreet signet ring.

"Nong, let me introduce you to Khun Tanawat," said Dang with his best polite smile firmly fixed on his face and a warning look in his eyes at Nong that he had better behave, however tired he felt.

"Good evening," mumbled Nong, deciding it was best not to offer his grimy hand with its blood-spattered, sweaty wraps in greeting.

"Good fight tonight. I can see something of your father in you. I remember Joi's first regional match; it now seems like a lifetime ago! Do you remember those days, Khun Dang?" asked Tanawat. "The 1990s were surely the golden age of Muay Thai! Not now, with the streaming services demanding shorter rounds and faster action. Do you know, boys, I've even heard rumours that some of the TV stations have started having crazy requests! Such as boxers being asked to perform tricks like fire breathing in the ring and female athletes being ordered to wear make-up and sexy outfits. The sport's going nuts!"

Dang shrugged his shoulders in exasperation and sighed. He had to train his students to focus on low kicks, elbows and punches rather than thinking too much about the strategy of a competition, especially for television-focused productions like *Max Muay Thai,* with its three-round bouts and matchmaking of Thai fighters against foreigners.

"You're right, Khun Tanawat," said Dang. "We all miss those days. But Nong here can make it to Lumpinee, don't you think?"

"Well, that's what I came by to chat about. Nong, I've got a space for a competitor next month in the first bout in a Lumpinee. You want to take it?"

"What?" said Nong in disbelief, switching his gaze from Tanawat's face to his friends to see if he had heard right. Suddenly, Somchai pinched Nong's right underarm, causing him to flinch. Getting the hint, Nong stood up and flashed the stranger his best engaging smile.

"Where's your manners, boy," snapped Dang. "*What* is not a response! I'm sorry, Khun Tanawat. I'm sure what Joi's boy meant to say is, 'I'd be honoured and HUMBLED! Thank you, SIR!'"

Tanawat roared with laughter. "I remember first chatting with you, Khun Dang. When you were, what, about fifteen? This boy's an angel in comparison!"

"That's not the way I recall how our meeting went," said Dang, laughing at the memory of their first encounter. He opened his mouth to tell the story but thought better of it. Now was Nong's time, and he had to make sure his friend's kid got his chance at fame.

Incredulousness did not prevent sparks of excitement from setting Nong's heart on fire. "Lumpinee?" Nong said hesitantly. "Lumpinee? Really, next month?"

"Yes," smiled Tanawat, genuinely delighted to have made this exceptional young boxer's night.

"Can I call my dad?" asked Nong. He wanted to deliver the good news before accepting.

"That would be a very, very wise action to take," said Dang with a knowing look at Tanawat, who turned away to better hide his laughter.

CHAPTER EIGHTEEN

THE unsigned contract lay on the kitchen table, the remains of the welcome home dinner congealing in the serving plates. Gan twisted the dishcloth in her hands, frowning as she listened to her husband unconvinced.

"What's the problem, Gan? He'll earn good money."

"What about his schoolwork? How's he going to do that? You can't even promise me that you'll travel with him."

"I'll do my best."

"What's that supposed to mean?"

The conversation went around and around like Sam chasing his tail. Eventually, they would tire of the sound of their own voices. Deep in her heart, Gan knew she was unable to prevent Nong from fighting in Bangkok. But she at least had to try and wrangle some concession out of her husband. Perhaps after the fight in the capital, Nong could spend the next few months focusing on his schoolwork. Exams were looming, and her son had to graduate from secondary school.

Outside, Nong crouched underneath the kitchen window, listening to his parents' negotiations. The shrill sound of the cicadas drowned out the rustling of nocturnal forest creatures. Woolly horseshoe bats darted and squeaked, hunting insects in the dark. Near his bare feet, small green and brown lizards scurried beneath the forest debris and up the concrete walls of his house. As he strained to hear his father above the whir of the metal kitchen fan, he slapped the occasional mosquito away. *If Mother really puts her foot down, Lumpinee will never happen*, he thought, uprooting the long blades of grass growing against the concrete wall and tossing them away into the night breezes.

By his side lay Sam, semi-dozing with his large head resting on his paws. His black ear was upright as if he were also attempting to listen. Through the open window, Nong heard his parents' voices become angrier and sharper. A door slammed. The familiar sound of his father's footsteps thudded in the night air as he stomped across the porch in the direction of his motorbike. As the engine roared off into the dark night, Nong put his head up over the windowsill to take a peek into the kitchen. His mother sat alone with her head in her hands, staring at the unsigned contract. *I want to go to Lumpinee,* thought Nong. He felt angry towards his mother because she always seemed to be doubting his abilities and trying to stop him. He had dreamt of boxing in the capital all his life, and what did it matter if he took his exams this year or next? "I am going to walk in and tell her I'm going and that they need to sign the contract today. If they don't, then I'm going to Bangkok alone," he muttered.

Stubbing his toe on a discarded piece of wood, Nong spat on the ground and cursed. As he crept along the side of the house, the light of the full moon was watery and pale, just bright enough to cast shadows. Against the grey wall, his own shadow crept behind him: ghoul-like in imitation of his crouched stance. Nong felt a brush of hair against his leg. Seeking comfort, he bent down to stroke Sam, but his fingers disappeared into dense fur much coarser than his dog's coat. "Tiger," he whispered as loud as he dared.

Tiger chuffed, her tail twitching ever so slightly. Eyes, a hard amber, met his. "Hello, Nong. I see you have arrived at one of life's crossroads."

"What do you mean?" asked Nong, uncomfortable at Tiger's piercing stare scrutinising him.

Tiger's gleaming eyes, with their lightning bolt flashes of gold, narrowed ever so slightly at the tone of his voice. Queen of the Forest, she did not appreciate being challenged. "Nong, where are your manners? Are you too important now to greet me properly? Careful: words once spoken cannot be unsaid." A faint hint of danger was implied by her irritably flicking tail.

The still night air seemed to be closing in, and the shadows behind Tiger darkened. The forest fell silent, waiting for his response. Nong felt the rising tension in the air as if every antennae, ear, tree, rock, stream and the very ground were listening and every sentient being holding its breath. Watching. Waiting. Wondering what he would do.

"No, no, no, of course not," Nong stuttered, his bravado faltering as her eyes, level with his, challenged him. "You look magnificent," he said in a clumsy attempt at flattery.

Tiger yawned. Displaying her four-inch canine teeth, her muscles rippling as she shifted her 318-kilograms body into a crouching position. "Cub, now is not the time to fight in Bangkok. You must wait another year. There are too many negative forces that await you there. More than this, I will not say. The path you want to take now to quick glory and success is scented with danger."

"But why? I've got to leave now. Let me tell—"

"No. Nong, you ARE NOT telling me anything! There is nothing you can say to me that I do not already know." Tiger replied, her tone both bored and disappointed. Already, her mind was transitioning to other planes and places she needed to be. Lifting her regal head, she sniffed the night air, and her long white whiskers twitched. Her pupils dilated to let more light enter her eyes to improve her night vision. She appeared to snarl but made no sound as she picked up a scent on her upper lip and curled it toward her nose for further discernment. Stretching her front legs, she briefly displayed her razor-sharp claws as she stood. "What you do is up to you. Just heed my warning. I can see danger on your path. It is blocked by tigers, lions, buffalos and rhinos."

"But I don't understand."

"All four of these animals are equally dangerous and fierce. If one had to choose which one to meet on a dark night, it would be a very difficult decision. Like me, lions eat meat, while the rhino has a deadly horn, which he uses at the first opportunity when annoyed. This just leaves the buffalo, which, if alone, should never be approached. If all four animals are together, it is a sure sign that danger is near. There are people around you that indicate trouble."

"Which people, who do you mean?"

"Use your eyes, Cub," replied Tiger as she turned away from him, gracefully moving towards the thick forest without a backward glance. The forest night chorus trilled, croaked and hooted as if welcoming her decision to enter its dark, shadowed embrace once again.

"But Tiger," he called, watching her as she became one with the forest, disappearing from view. "Why not now?"

But only the sound of the cicadas responded.

CHAPTER NINETEEN

PUNCHING his pillow and cursing under his breath at the encroaching daylight, Nong sulked as he considered his options. From the kitchen, he could hear the faint murmurs of his mother and father debating. Sitting up in bed, he gazed at the Chiang Mai gold trophy on his desk next to his neatly piled schoolbooks. He steadied himself for an argument, took a deep breath, and then bent down to retrieve his crumpled clothing from the floor. While pulling on his shorts, he spotted a small fluorescent-green praying mantis wavering back and forth. Irritated, he flicked the mantis into the air with his finger and thumb. On any other morning, he would have gently cupped the insect in his hands and placed it carefully outside his window. But not this morning. This morning, everything annoyed him.

The peeved mantis landed on the windowsill. Turning its head 180 degrees and raising its long, spiky front legs in front of its head as if in supplication. A small fly buzzed overhead. A lethal predator, the mantis snatched the fly from the air in a nano-second. While crushing its prey alive with its formidable mandibles, the mantis regarded Nong stomping from his bedroom. The praying mantis was much loved by the Thai people. Local folklore considered it bad luck to ill-treat the remarkable creatures.

"Nong, hurry up and drink your Milo, then go and get showered before we're late for training," Joi said without looking up from the kitchen table. Dressed in his coaching gear of a black and red sleeveless top with the Dragon's Gym logo on the front, he had been up for an hour already. As it was still early to leave for Dragon's Gym, he had offered to help Gan out with peeling vegetables.

"What's the point in training if I can't fight?"

Joi raised his head at the tone of Nong's voice and steadily regarded his son. Nong reminded him so much of his wife. He had the same rounded eyes, soft curve to his mouth and stubbornness when he believed himself to be right. "Sit down, stop your whimpering, and help me with these carrots."

"But. What. Is. The point?"

"Nong!! Here's your Milo." Gan recognised that Joi was giving Nong a chance to change his behaviour. "Drink it up, and then off you go."

"I AM NOT A CHILD!" he retorted, purposefully making as much sound as he could, stomping out of the kitchen and out to the front porch.

The electric fan whirred, its rusted metal frame shuddering every so often. *I must remember to tighten those screws,* Joi thought as he sipped his coffee. *Well, either that or see if I can find a second-hand one from the market.*

"Aren't you going to go after him?"

"What for? He will calm down, get bored and turn

up at the gym or be back here in five minutes' time. He wants to fight. No-one can dissuade him, certainly not you or me. A bit like someone else I know. Wouldn't you say?" Joi teased, pulling Gan onto his lap.

"Can't think who you mean!" retorted Gan, wriggling away from him with a smile and straightening her skirt. "You know, Joi, as long as you're with Nong then he can go. Just don't leave him alone to fend for himself. Bangkok is not Chiang Mai, and Somchai is not you. I'll sign the contract."

Joi's mouth fell open, and his eyes widened. Of course, he wanted Nong to compete, but he did not want the contract to be signed with bad feelings in the air. Attempting to better gauge her mood, he took a good look at his wife's face. What he saw caused him to wonder when he had last paused long enough to take the sight of his wife fully. The early morning sun streamed through the kitchen window and onto her face, highlighting the wrinkles around her eyes and revealing the slightly yellowish tone of her skin.

"What's wrong, Gan?" he asked, pulling out an empty chair in an invitation for her to sit.

"I'm fine. Just fine," she lied, wiping the back of her hand across her brow to clear the perspiration. "I didn't sleep well last night. That's all."

"Sure?" said Joi, his eyes seeing a completely different picture of the story she was telling.

"Yes! Stop making a fuss. Those eyes of yours make it seem like I'm undergoing an MRI. We can go to a hospital if you want a detailed image of my guts!"

Gan turned her face away from Joi. She felt as if he was attempting to read the health of every muscle, cell and bone. He was right. Of course, he was. But she did not, in this moment, wish to discuss her illness. So she turned to pots and pans, washing the breakfast dishes. The kitchen reverberated with the metallic sound of saucepans.

But Joi stopped her from evading him. Putting his hand under his wife's chin, he raised her face. Speaking softly, he said, "You know, if you're ill, then the boy stays. You could use some help around the house, and there'll be other opportunities."

Gan clasped Joi's hands in her own. "Stop fretting. I'm well, and it's not as if you'll be gone away for long now, is it? What's a few days? I'd like to go with you, but there's always so much work to do and..."

The sound of scuffling in the passageway brought a smile to her lips. Joi winked and put a finger to his lips.

"Nong, go and find a pen, will you," said Joi, smiling and shrugging as if to say, *told you so*.

Gan slapped him playfully on the arm. "Are you sure you're read—?"

"Yesssss," shouted Nong from the corridor, running into the kitchen to complete a circuit around the house before raising a fist in the air and charging off to his bedroom. "Bangkok, here I come!"

"What I was trying to say was, are you sure he can go?" asked Joi.

"Haven't I already said *yes*? Now, let that be the end of it. There's no need to—"

"Here's a pen," interrupted Nong, holding a chewed Arsenal United biro so high it almost pierced his father's nose. He hopped from foot to foot impatiently.

Joi threw a stern look at him, trying to suppress a smile. "Nong, butt in like a goat when I'm speaking once more, and you're not going anywhere!"

Nong withdrew the pen, dropping his hand by his side as he warily regarded his father.

Gan interjected, "Don't worry, Nong. Your father's fussing. Let's stop all this drama so early in the morning. Here, let me sign the contract so I can make a wish at the same time!"

Nong passed the biro, then hugged his mother's waist. No longer able to see over the top of Nong's head, she tilted her head to one side, smiled at her husband warmly and mouthed the words,

"It's all OK."

"You're going to be late," said Gan, as she unravelled herself from her son's embrace to sign the contract. No sooner had she done so, than a sharp, strong gust of wind blasted through the open window. The agreement shot up into the air and floated in the direction of the gas stove where a pork rib soup was bubbling away in an old steel wok.

"Grab it!" shouted Joi. "The promoter has already signed the other side."

"Noooooo," cried Nong, rushing round the table to try and catch the precious paper. But the page danced and twisted in the breeze, a mango leaf's width away from his fingertips. "Got it!" shouted Nong, grinning as he snatched the page a few centimetres away from the roaring gas flame, his sense of success dissipating when he saw the burnt corner. Trembling, he handed the paper to his father.

"Look at that!" exclaimed Joi, holding the damaged page up to the sunlight. "Those burns look just like claw marks."

"What's wrong, Nong?" asked Gan, worried by her son's horrified face. "It's just a burnt piece of paper. Here, let me see."

Shocked, she recognised the shape of the marks. The last time she had seen that particular formation of lines was when she had been a young girl of ten. Still to this day, she remembered her father pointing them out to her on a dawn hunting trip in the forest. The morning had been cool and damp. After tracking for miles, the only glimpses they had caught of the deer and wild pigs were flashes of teak brown and grey. As they picked their way through the forest, her father had shared stories about how every part of nature is inhabited or owned by unseen dwellers who are not visible to human eyes. In their local folklore, disasters such as famine, drought, flooding, typhoons and earthquakes are sent by the spirits when people no longer respect nature.

Suddenly, her father stopped talking mid-sentence. He had spotted four perfect curved lines carved in the bark of a dark red meranti tree, freshly made. A huge tiger was nearby. It had been marking its territory on the deeply fissured bark. No other animal could have left such damage. The two central scratches were slightly longer than the outer marks, which was a clear signal that the apex predator that had damaged the tree was a tiger. The sun bear was the only other animal that scratched bark, but its claws marked down the trees in a straight line.

Convinced that the burns were in the same formation as she had seen so many years ago in the forest, she slowly put the paper face down on the table, asking herself why these marks would appear now and for whom. For Gan, who had grown up with nature tales, acknowledging the spirits that occupy woods, oceans and the earth was just another part of life. The only possible link she could see between the marks and her family was the relationship her son had with the spirits as a child. Clearly, they thought going to Bangkok was a bad idea. She needed to question him, but carefully, as otherwise she would offend not only her family.

"Nong, do you still see your animal spirit friends? Monkey, Elephant and Tiger?" Gan asked. "Do you ever dream of them?"

"What?" snapped Nong, his eyes furious and face red with anger as he hid his fears. "Those games stopped long ago!" His narrow chest rose and fell. He hated lying, but his mother's animistic beliefs left him with no choice. He was going to Bangkok, whatever it took. Tiger never said he couldn't go, only that he shouldn't. In the certainty that the only road he wanted to take was the one north to Bangkok, Nong snatched the page from his mother.

"It's nothing. Just a burn mark! I'll post it. *Ouch!*" A flash of pain struck his cheek courtesy of Joi's palm. Holding his hand to his face, Nong glowered at his father defiantly and rubbed his jaw.

Dark, emotive storms whirled in Joi's jet-black eyes. Daring Nong to say just one more word, he stared his boy down. On his brow were frown lines reminiscent of Tiger's claw marks, his mouth drawn in a hard steel line. "Your mother's not feeling well—whatever she says. Now, hand that paper back." Joi considered his son and thought, *I'm going to teach that boy some respect this morning and show him he's not all he believes himself to be!*

Nong hung his head in shame, ignoring his still stinging jaw—he had received much worse punishment in the boxing ring, but he had never before felt the dark gloom of having disappointed his parents. Holding the paper with his two hands, he gave his mother a bow and handed her the singed page. His face flushed with shame because he had lied to his mother, shame because he had not respected Tiger and shame that his ego had got the better of him.

"I'm sorry."

"If you ever speak to your mother like that again, you're out of the house. Do you hear me?" said Joi in a low voice, his face granite.

"Yes," mumbled Nong, not daring to meet his father's eye.

"Now get to your room and meet me by the bike in

five minutes. Off with you!" said Joi, his eyes flitting to his wife for a moment, convinced she was ill. He helped Gan clear the garlic and other vegetables they had been peeling from the table and placed them on the draining board for washing. His hand caressed Gan's as she leant across to grab a tomato rolling towards the floor. They laughed as they narrowly avoided clutching the tomato simultaneously. Picking up the contract, Gan inspected it once again, looking at the two human signatures and one spiritual set of claw marks.

"Joi, you don't like it when I talk about the supernatural, but you know Nong is not telling the truth about his friendships with the spirits, don't you? I'm guessing they're telling him he should not fight. Look at the paper again; that's no ordinary burn mark!"

Joi inspected the page again with a sigh. It was hard enough fighting every day for a living, let alone having to deal with supposed creatures from another world. *Give me a break*, he thought. *It's not even 8 a.m., and the day's already been a killer!* But to his wife, he only said, "Look, I don't know about the truth of the tales our parents told us when we were kids, but I do know that you believe in the traditions and stories, and that's good enough for me."

"Ahh, so you don't believe, do you? So why is it that I sometimes see YOU putting fruits at our spirit house then most mornings? Or did you think a wife doesn't see everything?" teased Gan. "Only just the other day, I saw you put some bottles of strawberry Fanta on the house with a few biscuits!"

"Well, err, you know. It never hurts to protect yourself, now does it?"

"I guess not," replied Gan, smiling at her husband's refusal to acknowledge that he, too, believed that it was better to be wary of the spirit world than tempt fate by denying its existence.

"Look, about Nong. I'll leave the decision up to you as to if he goes or not. If you don't want him to, and now you say the spirits don't bless the trip, who am I to stand in the way? What I can promise is that if he does go, I will make sure he is ready to fight and stands a good chance of winning. And let's not forget about the fight purse. We're about to hit low season, and Dragon's Gym has not been as busy as it usually is. There are rumours that Lucy may need to lay people off. That fight purse would come in handy."

Against her better judgement and despite her doubts, Gan could not help but agree.

What was one weekend away in Bangkok? A month's lack of focus on his studies was not a catastrophe. But a seed of fear had been planted by the burnt contract. It was a bad omen. Talking a deep inward breath, she took a glance out of the window at the verdant forest beyond their small backyard. On the lower branch of the Bodhi Tree sat a monkey. She had never seen a macaque with such a solemn expression before. It looked just like a wizened abbot in grey monk's robes. It seemed to be staring straight at her as, if it were telling her to think very carefully about what decision she would take. Gan shook her head, *I'm going quite mad,* she thought. *Next, I will be thinking the trees are sending me messages!* But the monkey stayed still, staring at her as motionless as a temple statue. Putting the uneasy feeling she had down to a mother's protectiveness, she gave her husband's shoulder a squeeze. She bent down to retrieve a basket for the spirit house, calling Nong as she did to return to the kitchen and take the incense sticks and offerings.

"Hurry up, Nong. Do what your mother says," shouted Joi, "and not in twenty minutes' time either!"

Nong collected the reed woven basket carrying fruit and small cakes, a lighter, and the incense sticks and went outside to the miniature shrines housing the tutelary deities. He put the basket on the earth underneath the palm tree and carefully placed the mangoes and oranges on the silvered, worn offering plate below the roof of the tallest house. Next, he folded back the banana leaf fronds encasing the sticky white rice so the spirits could eat the grains easily. Then he lit the incense sticks and, holding them between his palms, bowed his head three times. When he had finished his prayers, he glanced around the yard to see if he could catch a glimpse of the spirit animals. Suddenly, there was the rustle of a large animal behind him. "Tiger!" he exclaimed under his breath with relief. He turned his face away from the house in case he was being watched.

"I'm so happy to… Oh, it's you."

Sam, now a slightly mature dog of four, stopped scratching in the dirt, looking for discarded food at the sound of Nong's voice, his tail wagging and ears upright. Padding forwards, Sam sniffed for treats. Finding nothing, he ambled off in the direction of the rubbish bins.

Nong exhaled a deep breath. Behind him, an Asian koel landed on the spirit house and began to peck at the soft white rice on the banana leaf. Nong was not a fan of koels. The male koels had a distinctively loud, repetitive, high-pitched "ku-oo" mating call, which they made from dawn and sometimes repeated at dusk.

"Stop it. STOP! Shooo," Gan shouted.

"What?"

"The bird, the bird."

Confused, Nong turned to where his mother was pointing. The cuckoo was now pecking at the altar's little, smiling boy doll or *Kuman Thong* (golden little boy) wearing traditional Ayutthaya clothing with his hair in a topknot. In his hand, the toy carried a small bag of gold. *Kuman Thongs*, like most children, were thought to prefer sweets like cookies and candies. Nong's aunt had taught him that for a drink, the dolls almost exclusively desired *Nam-daeng,* which means 'red water.' This was made using bright red artificial food colouring and the flavouring of local *sala* or snake fruit. If traditional *Nam-daeng* cannot be obtained, red Fanta was the next best thing. His aunt said that the belief the idols preferred red beverages stemmed from the ancient tradition of offering spirit animals' blood.

The koel pecked at the spirit figurines with its hard-black beak, knocking them over. Gan shouted frantically as she waved her arms, shooing the cuckoo away to prevent it from drawing bad luck down onto her family. The cuckoo turned its head and glared at Gan with its left red eye before taking to the air, lazily flapping his wings. Squawking in protest at being disturbed, the koel flew to the lowest branch of the nearest palm tree, where it perched and recommenced its repetitive, high-pitched "ku-oo".

Nong and Gan contemplated the carnage. The illustrious pearl-coloured rice grains were now covered in excrement, and the figurines were either on their sides or had been knocked over the side of the spirit house and now lay in the mud.

"Nong, promise me you'll go to the forest temple before you leave and ask Abbot Anurak to bless your trip."

"Sure, I'll go tomorrow."

"Good. I'll let your father know. He'll be pleased to have one less thing to organise while you're in Bangkok. He'll have enough on his hands without having to visit a temple!"

Chapter Twenty

NONG stared up at the paint peeling off the hotel room ceiling, waving his toes back and forth as he listened to his favourite rock band. On the bed next to his, Somchai lay face down, snoring loudly. The early morning sun filtered through the thin, dusty grey curtains. Even though the windows were shut tightly, the cacophony caused by the Bangkok rush hour traffic reverberated around the room. Frustrated drivers, incapable of doing anything about the traffic jam, signalled their annoyance by dutifully beeping their horns. Intercity trains *whooshed* along the tracks behind the hotel, causing the walls to shudder. Throughout the night, police sirens had wailed. One-kilometre northwards, Bangkok's famous river, the *Chao Phraya*, always jam-packed with ferries and tugboats pulling enormous black rice barges, wound its way past the stunning, asymmetrically designed Rama VIII bridge with its lotus motifs. On the opposite side of the *Chao Phraya*, to the south, the soaring silhouette of *Wat Arun*, the Temple of Dawn, could be seen.

Lying back with arms under his head, Nong visualised himself celebrating a resounding win against his opponent Agung. He imagined himself doing a cartwheel that caught Agung in the head despite his clear height advantage. Taking a deep breath, he thanked his father for his patience, guidance and willingness to share his experience.

There had been moments he had caught Somchai watching them work together with an annoyed look. At other times, Somchai had teased him about being the favourite, but Nong was not so easily goaded and would just shrug his shoulders and say, "It is what it is."

Joi had devised a clear fight strategy with him. He would use lots of kicks and *teeps*, changing angles to make sure he would stay out of the bigger and stronger Agung's clinch range. Big punchers and clinchers were very predictable for Nong, being a Muay Femur style fighter. His secret was to create angles and lateral moves rather than just moving backwards to avoid an attack. If they had his game plan right, then his opponent would completely miss him. The trick was to find Agung's strong side and remain near his weaker one.

Joi taught that one hundred per cent of the time, boxers use their best weapons in the first few moments and stick to the style they are confident and comfortable with. There is no way they can save their best techniques for rounds three and beyond. In general, foreign fighters had good punching and quite good leg kicks. Nong needed to be extra careful to avoid punches and make sure his counterattack was solid. Every day, he worked on the shuffle which he planned to use in the ring to confuse his opponent as to whether he was going to kick with his left or right leg.

Nong not only trained with Joi and his team of *krus* but also practised with the champion boxers who came down from Bangkok for a change of environment. When he could, he would spar with them. As Nong grew in experience, he added more technical elements to his arsenal. *Farang* fighters were typically much bigger than Thais, and Nong had had to change his approach. What's more, he also had to adapt his style of boxing to the demands of the promoters. They encouraged fighters to use sharp and powerful kicks rather than clinch techniques because, they argued, international audiences did not like to watch wrestling matches.

Boxers fought for two reasons. The first was because they had no choice; their families pushed them into the sport to make money. The second reason was because they loved to fight. Nong loved the sport of Muay Thai, and his strong character meant that he trained hard and was willing to study and learn from more experienced champions. His father warned that he had seen many incredible fighters who never quite made it because of a lack of self-discipline and dedication. They got distracted by life's pleasures and did not study the champions and have the commitment it takes to get to a world-class level. When his father fought, it was very difficult to get a championship belt. Now, boxers only had to win four or five fights to earn one in the regional stadiums.

Joi alternated Nong's training sessions between Somchai and Ram, who did not have major fights coming up. They did not work in rounds but just kept going until Nong was exhausted. Sometimes, they did pad work for endurance. Sparring was the best way to prepare for a fight, and they battled at about seventy to eighty per cent of their strength. Each fighter at Dragon's Gym always tried to dominate, as sparring was very close to actual fighting. Sparring gave boxers tactical experience. The month had been hard, really hard, but not once had Nong complained about the intensity of the training. He had done just enough schoolwork to enable him to follow the classes, and every other waking moment had been spent preparing for Bangkok.

Lucy had been running an online campaign on the Dragon's Gym Instagram page, telling the story of what it takes to get ready for a fight at Lumpinee. Seeing all the likes and positive comments boosted Nong's confidence. He didn't share the secret pleasure he took from the growing media exposure with Somchai and the rest, not wishing to tempt bad luck as a result of making them jealous.

When Joi confirmed he would be flying to Bangkok along with Somchai, he felt an immense sense of relief. Nong's days were filled with the demands that he trained harder and responded faster defensively and offensively during the sparring sessions. He had incorporated more weight training into his daily workout routine to help him dominate when clinching. The fight would not be like the shorter *Muay Xtreme* events but a full-blown Muay Thai fight of five rounds of three minutes each. Time and time again, Joi told Nong it was important to engage with the crowd and show a deep level of skill to the Muay Thai aficionados in the audience, as their shouts and cheers helped persuade the judging panel to vote in a particular direction. This was especially important when he and his opponent were evenly matched. As the fight would be won by the boxer who had displayed the best sense of Muay 'Thainess', which is to say, the aptitudes of a Muay Thai fighter in the areas of mind, body and spirit. Mind refers to a fighter's technique and fight intelligence: their skill, tactics, awareness, range, and timing. Body refers to a fighter's strength and condition, movement efficiency, balance as well as robustness and is the physical component of a Muay Thai fighter. Lastly, spirit refers to a fighter's attitude and heart—their emotional fortitude, resilience, psychology and 'mindset', the emotional side of a fighter's game. Mercifully oblivious to horns and sirens outside his hotel room, Nong dreamt of showing the whole world how beautiful and deadly Muay Thai was, of travelling the globe to educate people about his country's national sport.

"Ouch, what's that for Somchai," moaned Nong, holding a hand to his head. "I was just getting to the best bit in the film, where I get the supermodel."

"Too slow, Nong. Too slow! We gotta get going. Here, hand me my Adidas, will you?" yawned Somchai as he stretched his arms up over his head. "It's 8 a.m. already, and we've got the weigh-in at eleven. Get the door, will you, or your dad's going to knock it down."

Nong opened the door latch. Outside the door, his father stood dressed in jeans and a blue shirt.

"Good morning, Nong," he said. As he looked around the room, he couldn't help but notice the mess. Clothes jumbled up on the floor, empty bottles of Sprite, which Joi hoped belonged to Somchai given the high sugar content, mobile phone chargers and rucksacks with their contents spilling out. The open wardrobe doors revealed an empty interior.

"You two do know what clothes hangers are for, don't you?"

Nong and Somchai exchanged glances, silently agreeing it was best not to answer. "Nong, you go and shower first. Give me a shout when you're done."

Once Nong had closed the door behind him, Somchai asked, "So what's the game plan?"

"We're heading out straight from here. We've got no time to be hanging around. You know what hell Bangkok traffic is! Getting to Ram Intra Road in Bang Khen could take an hour. You can grab something to eat once we've done the weigh-in."

"What?" protested Somchai. "There's—"

"No," cut in Joi. "We've got to get going. Call Tanawat and ask him about the cape Nong's gotta wear. It should've been delivered here. Let's hope for Nong's sake that they don't make him share the same cloak the other boxers have worn. When I fought at the old stadium, all the fighters had to use the same branded ones. Which is fine if you were first on, but if you were on last, it felt like wearing a sweaty old pair of boxer's shorts and stunk just as badly."

"Will do."

"Did you remember the long-sleeved jumpers? The stadium's freezing! Hang on a minute."

"What?"

"Nong! STOP singing and GET moving!" ordered Joi, banging the bathroom door several times with his fist. "Look, I'll meet you downstairs in ten minutes. Hurry up, the next contender for *Thailand's Got Talent*, will you?"

CHAPTER TWENTY-ONE

JOI got in the front of the taxi. Somchai and Nong sat behind. A walnut has fewer wrinkles than the taxi driver who cheerfully bid them good morning. His wide grin revealed his tombstone teeth, all jagged and chipped, leaning to the left or right and covered in yellow lichen. His front middle tooth was missing.

As the taxi pulled out into the crawling traffic, Joi said to the driver, "No turbo meter, please," referring to the little blue switch installed right next to the gear stick, which some taxi drivers switch on so the meter fare ticks up faster than Nong could sprint. The cabbie laughed and protested that no mechanical alterations had been done to his car while covering up the switch with an old grey rag. After declining the taxi driver's entreaties to visit the Golden Temple of the Emerald Buddha and the Grand Palace, which for more than two centuries, since the founding of the Chakri dynasty, have represented the heart of spiritual and royal power in Thailand, they finally set off in the direction of the new Lumpinee stadium.

Twenty minutes later, they were edging their way through the Bangkok traffic bantering with the driver, who refused to turn on the air conditioning, insisting they wound down the windows in the mistaken belief it would save his fuel. It was only when Joi explained that Nong was fighting and didn't want to lose a lung from the pollution before his big night that the driver relented.

"Look at that!" cried Nong as the car approached Lumpinee Boxing Stadium. "Yesssssss!" He jumped out of the taxi before it had even stopped. Round and round, he spun, celebrating that he would soon be competing at the most famous Muay Thai stadium. Putting his palms together, he said a short prayer under his breath. Then he realised he had not kept his promise to visit Abbot Anurak. What to do? He could hardly go and ask his father if they could go and visit a temple now, could he? He'd be annoyed, and they couldn't waste time charging around to find the right monk in Bangkok. There were important people to meet.

The three generations of boxers stood contemplating the silver metallic space-age oval stadium that bore no resemblance to the old venue on Rama IV Road, with its concrete walls and corrugated iron roof. Joi put his arm around Nong's shoulders and gave an audible sigh of pride. Today, not only were Nong's dreams being realised, but Joi's too. He had long since retired when the new stadium was opened in 2014. Joi had fought at the old stadium and fondly recalled his time there and events such as history-making fights, mafia assassinations ringside, and a cat somersaulting through the roof and crashing onto the ring in the blue corner during a break in the action. At the old stadium, the fighters' changing rooms were open to the public and the media. Television cameras would try and interview the boxers even as they warmed up. Somchai had told Nong that here, the fighters' changing rooms were away from the audiences, clean, with lavatories and showers. And most importantly, they had a door that could be locked.

"Come on, let's get the weigh-in done," said Joi. "Lead the way, Somchai."

Nong trailed behind the two of them. "You're going to win; you're going to win," he repeated to himself as he fought back a sense of dread.

Ten hours later, Nong peeked through the changing room door. Already, the corridor was filled with match officials, stadium staff and boxing fans. The menthol smell of the *Namman Muay,* a type of Tiger Balm covering his limbs and torso, both warmed his muscles and helped him get in the right mindset for the fight ahead. He didn't use the oil when sparring, so its scent meant one thing, it was time to meet his adversary. At the end of the corridor, he spotted two familiar people talking to Tanawat. Bhan and Aye. They seemed to be arguing. Tanawat was shaking his head and waving his hands in a definitive no movement. Nong quickly ducked his head back into the changing room to avoid being seen. Not wanting to unsettle himself with concerns about the two men and curious as to why they were there, he decided to let Somchai know.

"You'll never guess who I've just spotted," he said.

"Probably not, no," replied Somchai. "Do I need to play guessing games now?"

"It was Bhan and that guy, Aye. You know, the rich

kid I first met in the temple and then saw again in Chiang Mai with his friend?"

"Oh, right. Well, they said they were involved in boxing, somehow, didn't they? What's the problem? Don't you know that Aye is a gangster?"

"A what?"

"The important guy, the one that technically acts as the 'House' at Lumpinee. He's a rich and powerful man, the one that calls the odds."

"But how does that work?"

"It depends on who is winning the round, doesn't it, stupid? The odds change almost every round. It's difficult to explain how odds are made, and often, you'll look around the stadium and see the other gangsters calling out different odds for their own section of gamblers. Given how important he is, perhaps you should've been a bit nicer to him in Chiang Mai?"

Nong assessed him quizzically. Somchai had been behaving rather strangely all day as if his mind were elsewhere. He knew his father had noticed by the questioning glances he had been sending Somchai's way. He suspected that before long, Joi was going to have a few words with him. Ever since Nong had told Somchai that he was up for the *Muay Thai Fighter of the Year* award by the Sports Writers of Thailand for winning ten consecutive knockouts, he had been cold and distant towards him.

"I'll go and say hi. I need to get us some more towels for the fight anyway," Somchai said as he walked out, his eyes to the ground, hands in his pockets and shoulders slightly hunched.

Joi looked up from his paper, scrutinising Somchai as he left.

"Where's he off to, Nong?"

"He said he had to get towels."

"Why? There's a pile over there in the corner."

"Probably didn't see them."

"He hasn't been himself at all today. Good job your dad's here, Nong! Here, get back on the table. We need to give those muscles a bit more of a warm-up."

Nong went over to the red plastic-covered massage table and lay face down. Joi kneaded the back of Nong's thighs, watching the door for Somchai's return, thinking he would pull him aside for a few words and ask not only what was wrong but also tell him to pull it together. Now was not the time to cast doubt in Nong's mind. If Nong stood any chance of winning, he had to stay calm and focused.

Twenty minutes later, Somchai returned with a few white towels and bottles of water in a Seven-Eleven plastic bag in his left hand. In his right, he held his mobile, which he was talking into as he walked.

"You took your time?" snapped Joi. "We don't need more towels and water. There are enough over there!" He was about to berate Somchai when a middle-aged, attractive woman wearing neatly ironed blue trousers and a white polo shirt interrupted him from the doorway. Around her neck hung a security tag fixed onto a red lanyard printed with the stadium's logo.

"I've got the cape for Nong. Sorry you can't use your own gym's this time around, but we've got some special sponsors backing tonight's fights."

"Thanks. When you say special, I hope they've stumped up a bit more cash than usual," said Joi, smiling at her. "How are you?" He recognised her from the old stadium. Forgetting all about the towels, they chatted for a while as he took the cape.

"You know," she said, "I can remember those sweat rags from years back too. It can't have been nice you all having to share the one cloak!"

Eventually, Joi excused himself, seeing it was almost time to go.

"You already look like a winner, Champ!" said Joi as he tied the black faux satin cloak around Nong's neck, joking that they should make it fur-lined, given how cold the room was. But Nong did not smile back. He was focused on the fight ahead, his mouth drawn into a thin line and his jaw clenched.

"Here, let me recheck your gloves," said Joi, taking both of Nong's hands in his own. He turned Nong's palms facing upwards, expertly testing the tautness of the laces and wiping them clean of the Namman Muay, which had become smeared on their surface. Lastly, he tied the *Pra jiad,* which Gan had made for Nong, around his upper arms. Standing back, he looked at his boy. "Here, Somchai. Take a picture, will you?"

"Sure. Stand over there, next to the wall where the light is better."

Nong opted for his southpaw boxer stance, held up

both his gloved hands and stared into the camera phone, looking every inch a prize fighter. His taught stomach muscles glistened with oil. To his right, Joi stood with his legs slightly apart, giving a double thumbs-up signal. When Gan saw the image later, she would be struck by how much alike they were. Both had the same clear-eyed look and determined soft jawline, which was deceptively tough.

"Hey, guys," announced Tanawat, entering the room. "Let's go, it's show time. Nong, you walk out first, and Joi, Somchai and I'll follow just as we rehearsed earlier. Ignore the media milling around outside, and DO NOT stop to talk to anyone! When you're through the curtain and at the start of the ramp, we'll line up and have a few shots taken. You should strike a few poses alone for the cameras before running into the centre of the ring. Magazines love those poses. Don't forget to wave to the crowds and the TV cameras. If you've any special little dances to make the crowd laugh, cut a jig before running down the ramp. Once you're in the ring, then be still. Joi, have I left anything out?"

"Nope, Nong's golden."

"Let's be off then."

Tanawat lead the way, with Nong and Joi following closely behind. Somchai trailed last, still holding the bag of towels in his left hand so tightly his knuckles were white. Nong half-jogged his way down the corridor, shadow-boxing. As he moved, he imagined the strength of his father supporting him. Tanawat was saying something to him, but the only voices he could hear were the one inside his head and the low tones of his father. He focused on calming his nerves and settling his mind. Shifting from foot to foot, Nong took deep breaths and wished the organisers would hurry up and open the curtain. The BOOM BOOM of the techno music reminded Nong of the war drums in his favourite Siam martial art fighting movies.

Finally, two girls in hot pants pulled the white, stained bell ropes of the crimson-red curtains. For the first time, the stadium interior was revealed to Nong. He struggled to stop his mouth from falling open. The stadium was awash with blue and diamond-white neon high-tech lights and enormous TV screens. Red, yellow and white spotlights flashed back and forth over the audience, some of whom were up from their seats, cheering and applauding. The whole experience felt unreal, as if he had stepped through the television and onto a movie set.

"Give it up for Sirachaipet! Heeeeeee's from a long line of boxers," screamed the emcee in a high-octane voice. "Sirachiapet's father, Joi, is here tonight. Yes, that's the handsome man on the right. He fought in his day at the old Lumpinee! Welcome back to Bangkok, sir! Awesome! Let's hear it for the Muay Thai family!"

Joi acknowledged the crowd's roar with a wave. This was not his night but Nong's. Nong gulped down a mouthful of the Arctic air, as he let his brain absorb a sight, he had imagined all his life. Nong was always quite nervous warming up but as soon as he got in the ring that would all go. Nong slapped the upraised palms of the crowd for good luck as he led Joi and Somchai up the ramp to his corner. As Nong climbed over the top rope, his pride in his achievements grew. He couldn't help but ignore Tanawat's instruction to stand quietly and wait for his opponent to join him in the ring. The media wanted to focus on each fighter without any distractions. But tonight was his night. He ran around the circumference of the ring, leaping into the air and punching it with his fists. The crowd roared its appreciation of his antics, which the referee quickly stepped in to truncate at the same time as his opponent Agung was announced with a deafening drum roll.

"Hereeeer's Agung Iron Fist," screamed the manic emcee into his microphone: first in English, then Thai. Agung bounced on the balls of his feet. As he shadow-boxed his way along the ramp, he performed a series of set pieces: cross, jab, uppercut cross. Not once did he reach out to the crowd or even acknowledge their presence. Agung's eyes focused on Nong. His proud, lean face showed no emotion, no glimmer of excitement. His mouth a thin line like a rock fissure. Nong hated him on sight.

After they had completed the ceremonial *Wai Ram*, the referee gave the instruction to "Keep it clean." Finally, he slashed his arm downwards to signal they should start. Just as the *Samara* musicians picked up their tempo, Nong struck out with a straight blast attack with his right foot, hitting Agung in the stomach. "Yes, you arrogant bastard, this is my night, not yours," snarled Nong. Immediately, Agung retaliated, taking a small hop forward on his back left foot, aiming a side *teep* at Nong's solar plexus with his right. He failed to make impact, however, as Nong whipped around to his left, side-stepping away. Circling each other like two lions, they assessed each other's strengths with a series of feints, the noise of the *Samara* and audience cries having faded in each of their minds to nothingness. They only sensed one another, testing the walls of each other's defences with jabs and low kicks, blocking and making counter-offensive moves as they went. They regularly reset to the standard Muay Thai stance that was more squared than the common, parallel stances of boxing, karate, *tae kwon do* and other martial arts. To move explosively and change directions quickly, they drove their feet hard into the mat. They always kept their guard up as they would be momentarily stance-less when moving, and a sharp opponent could take advantage of the transition. The reason for a more squared stance was so they could properly defend and deliver Muay Thai kicks.

Each boxer left the back-foot heel off the ground to assist in fast movement and quick changes of direction. Agung attempted a left roundhouse kick. Nong responded by grabbing the heel of Agung's foot, unbalancing his opponent just enough to be able to push him back and then hit him in the side of the head with his foot. They reset. Agung smashed his foot sideways into Nong's upper thigh, but Nong did not flinch. As they settled into their deadly cobra dance, weaving and swaying, exchanging *teeps*, low kicks, and effectively blocking one another, the bell sounded. It seemed to Nong that Agung was holding back and giving him an advantage, but he pushed the thought straight out of his mind.

Nong spat his mouthguard out into Somchai's waiting hand. Somchai took the mouthguard, rinsed it with water from one of his bottles and carefully dried it while Joi massaged Nong's arms and poured ice-cold water on his limbs, telling him that he needed to start drawing his opponent in. As Nong sat on the plastic corner stool, he heard his father and readied his mind for the offensive strategy he would put in place. Behind him, the gamblers gesticulated, waving their hands, making it clear that Nong was the favourite and that all bets had gone his way. Near the bar stood Bhan and Aye, laughing and looking thoroughly smug. The bell rang, but still Somchai had not returned Nong's mouthguard.

"What the fuck are you doing? You idiot," snapped Joi, grabbing the mouthguard.

Judges did not like to be kept waiting. Joi pushed the rubber shield in Nong's mouth, gave him a thumbs up and slapped his son on the back as he turned to face the centre of the ring. Advancing within two arms reach of Agung, Nong immediately struck him with a hard low kick to the inside of his right leg, drew his leg back again and quickly followed up with a left kick to the side of his head. Agung struck back with a punch, hammering into Nong's face. Nong went to kick again with his left, but Agung responded by grabbing his heel and yanked his foot back and forth to throw him off balance. Nong managed to free himself. They reset, measuring the striking distance between one another by stretching their arms and tapping the shoulder. Agung struck out with a jab, but Nong leaned back, causing his glove to meet thin air. Nong *teeped* Agung with a toe jab that felt as if someone had thrust the end of an iron bar into his stomach and sent him flying backwards. Agung advanced with a kick to the ribs followed by a jab that Nong barely managed to block, staggering sideways, suddenly disorientated.

"Something's not right," said Joi from the sidelines to Somchai. "Why's he wavering? As he looked on, he saw Nong take a sharp blow to the head without even attempting to protect himself. "He's fighting like a fly stuck on sandpaper. What the fuck?"

Blood poured from a deep cut on Nong's forehead. He had taken an elbow to the head and was receiving a battering. In under thirty seconds, the fight had turned into a massacre as Agung smashed into Nong's body, mercilessly driving into him with every bone and sinew. The crowd booed.

Nearby, a man shouted, "He's been drugged."

Something was wrong. Seriously wrong.

"Stop this fucking shit," screamed Joi, jumping into the ring as Nong collapsed on the floor lifeless. The referee gave a whistle, calling an end to the fight, not bothering to count Nong out as he stepped out of the way for the paramedics.

"Somchai, you fucker! You've drugged him!" Joi bellowed, charging to the red corner.

"Err, what, me? No way!"

"Give me those water bottles!"

"Why, what for?"

Furious, Joi shoved Somchai backwards, causing him to stumble, and grabbed the opened bottles and towels, stuffing them into the bag. "I'll deal with you later," he snarled over his shoulder as he climbed over the ropes and ran towards Nong, who by now had had his head fitted into a brace. Behind him, two match officials were already approaching Somchai, having seen the altercation between the two of them. Knowing Somchai would not be allowed to leave, Joi focused on getting to his son. The crowd booed, jeered and whistled. Judges, media, journalists and members of the audience had crowded into the ring, and bedlam ensued as people shouted at one another to get out of the way.

Joi ploughed through the mob, pushing people aside. He knelt down beside Nong. Opposite him crouched Agung; his face was crumpled in concern.

His coach, Desnee, said, "This is not on us. You know that. I give you, my word."

"I know. You don't need to tell me," said Joi, keeping his voice calm and hiding the fury inside. "I'll talk to the officials." He had known Desnee for over twenty years and understood the concern. No fighter wanted to win a match in such a dishonourable way, and if implicated in the drugging of a boxer, would be banned for life.

"Nong, can you hear me? What do you feel?"

"What's going on? I lost, didn't I?"

"No, no, you didn't."

"But I felt so weak, it was as if I couldn't move and…" Nong started to struggle to sit up, tracks of red blood running down his face. Joi gently pushed him back down.

"No, let's get you to hospital. We need to know what caused this and run blood tests."

"OK, guys. You heard Joi. Get going," instructed Tanawat, who, while he was concerned for the boy, needed to get the night's fight schedule back up and running. "Joi, call me when you get the results, will you? I saw you arguing with Somchai. What do you want me to do there?"

"Arrest the fucker!"

Nong was carried off on a stretcher with the media following. Some of the crowd cheered and clapped. A fight broke out between the gamblers, who always stood in groups throughout the stadium. Normally, they wanted to see a knockout as they could get their money faster and move on to the next fight. Fists flew, and drinks were thrown. A number of the tourists could be seen making for the exit, while others went to the box office to try and get a refund. There was little point in watching fixed matches.

Joi felt a tap on the shoulder. A tall, thin, grim-faced man reached out a hand. Joi took it, recognising Colonel Mongkol Siriparu, Director of Discipline and

Preventive Measures against Match-Fixing.

"I apologise on behalf of the Royal Thai Army," said the colonel.

"Thank you, Sir," replied Joi.

"I will not detain you; I understand you must go with your son. But please take my business card. There will be an investigation, and we will see the medical reports. The ambulance had been directed to take Nong to the nearest hospital, and the medical team is on standby."

Joi took the card with both hands and gave a slight bow of his head before hurrying away. He understood that the military were keen to solve what happened so they could make an official report, but he wanted to deal with Somchai first. This was personal. And anyway, who knew who had earned money from Nong being poisoned? It might even have been the colonel himself.

Later, in the stark hospital waiting room, he racked his brain as to why Somchai would take the money from gamblers to fix the fight. Hadn't he done enough for the boy who was now his enemy? Somchai wasn't stupid. He understood that if caught, he was in very real danger of disappearing for good. The military did not mess around, and neither would he. The poisoning of fighters was a disease in the sport, and he guessed that Nong would test positive for a sedative. He comprehended what had happened and considered whether the match officials knew too. Nong was going to take a couple of months to make a full recovery. He would be on an IV drip for a while and be prescribed long doses of medicine. Joi almost hoped he would never see Somchai again. He had been long enough in the business of Muay Thai to have heard all the stories, and it was always someone who was known to the boxer who administered the poison. More often than not, it was a person who was very close.

The doctor handed Joi the medical reports and confirmed his suspicions. Nong's blood had tested positive for a cocktail of Nordazepam, Temazepam, and Oxazepam, as had the water bottle.

Seeing that Joi was struggling to read medical jargon, the doctor said, "The results show that your son was given a mixture that, in overdose, could have been lethal. In some ways, he is lucky to be alive."

Joi bowed his head slightly and thanked the doctor.

"Let me know if you need anything else."

"Thanks, Doctor. Where can I find you in ten minutes? I just need to make a call back home."

"Just ask the receptionist to page me. I am incredibly sorry this has happened to your boy."

Joi waited for the doctor to disappear before taking out his phone. He thought *I'd better get this over with.* He took a deep breath before tapping in the colonel's cell number.

CHAPTER TWENTY-TWO

BACK at Dragon's Gym, only hours before, everyone from the youngest child to the oldest villager, who had gate-crashed the event at the ripe old age of ninety-five, was in a *Songkran* mood. Lucy had sponsored a pre-match barbeque for the gym employees, their families and the foreign boxers staying at the camp. There was enough beef, fried chicken, pork satay sticks, rice, fresh fruit and locally caught red snapper, grouper and tiger prawns for the whole village, and many uninvited guests arrived. Everyone wanted to celebrate.

Nong, Joi and Gan were popular community members, and people welcomed not only the opportunity to drink and eat at someone else's expense but also to catch up on gossip, forget their woes for a while and have a bet on what seemed a sure chance to make some money. Baht notes exchanged hands. Everyone punted on Nong winning but vehemently disagreed over whether he would win by a knockout in the second, third, fourth or fifth round. Proud parents showed off babies, grandparents fussed and played with children kicking footballs, while groups of men and women stood around chatting and smoking. The clouds of blue smoke over their heads kept away the mosquitos. Even Abbot Anurak and a couple of the monks from the *wat* had joined the evening's festivities to watch Nong's fight on the large white bedsheet that had been suspended between the roof rafters and two huge tractor tyres to serve as a film screen.

Raucous beer-fuelled shouts and screams of encouragement in English, German, Dutch, Finnish and Thai greeted Nong's appearance. Where the bedsheet had not been ironed properly, creases caused distortions on his face, making him look like he had multiple bumps and three ears, to the delight of the children who started making impressions of his altered image, flattening their noses and ears in parody. People called out "superhero, champ and *chok dee*." They clapped and banged drums.

Their cacophony frightened birds in the nearby forest and sent small mammals scurrying away deep into the woods and into the tree canopies. Soi dogs milled around the children playing chase and the adults shouting, scavenging for any food that Sam had not gobbled up already. In the first round, frenzied applause greeted each blow that the seven-foot projection of Nong struck. Warit and Kritsada punched and kicked the air along with the children imitating the competitor's low kicks, jabs and crosses.

Then, swift as a thunderclap, the mood changed. "Nooooo, What! Murderers!" wailed two hundred voices in unison. Hands covered horrified expressions, and babies started to scream, feeling their parents' anxious response to the sight of Nong stumbling around the ring. The confused look on his ashen face caused one woman to weep and others to fall silent, their mouths open, while others booed and whistled.

"You corrupt bastards," Warit screamed, recognising that the month's wages he had gambled were lost and fearing the worst had happened.

Gan, too, had risked her meagre savings on Nong winning, as had all her friends and neighbours. Aghast, everyone witnessed the effect of the sedative in real-time. Nong's legs collapsed from underneath him, and then he crumpled into a heap on the mat.

The villagers' horror at the money they had lost dissipated as the injustice of what had occurred enraged them. Later that evening and tomorrow morning, they would feel different. Everyone would be out of pocket. Gan, like her neighbours, had gambled money her family could ill afford to waste. Hospital bills, children's school fees and loans would remain unpaid. Arguments would break out between families who would now not be eating well for a month. The poisoning would not only impact Nong's health but that of the whole village, which struggled to feed hungry mouths at the best of times. Parents held onto their children's hands. The smaller ones continued to cry, not able to understand why their mothers and fathers were so upset.

Hearts wrenched for the onscreen Joi when he knelt by his son's side and tenderly wiped the sweat off his face and the drool from his mouth. The sight of the man they knew and loved looking heartbroken, grieved woman, man and child alike. In silence, the audience watched as the Lumpinee medical officials carried Nong from the ring on a stretcher. The TV pulled away from its close-up of Nong's face, and the camera briefly flitted to Nong's corner. For all to see was Somchai, looking over his shoulder back at Nong with an expression of hatred.

"It was Somchai," Gan screamed, one thin hand clasped to her chest and the other pointing at the screen. "He poisoned my—" Angry shouts, boos and hisses drowned out the end of her sentence.

At the back of the gym, Lucy watched in silence, turned on her heel and left. She needed to speak to Joi and offer whatever support she could, as well as stop him from going on a vendetta. Sometimes, Thailand is more a land of corruption, conspiracies and coups than a land of smiles. Shaking her head in frustration at the amount of effort everyone had wasted, she focused her mind on damage control. The company and what could bring the whole company's name into disrepute had to be her first concern, for all of them Lucy needed to protect the Dragon's Gym brand and could not risk Joi taking matters into his own hands. Retrieving her mobile phone, she headed into the office and locked the door behind her. Any mess left from the barbeque could be dealt with tomorrow.

Back outside, Gan's head swam, and her knees buckled. Warit caught her just before she collapsed on the gym floor. As Warit gently supported Gan, his hands under her arms, Natcha and Neuy consoled her as she wept.

"It's my fault, I should've listened. It's my fault. The spirits warned of the danger. The trip was cursed."

"Hush, it's not as bad as it looks, I'm sure. Nong's in good hands," said Neuy, gently stroking Gan's back. "He'll be sent to the best hospital, and Joi's there."

"You don't understand," wept Gan. Tears fell through her fingers. "I knew he shouldn't have gone, but I still let him go."

Natcha and Neuy exchanged baffled looks over the top of Gan's head. Neither of them knew how best to comfort her. What on earth did Gan mean by 'the spirits'?

"Is it okay if I go?" Natcha asked quietly.

Neuy gave her a quick nod, trusting that her daughter had some urgent errand and turned her attention once again to Gan. No sooner had Natcha stood than another woman took her place, offering sympathetic words.

Natcha cut through the crowds and exited the gym, determined to find Ram and the boys. Outside, she spotted him, beer in hand, laughing and joking with a very upset-looking Mongkut and Prasert. Mongkut saw Natcha first and waved, his face in a state of shock. Immediately, though, he lowered his hand as one of the spotlights from the gym revealed the fury on her face. Instinctively, he took a step back, causing Ram to turn and check what the problem was. Before he had a chance to even say hi, Natcha screamed in Ram's face,

"What do you know?" Turning to Mongkut and Panit, she repeated her question, and their shocked faces and wide-open eyes told her all she needed to know.

Ram met Natcha's question with a silent stare and shrugged. His calm, nonchalant expression decided his fate. Furious for Nong, her *kru* Joi, friends, family and neighbours, she met his patronising look with the response she felt most appropriate. She pulled back her left arm and punched Ram in the face. Her sharp knuckles smashed into his jaw. Ram, unable to block her cross punch in time, took the blow side on and went down. A lined, sinewy hand reached out and grabbed him under the arm, pulling him up.

"Get some ice on your face and go home," Kritsada instructed Ram, shoving him away in the direction where he lived and indicating that Panit and Mongkut should go with him. "Natcha, STOP RIGHT NOW."

"*Kru*, let me…"

"I said STOP! Find Prasert and tell your mother she should be leaving too. The two of you need to help Gan get home."

"Yeah, but I can—"

"Can do WHAT? I said, right now, Natcha! Warit and I've got to organise getting this place cleared up. Most folk have drunk more whisky than they can handle."

No sooner had Kritsada spoken than angry shouts and swearing sounded from within the gym.

Kritsada sighed. *It's going to be a long, long night*, he thought, glancing in the direction of his fighting cockerel to make sure he was safe. Seeing the bird perched proudly on the handlebars of a motorbike like the figurehead of a ship, he nodded his head at Natcha to signal that she should follow him. Shielding his eyes from the glare of a security light, he stared into the gloom of the gym interior, searching for the cause of the shouts and hollers.

"OK, I'm off to get Sert," said Natcha, not unproudly inspecting her hand's bruised knuckles.

"It just had to be them fighting, didn't it?" said Kritsada with a knowing shake of his head.

"Who?" replied Natcha, peering into the dingy interior.

"My stupid cousin and that neighbour of his! Probably still arguing over last night's football results. The pair fight like fat old water buffalos! I'm going to need to bang their heads together!"

"Best of luck with that," Natcha said with a grin as she ambled away to rescue Sert from the whisky bottle that their neighbour was thrusting in his face just 10 metres away.

The drunken crowd protested as Kritsada split up the fight. Enjoying himself, he considered throwing a couple of punches for fun. But reflecting on what Joi would do in the same situation, he opted to smile and wave, acknowledging the cat calls. He shouted back a couple of friendly insults and helped the beer-enlivened, staggering old bulls down from the boxing ring. Then he spotted a group of chatting *farangs* idling, so he approached them to ask if they wouldn't mind removing the projector, clearing away the food and taking down the bedsheet.

Villagers were still milling around the gym. Some of them tried to detain him to ask his thoughts on what could be happening to Joi and Nong in Bangkok, but he avoided answering any questions with a shrug. Kritsada loved the art of Muay Thai as much as he loathed the cancer of gambling and was probably the only villager who had not bet on Nong. Not because he did not believe he could win but because he refused to feed the betting beast devouring all that was good about the sport. He had even heard a story the week before about a trainer drugging his own student. Suddenly, the gym was as bright as noon and a lot quieter. Lucy had turned on the ceiling light's full beam and turned off the industrial cooling fans.

"Shall I say a few words?" asked Lucy, assessing the mood of the crowd. She had managed to get hold of Joi, briefly speaking to him to offer her support, but the line had died when she had broached the subject of repercussions. Suspecting that Joi had hung up on her, she was furious and had sat at the office desk debating whether to call him back. Finally, she decided it wouldn't get her anywhere. Even though she had lived in Thailand for many years and spoke the language, it was at times such as this she still felt foreign. Naturally, the Thais had their own way of dealing with problems. Steeling herself to go back in the gym, she thought the best thing she could do now was make a public announcement informing people of the Dragon's Gym view and what would happen next. But she couldn't have been more wrong.

"Not now," replied Kritsada. "Best that everyone goes. A lot of people lost a lot of money. They should take themselves off home. No-one cares about anything else but family and retaliation right now."

"Are you sure, Kritsada? A few soothing words and direction from me could help people."

"Best not to speak, Ma'am. Don't worry. We'll deal with this."

"What do you mean by *deal* with it? Do you really think Somchai's guilty? Could he have poisoned Nong?"

"Let's wait for Joi. He'll know what to do."

Lucy considered Kritsada for a moment, controlling her anger. She hated it when her own employees shut her out. Observing the set of his mouth, the frown and the blank, non-committal stare, she knew she wasn't going to get anywhere. In an attempt to appear as if she had the final word and to salve her bruised ego, she issued a last instruction, "OK, let's get this place cleared up."

"Sure, see you tomorrow," said Kritsada with a nod and bland smile.

"Okay, then, I'll call Joi again in the morning," she replied, ignoring the voice in her head saying Joi would be unlikely to pick up. As she walked back to her car, she reflected that she had never felt so foreign. While she was their boss, there was clearly a barrier she could not cross, the wall which the boxers built around their culture and way of managing the sport. Turning the key over in the engine, she took one last long look through the tinted glass at the scene in the gym. The carnival atmosphere, with its smiling faces and delighted children, had been crushed by Nong's collapse. Lucy doubted she would ever see Somchai again. Feeling bereaved as she backed the car out slowly to avoid the potholes, Lucy made a wish that Somchai was not guilty, but the words just fell from her mouth like heavy stones. She imagined each syllable falling into her lap, and the truth hit her hard. Somchai could not come back from this. The guilt was written all over his face. Lucy rested her head for a moment on the steering wheel, then sat back upright. Turning the wheels to the left, she drove cautiously off into the dark night, contemplating what Joi would do.

From that night on, when Somchai's expression of hate had been broadcast from Bangkok, Kritsada and Warit had watched and listened to the conversations of Ram, Mongkut and Panit. Privately, they had asked the Thai staff to report any snippets of gossip or suspicious behaviour as they calmly went about their business. Warit told Kritsada that Gan had not left her house, nor was she answering her phone. Her neighbours had taken it upon themselves to force the front door open and found her in bed. She had not eaten for forty-eight hours. Kritsada deliberated about going to see her but thought better of it. The whole village must have been knocking down her door to see how she was feeling, not just out of sympathy but also to get the inside scoop. Even some journalists had turned up on Gan's porch. Luckily, Natcha had been collecting the dishes used for the lunch her mother had sent and prevented them from entering the house. That same afternoon, Natcha moved into Nong's room.

CHAPTER TWENTY-THREE

JOI walked into Dragon's Gym, taking stock of the scene before him, his emotions a soup of sorrow, fury and determination, flavoured heavily with revenge. And guilt. Guilt for not listening to Dang when he called to express his discomfort with Somchai. He thought it was just professional jealousy coming from a retired boxer towards one whose star was rising. But he was wrong and should never have doubted an old friend. He could have prevented this all from happening if only he had not been so arrogant. On the flight home, he had berated himself for not seeing what was right before his eyes. Joi pushed the thoughts of the stressful past half an hour he had spent with Gan, Natcha and Nong to the back of his mind, noting with grim satisfaction who was now before him training. *Now's the time*, Joi thought, *to cleanse the cancer of corruption from this gym.*

As Joi compartmentalised the events of the past few days, from the horror of seeing Nong drugged to the shocking sight of Gan's drawn face and thin frame, he took a deep breath. This was not one of those days when he rolled with life's punches, calmly accepting life's ups and downs. No higher power had caused Somchai to poison Nong. Only human frailty, jealousy, greed and spite. Now was the time to start rebuilding and crush any remaining cuckoo eggs.

Earlier that morning, when he clambered from Lucy's car with Nong in tow, Gan stood in the doorway of their home. Her arms folded across her chest and eyes blank. She did not rush to welcome them but waited for her husband and son to approach. She looked tired and thinner, her skin shallow and aged. Ignoring her husband, she encased Nong into her arms and led him into the house. She asked how he felt as she ushered him in the direction of the kitchen. Joi caught her accusatory sideward glance, letting him know he had failed to protect their son. Her look punched his gut harder than the toughest body blows he had felt in his entire career.

Now he had returned to the place where Somchai had decided to betray them, Joi looked anew at the gym he knew so well, like a hawk riding a thermal observing its prey. His sharp, hunter's eyes observed Warit holding the pads for Panit in ring two. Next, he critically considered Ram and Mongkut, practising their clinching techniques in ring four. Around the periphery of the training rings, the local children were either kicking and hitting the black, worn leather punching bags or playing near the weights room.

I'll need to ask the children to leave before I act, thought Joi, waiting to see how Warit and the boxers would respond to his arrival. Joi had yet to decide the fate of the three boys, whom he considered to be adopted sons. In the Bangkok hospital, Joi had sat by Nong's bed, holding his hand, and had taken an oath to do what was right and fair by Dragon's Gym's owners, his team and everyone who trained there. But no-one was going to tell him to be soft or give anyone involved a second chance. He was the head trainer and, as such, had to act, however hard, to protect not only his son's boxing future but the other trainees, his coaching team and the reputation of the gym.

Warit noted Joi first. Immediately, he took off the boxing pads, jumped down from the ring and walked over. Warit did not attempt any banter with his boss and lifelong friend and only gave him a slight nod in greeting, which Joi barely acknowledged. Warit then turned back towards the boxing rings and stood to the right of Joi.

"Ayy, Somchai," Warit sighed with a sorrowful shake of his head. "We watched, trained and nurtured you, but you've failed everyone. Me, your trainers, your gym brothers and sisters, the owners. Everyone, including yourself and now your gym brothers, is going to pay the price of your treachery." Taking a deep breath, he shouted, "Ram, Mongkut, Panit get over here! It's time to talk."

Panit, who had whipped round to see what had caused the abrupt end to his session and seen Joi, was already removing his gloves. Ram and Mongkut, however, remained entwined in a clinch. Twisting around and kneeing one other in the side as they goaded each other to fight back harder, they ignored Warit's call. Then, Ram shoved Mongkut backwards as he felt the hairs rise on the back of his neck. He looked round the gym, searching for the source of the bad feeling overwhelming him, freezing when he spotted Joi.

"What?" said Mongkut, irritated that Ram had stopped sparring just as he was about to gain the upper hand.

Ram nodded in the direction of where Joi stood. "Joi's here," Ram snapped, yanking off his gloves.

"Oh, shit," exclaimed Mongkut ripping open the Velcro on his own well-worn pair and glancing over to where Joi stood with his hands behind his back and feet slightly apart, as solid as an ancient Buddha statue and similarly worn by time. Like Nature's forces on stone, life had worn away at Joi. His face had been furrowed by the years. Today, there was no benevolence in his eyes, not a hint of the usual kindness, just cold hatred. At Joi's side, Panit and Warit waited as still as well-trained police dogs, looking at their handler for a command out of the corner of their eyes.

Ram attempted a smile and greeting. "*Sawadee kap, Kru* Joi," Ram began. "It's so—"

"So what, Ram?" said Joi as softly as a panther's tread, noting Ram's hunched shoulders, badly bruised eyes and broken nose. "What happened to your face?"

"Ahh, it's nothing. Natcha and I had a disagreement. But Nong, how's Nong? Everyone was here watching the fight and—"

"She's a good girl, Natcha. One of the best," cut in Joi. "Wouldn't you agree, Mongkut?" Joi knew full well that Natcha had smashed her fist in Ram's face.

"Err, yes, she's great," replied Mongkut, shifting his

weight from foot to foot.

"Warit, get chairs from the office. Next, go find Kritsada. Everyone else, clear OUT. I'll see you all back here tomorrow at 7 a.m.!"

With a look of relief on his face, Ram said, "OK, right, we'll see—"

"No! Not you," snarled Joi, each word as sharp as a sword.

As Joi's words sliced through the gentle hum of good-natured gym banter, even the youngest children lying amongst the weights in the fitness corner colouring in their paint-by-number books stopped playing. A five-year-old boy started crying and protesting as his older sister pulled him to his feet. No-one needed to be told twice. Students stuffed their kit into bags and grabbed water bottles, purses and mobile phones as if their very lives depended on them getting out of the gym as quickly as humanly possible.

Curious children from the age of six to 15, eager to know whether Nong was recovering, tried stopping to ask Joi for news. But Joi was focused on the fight ahead. Each enquiry after Nong's health was met with a polite monosyllabic "fine," followed by instructions to be punctual in the morning.

As soon as the last child was out of earshot, Ram nervously attempted to set the tone for the conversation. Still, he only managed to stutter, "*Kru* Joi, I…err... just... um…err want to…"

"I care what you want because?" asked Joi as he stared emotionless at Ram.

Ram's usual cocksure nature collapsed. This was real, very real. His career was at stake, and his head was on the executioner's block. Raising his head, he smiled wanly at Panit, whose face was white, his eyes downcast. As with Mongkut and Ram, Dragon's Gym was the only home he had ever known. He had no idea where he would go and live if Joi ordered him to leave. The Muay Thai world was a small one, and there wasn't a gym that would touch him if Joi blacklisted him.

"Fuck it, Somchai," Ram swore to no-one in particular, "Why the fuck did you have to go and blow everything up for all of us?"

Mongkut stayed silent, wishing Ram would shut up. More sanguine than Ram and Panit, he knew Joi did not want to throw the three of them out on the street but would do so at the slightest indication of a lie. Joi was a ruthless competitor but a good man. He followed the ways of Buddha and often made merit at the local *wat*. Mongkut had never seen him say an unkind word to anyone that did not deserve it. Joi was like a father to all three of them.

Mongkut sighed with the realisation that the conversation was only going to go one way, just like a huge tree that had already started to crash to the ground. Nothing was going to alter the path of Joi's decision. The question was, who was going to get crushed? All three of them, or just the person closest to Somchai?

Joi pointed to the side of the centre boxing ring, indicating they should sit. As he did so, he took another sideward glance at Ram's spectacularly bruised purple eyes and the white plaster across his nose. For the first time that morning, Joi smiled and gave thanks to the women in his life. Gan, his boss, Lucy, and, besides Nong, his best-ever student Natcha.

Ram, Panit and Mongkut arranged themselves in a line and perched on the three-foot-high edge of the ring, nervously waiting for Joi's decree. Ram's feet swung back and forth as he busied himself inspecting his hands while Panit and Mongkut sat in silence, awaiting their sentence. Covertly, they glanced to where the head *kru* stood checking his phone for messages, desperate to learn their fate. Mongkut, who was mentally the strongest of the three, sat stoically upright. The tense silence was punctuated by warm tropical rain drumming on the metal roof. Raindrops the size of ten-baht coins reverberated like thousands of tiny hammers striking cymbals against the metal roof.

A large black and white feral cat jumped on the gym wall to shelter from the downpour. Her haughty green eyes looked first at the bunch of boxers, then contemptuously at the rainstorm outside. Normally, she slept contentedly beneath the banana leaf tree by the reception, where an icy breeze from the office air-conditioning units would blast through the doors each time someone entered or left the office. The huge storm raged on, but compared to Joi's angry aura, it was no more consequential to the atmosphere in the gym than the sand on the beach.

Joi glanced over at Kritsada jogging in the distance and hid a smile. A short, late-middle-aged man with a slight paunch, he was still incredibly fit and a favourite amongst the students. Preferring a bachelor's life, he had never married. He was a fair coach and quick to laugh, but stern. Kritsada knew everything there was to know about Muay Thai as well as Muay Boran, which he taught to mostly foreigners, the Thais not being as interested in the ancient art that no-one paid to watch apart from the tourists. In his left hand, Kritsada grasped an enormous bright-green ruffled fan palm leaf, from which the rain poured down in rivulets. Tucked under his right arm, his favourite fighting rooster. When Kritsada reached the motorbike shelter next to the reception, he discarded the makeshift umbrella, threw it over the short hedge and tied the fowl's leg with a piece of string to a post. Soothing the rooster with soft words, he lovingly stroked its brilliant plumage and cooed that he would soon return. The rooster, for its part, oblivious to Kritsada, started to peck away at a cigarette butt.

Kritsada picked his way around the huge puddles, slipped off his flip-flops and entered the gym, where the sad sight of an estranged family caused him to shake his head in sorrow.

"How quickly life changes," he sighed. Forcing a smile, Kritsada greeted the group with a wave of the hand and a polite, "S*awadee kap*!" With a slight motion of his head, Joi invited Kritsada to join him and Warit. The three *krus* arranged themselves on small red dusty chairs facing Ram, Mongkut and Panit. The judges empanelled, each sternly read the micro-expressions flitting across the blank faces of the accused. Relentlessly, as sharp and cutting as a machete sheering through the forest foliage of their tall tales, Joi slashed questions through their mumbled excuses, lapses in memory, and ill-concealed guilt. "Who had Somchai been speaking to? Had he been seen with Ray? Did he complain about Nong?" Gradually, the picture emerged of Somchai's frustration, jealously and seething resentment. Finally, Ram admitted he had heard Somchai complain his career was suffering because of Nong. But still, Joi continued, switching his interrogation between Panit, Mongkut and Ram to see just how far the rot of jealousy had spread. At last, Ram erupted; his pride could not take the onslaught. Ram muttered to Mongkut to his left.

"Give me a battering in the ring anytime over this."

"What did you say?" snapped Joi.

"I said, I'm sorry this happened, but it wasn't us, you know."

"You're lying. I can tell you're lying," retorted Joi.

"But… errr… it wasn't us, you know, us that…"

"You knew that Somchai had issues with Nong and me, didn't you?"

"Yes, but—"

"But you said nothing. Not one word. Now get the fuck out of my gym!"

"Hang on…" said Warit, daring to interject. "He's got nowhere to go. It's not as if he drugged Nong. Who is going to hire him if we do this?"

"Want to follow him?" challenged Joi, stepping into Warit's space.

"No, I don't, but come on," said Warit, taking a step back. "I—"

"Okay, let's calm it," Kritsada said with a worried glance at Joi. Five years ago, Kritsada had worked in a Bangkok gym. At that time, one of the boxers had also been poisoned. But unlike now, one of the coaches was responsible. Nobody had ever seen the trainer again. Rumours of screams in the night near his house circulated. The underworld side of the sport had its own way of dealing with these crooks. If Joi didn't throw Ram out, he would, along with the other trainers. The best-case scenario right now for Ram was for him to leave and get some kind of reference. The court was out as to whether Panit and Mongkut should pack their stuff too. Nong was Joi's son, and the head trainer had every right to issue his judgements.

"Warit, would you want Sert to fight with a corrupt guy in his corner?"

"Sert's not the best good example," snorted Warit. "He's got more chance of getting to Mars than Lumpinee."

"Ram knew Somchai was gunning for Nong and said nothing," snapped Joi.

"Joi's right," agreed Kritsada, knowing there was only one way this conversation was going to go. "What's more, these guys are men. They aren't children anymore. Perhaps we made a mistake not sending them off a long time ago?"

Warit met Joi's gaze and said, "Yep, I agree."

"Go pack your stuff, Ram," said Kritsada, adding support to Joi's decision.

Ram let his chair fall over backwards as he stood up. Where would he go? He had earned some money winning fights, but it was nothing compared to the income from teaching the private classes.

Before Ram was even out of earshot, Joi looked first at Panit and then Mongkut before asking coldly, "So, tell me, why should I keep either of you two here?"

CHAPTER TWENTY-FOUR

IN his hospital bed, Nong had opened one eye and stretched his aching body. It was late afternoon, and the noise of the Bangkok rush hour traffic had woken him. The three days since his poisoning passed in a blur. Doctors, the colonel and an endless stream of representatives from the Muay Thai community popped by his hospital room. His father had dealt firmly and politely with everyone. Some of the older men Nong recognised from the television as being famous ex-boxers and promoters. Every time he woke from a fitful sleep, he saw his father either talking to someone or sitting quietly in the worn blue chair next to his hospital bed. The fight tasted as bitter in his mouth as unsweetened lime juice; his dreams were shattered, and as far as he was concerned, so was his boxing. All the training and for what? Why bother when it just brought misery? Somchai's treachery puzzled and hurt. He had been like an older brother to him, and he was someone he looked up to and admired. How could he have sided with the gamblers?

As he lay on the thin hospital bed mattress chained to an IV drip, his foggy mind attempted to understand why he had been poisoned. He heard Joi talking quietly on the phone in the white echoing corridor outside his room while he pretended to sleep. From piecing together snippets of conversation, he had built a tapestry of events. The military police had arrested Somchai trying to board a plane back to Khao Lak. Repeatedly, he asked Joi about Somchai's motives, but he would always receive the same curt reply, "Don't worry, I'm managing it."

The only piece of news Joi would share was that Nong had won the *Muay Thai Fighter of the Year* award. But even the glory of that award did not dispel his disdain for fighting again. What was the point? Nong replayed scenes of growing up with Somchai Thinking back to how Bhan and Aye had just happened to be in Chiang Mai, he wondered if it was all a setup. Had they really been there to meet with Somchai?

Luckily, Tanawat covered the hospital bills and accommodation. On the first day of Nong's hospitalisation, his father told him that the colonel had issued strict instructions not to talk to the media. All journalists had to be referred to the military public relations executive. This official would shield those in the top brass, who knew all about the case, and instead refer the media to junior military personnel, who would be willing to talk but were kept entirely in the dark.

Nong was irritated at missing his chance in the media spotlight, but Joi insisted some things were better left to the authorities. Again and again, Nong had asked after Somchai, desperate to ask if it was true what the media was saying, but Joi would only shake his head and say Somchai had been dealt with, and that was that. Nong wasn't blind to the anger beneath his father's calm exterior. Still, he repeatedly told Joi that when they arrived home, he wanted to go to Dragon's Gym himself to meet with Ram and the others. On their return home, it wasn't Joi but Gan and Natcha who sent him to bed.

Despite still feeling weak, Nong's heart jumped, and a smile as bright as the midday sun broke out on his face as he walked through the Phuket arrival gate. Amongst the group of fifty people welcoming him home were Lucy, Natcha, and Sert, any trainers that could be spared from the gym, and an assortment of aunts, uncles and neighbours. Cheers of "Champion" greeted him. He fought back tears at the sight of crayoned placards with his name, featuring drawings of animals and stick men, women and children. One of the placards had been made out of a boxing promotion poster with his image and his competitor whited out. Everyone asked how he was feeling, and tourists heaving suitcases glanced curiously at this local hero. Thais pointed at him, recognising his face from the TV news stations and social media.

"Thanks for coming," he said, greeting Sert and Natcha with a warm hug and a weak hand slap. "Has Somchai returned to the gym?" he asked.

Natcha shook her head and replied, "No way, not if he wants to live. Anyways, he's most likely wearing a pair of cement boots at the bottom of a Bangkok construction site."

"Your dad, prob—"

"Sert," admonished Natcha, aware that Lucy and Joi

could overhear their conversation, "There's no need to go there! Come on, let's get back to Khao Lak—"

"Okay, everyone, let's GET GOING," shouted Joi, interrupting Natcha's reply. "Classes start in a couple of hours, and Gan's going to be wondering what's kept us!

* * *

The old bedroom clock showed he had been asleep for three hours. Despite not eating since the early morning, he didn't feel hungry. But his mouth felt as dry as December in the hot season. The disappearance of Somchai felt like a bereavement, and he tossed and turned in his bedsheets, his mind exhausted from coursing through a never-ending emotional labyrinth.

Suddenly, there was a rustle at the window. Monkey hopped onto the floor, looking as pleased with himself as a child who had just won the first prize in athletics and a treat of a bowl of chocolate ice-cream. In his left paw, he clutched a plant the size of a small mint bush, which he brandished before him like a medal to be admired by all. Nong pushed himself upright, setting depressing thoughts aside and ignoring the macaque. He stared into the forest silhouetted through the window to see if he could catch a glimpse of Tiger, hoping and praying she would appear. Since that night before leaving for Bangkok, he had regretted not showing her respect and was desperate to thank her for trying to warn him. However, there were only the sounds of the forest and the sight of the evening darkening as the leaves lost their golds and silvers and turned to a palette of ash and ivy greens. Sighing, he got out of bed, the weight of shame heavy on his shoulders.

Well, buddy, it's good to see you, thought Nong as he pondered on how much he was glad for a diversion from the dull day. He wondered what Monkey was up to this time and hoped it had nothing to do with his latest girlfriend. He still couldn't unsee the last time Monkey had felt it necessary to enact his ghostly encounters with the opposite sex. Curious but tentative, Nong sat on the floor cross-legged opposite Monkey, who was crouching on the floor with his precious vegetal stash held firmly in between his back paws. Monkey's eyebrows waggled and wriggled like caterpillars receiving electroconvulsive therapy. His mischievous macaque eyes glanced from Nong to the leaves and back again, checking Nong was paying attention. Satisfied his audience was sufficiently engaged, he shredded the heart-shaped leaves into one-centimetre pieces.

Nong sat as still as a boulder in the middle of his bedroom, feeling good about himself for the first time since the fight. Monkey chattered and bobbed up and down on his strong hind legs as if he were putting on a theatrical performance to entertain and cheer Nong. Then, Monkey jumped up on the desk and emptied the blue and white mug where Nong kept his pens, by simply turning it upside down. Not bothering about the coloured pencils falling on to the floor, he leapt to the leaf fragments. Next, he collected the little heap of torn leaves and tipped them into the cup. Finally, he mimicked the pouring of a liquid and drank the imaginary concoction. Tiny leaf particles covered his face as he tipped the cup, sticking to his forehead and eyelashes. Throughout the theatrical display, Monkey chatted and nodded, raising his eyebrows each time at Nong to check he understood.

Nong felt lighter as he laughed with the now green-freckled macaque, who grinned back at him, revealing yellowed teeth. Nong did not notice, but Monkey slyly and, ever so slowly, picked up leaf particles from the floor. Suddenly, the macaque was as still as the three see-no-evil, hear-no-evil, speak-no-evil monkey statues at the forest *wat* entrance. Looking at Nong intently, Monkey opened his mouth in a tremendous, gaping yawn. Instinctively, Nong yawned too, and just at the point his mouth was at its widest, Monkey leapt forward at lightning speed and stuffed the torn leaves into Nong's mouth, almost causing him to choke. When Nong had finished coughing and spluttering, a realisation hit him. Smacking his hand to his forehead, he knew what Monkey wanted.

"You want me to eat these?"

Hopping from his left foot to his right, Monkey grunted, squeaked and trilled, stuffing leaves into his own mouth, gesticulating wildly.

"Ouch!" Pencils started hitting Nong on the head. Monkey poked out his tongue, provoking him from the final stages of his stupor.

"That does it," Nong roared, thoroughly pissed. He swiped at Monkey as he scampered and darted around the room, springing off the table, bed and even his own head to avoid being captured. Catching the sprightly beast was harder than swatting a mosquito. At least a mosquito rested once in a while. "Monkey," gasped Nong, feeling queasy. "I—"

"WHAT's going on in there!!?" shouted Gan, storming down the corridor to his room. Wiping her hands on her apron, Gan flew into the dishevelled room and gasped in amazement at the chaotic state of the floor, bed linen, the upturned desk chair and strewn pencils, paper, and leaves. *Leaves? Why on earth are there leaves everywhere?* Puzzled, she turned to Nong in search of answers, prepared to combat his ability to evade questioning better than a member of the Thai secret police. She measured Nong up and down for signs of weakness, before shrewdly asking the question she thought would help to elicit the facts. "How come there's a leaf on your face when you are supposed to be in bed?" she asked with one eyebrow raised and her thin arms crossed in front of her chest, waiting for Nong to formulate a believable response.

"Well, err, you see—"

"No, I don't see—"

"Well, the wind."

"The wind tore up pieces of leaves and stuck them on your face? The wind upturned the coffee mug and scattered pencils round the room so hard that some of them broke. Is that what the wind did?"

"I don't feel well."

If Nong had not been poisoned only a few days ago, Gan would never have accepted such a line, but she refused to take any chances on his health and decided to give him the benefit of the doubt. The sweat running down his face made Gan worry he might be suffering from delusions caused by a fever. Feeling guilty for shouting, she put her arm around Nong and gently guided him to the bed, carefully making sure he lay down slowly and pulling the Arsenal football club bed sheet over him. She put her hand on his forehead to check his temperature. Satisfied he wasn't that hot, she proceeded to pick up the paraphernalia from the bedroom floor. She drew in a sharp intake of breath when she saw sandy paw marks in the dust.

"Nong, did an animal cause this mess? Were you playing in your bedroom with a cat or a dog?"

"Sorry, Mum, I really don't feel well," came back the mumbled and somewhat sulky reply from beneath the bed sheet.

"Well, you didn't seem that way just a moment ago?" she snapped, losing patience and suspecting there was more to the chaos than Nong wanted to explain.

"I know, but it was a, a.… a monkey, you know? It just came into the room. What was I to do? It started charging around, and I tried to catch it." Nong listened to his own voice telling half-truths and cringed. Rolling onto his side, he faced the wall. "I'll go back to sleep now," he muttered, pulling the bedclothes more tightly around him as if they could shield him from his mother's Superman laser eyes.

"No! You don't!" WHY are there leaves on the floor ripped up and stuffed in this cup?"

"You won't believe me," sighed Nong, feeling the burning sensation of Gan's glare between his shoulder blades. Desperately wanting to avoid any conversation about spirit animals, he gave an exaggerated, loud yawn. "I need to rest, Mother. I don't feel well," he said, thinking *I'm in trouble if I tell the truth and if I don't!*

Gan moved over on the bed, plonking herself down with a heavy sigh. *The past week has aged me one hundred years*, she thought. *I didn't heed the warnings before, and whether the boy likes it or not, he has to explain the monkey, the state of this room, the leaves in the coffee cup and what's going on!*

Gan peeled back the bed sheet from Nong, which was not the easiest of tasks. Like the skin of an unripe avocado, the bed sheet did not want to come free because Nong had mummified himself. Finally, fed up with the gentle mother approach, Gan yanked down the bedsheets. Nong turned to face Gan and looked into her clear brown eyes and raised brows, expressing that not for one minute did she believe a word.

"Out with it, Nong. Now."

Nong rolled his eyes and sighed. *Well, here goes. No escaping this one.* As he spilt the beans, Gan listened intently, holding Nong's hand the whole while.

She cleared her mind of any bias and made sure not to interrupt him. The anger that she had once felt towards his childhood games turned to gratitude.

When Nong finished his story, she leaned forward and kissed him on the cheek, saying, “Let’s keep this between ourselves. I was wrong too, you know? I put away the stories of my own mother as childish tales and did not listen to the voices of the forest. Mother Nature does not need us, but we need her. We were arrogant in thinking that we shouldn’t accept her advice. Go to sleep, Nong.”

Before leaving the room, she picked up the cup and gathered the fallen leaves. Then she went to the kitchen to make an infusion. Gan retrieved the grey stone mortar and pestle from the shelf beneath the window, pulled out a chair from underneath the table and sat down to grind the leaves. A soft breeze blew through the kitchen, and for a brief moment, she felt calm and the tumour which was causing her so much pain and bad temper stopped hurting. Turning round to face the breeze, she looked out the window and saw that the kitchen shelf was covered with small garlands of green, heart-shaped leaves on a piece of bright gold silk. Placing the palms of her hands together, with her fingers extended at chest level and close to her body, she bowed and raised her fingers to the level of her nose, making the shape of a lotus bud, as she thanked Lady Ta-khian with a promise to visit the rock pool in the morning.

CHAPTER TWENTY-FIVE

DISILLUSIONED, Nong did not go back to the training camp for weeks. What was the point? He attended to his schoolwork, did his chores and hung around with Sert. Finally, for a number of reasons, not least economical, Joi decided not to throw out Mongkut and Panit from Dragon's Gym. He had many heated debates with Lucy about fight purses and what they stood to lose if Ram, Mongkut and Panit were evicted. Not a single person had heard from Somchai, and Joi knew the reason why. The colonel had texted from Bangkok that everything had been sorted, and Joi knew what that meant. To have tarnished the name of the Lumpinee stadium was a stupid thing for Somchai to have done. Joi wasn't naïve. He knew it was not just his son's health that was at stake but also the reputation of Muay Thai boxing. Many people made their livelihoods or topped up their monthly salaries through kickbacks and gambling, not least members of the military. Joi had felt comfortable expelling Ram, but his instincts told him to consult with Lucy about the other two, who were younger and not as close to Somchai. Lucy had raised them from young kids.

Slowly, the web of deceit unravelled to reveal Somchai's increasing jealousy, the frustration he felt at never becoming a Lumpinee champion and his burning desire for money. Panit and Mongkut had sworn fealty to Dragon's Gym and admitted that they had worried something was going on but were unsure exactly what. Lessons were learnt and now everyone needed to move forwards.

But Nong? Well, Nong couldn't forget. His eyes clouded over whenever Joi tried to encourage his son to return to the gym and train. On the two occasions he had acquiesced to train, he was pathetically slow and listless. Half-hearted, he had moped his way through the pad work and sparring until Joi couldn't bear to watch. Not wanting his own son to show them both up, Joi had sent Nong home. Also, Joi had no patience for people feeling sorry for themselves. Yes, it was a terrible thing to have happened, but life moves on, and Nong had to, as well. Gan, though, was a different matter, and her continual ill health worried him.

Only the other day, Joi had seen Gan holding her abdomen and coughing. Concerned by her pained expression, he had asked her what was wrong, but Gan waved him away, telling him not to fuss. Leaning against the kitchen door frame, with a boxer's eye for a body in pain, he did not say another word. Despite her protestations, Gan was unable to hide her enfeebled stance and slightly hunched shoulders from a gaze that was finely tuned to searching out weaknesses.

The following evening, Joi tried to encourage Gan to eat more. She refused, even though she had only picked at the pork and basil curry, complaining she felt full and that there was discomfort in her abdomen above the navel, which she put down to women's troubles. But her sallow complexion and the new lines around her eyes told a different story. Ignoring Gan's insistence that he stop fussing, he called a clinic in Phuket, the nearest city. A few days later, he drove Gan in the neighbour's borrowed car to the hospital for some tests. In Khao Lak, the public medical facilities left a lot to be desired, and there was no way they could afford private health care.

It was about a two hours' drive along the new motorway to reach the island, a famous tourist draw for its beaches and warm waters. Joi detested Phuket centre, with its tourist noise, traffic mayhem, drugs, and overcrowding.

* * *

The warning alarm on the clinic entrance door bleeped every few minutes as visitors, hospital staff, people who had popped outside for a smoke, or a chat on the phone, passed by. Tourists with head injuries from riding hired mopeds were rushed through to the Accident and Emergency rooms. Others with minor cuts and bruises from bar fights, pavement stumbles and sports activities, sat staring sullenly ahead or chatted with their companions. Once registered at the reception desk, Joi and Gan sat on the last two empty blue plastic chairs to wait for Gan's name to be called.

One hour later, Joi took off his sweatshirt and wrapped it around a shivering Gan. *Why do they always have the air-conditioning set so high in these places?* he wondered, cursing that he'd forgotten to bring a jumper and wear long trousers. Another polar hour passed before the receptionist called Gan's name and indicated that she should proceed to see Doctor Gop in room six. In case the diagnosis was bad, Gan asked Joi to wait outside.

The request fell on deaf ears. Joi picked up Gan's handbag and, impatient to discover what was ailing his wife, urged her to hurry up. Placing his hand on the small of Gan's back, he walked by her side down the wide clinic corridor, sharing the latest gossip from Dragon's Gym, until they came to room six and entered. Behind an ostentatious dark teak desk sat a well-fed, middle-aged man in a crumpled shiny suit and blue shirt. Brusquely, he waved one hand, indicating they should sit, whilst he finished sending a text message, a smarmy grin on his face. Joi reminded himself that what mattered most was Gan and sat in silence waiting patiently.

Subconsciously, Gan rested her hands on her stomach, recognising that something was amiss. The doctor pushed his gold-rim Cartier glasses firmly to the top of his nose, unclipped his limited-edition Oyster steel and platinum Yacht-Master Rolex, and placed it in front of him on the desk. Without moving a single muscle on his face, Joi read the motifs of corruption and feared the worst. This was not a boxing arena where he could manage the power structures and wield influence; this was a hospital where the doctor, with a stroke of a pen, would decide Gan's fate.

The doctor opened a manila folder with Gan's health records and hummed and hawed while flicking with a bored look on his face through the notes. *What can be taking him so long?* seethed Joi, glaring at the man who had barely acknowledged their presence. Concealing his annoyance, he took Gan's hand and turned to smile at her reassuringly. Relief at the small display of support, flitted across Gan's tired face.

Doctor Gop snapped the file shut and then tossed it across the desk. "I understand you have stomach pains, correct? OK, let's take a look at you. Go lie on the bed, face up."

Joi reacted first, noting Gan's flinch at the informal tone. "Come on, it's going to be okay," he said giving her a gentle push of encouragement to stand.

A nurse pulled down the metal grill that prevented patients from rolling off the thin, plastic-covered mattress. Gan lay down with her arms by her side, a nervous expression on her face. After much prodding and poking, as well as wincing from Gan, Doctor Gop said the examination was finished and returned to his desk.

Without waiting for Gan to finish rearranging her clothes or giving any preamble to soften his message, Doctor Gop delivered his verdict. "There are a variety of techniques to identify tumours. The key to an accurate diagnosis is determining if a growth is benign or malignant. Only laboratory tests can determine this with certainty. Benign tumours are noncancerous growths in the body. Cancerous tumours differ in that they metastasize to other parts of the body. Myomas grow from muscle or in the walls of blood vessels. They can also grow in smooth muscle, like the kind found inside organs such as the stomach, which is where you have a lump. Do you follow me?" asked Doctor Gop without showing the slightest interest in receiving a response.

Joi and Gan nodded affirmatively, so he continued in the same patronising tone.

"Tumours can form anywhere. I advise people that if they discover a lump or mass in their body that can be felt from the outside, they must not immediately assume it is cancerous."

"So, there's no need to worry?" asked Joi, a note of disbelief in his voice.

"That is not what I said," snapped Doctor Gop, "I thought you could understand? Do I need to explain myself again or perhaps write my explanation down?"

"We follow you, Doctor," said Gan, tightly holding on to her husband's taut upper arm.

"Good. Nurse, come with me while the patient waits here," said Doctor Gop, stepping aside so she could pass and he could walk behind. He waited until she was three paces in front of him and followed her out of the door, his eyes fixated on her slim, swinging hips.

For twenty minutes, they whiled away the time, talking about Nong's schoolwork and recovery. Joi nodded in agreement with Gan, knowing she spoke only to keep her mind off the tests. *I bet Doctor Gop is still harassing the poor nurse*, Joi thought, as he held Gan's hand to stop her from chewing her nails, which were already bitten down to the hyponychium. Frozen and frightened, Gan was startled by the doctor throwing the door open with a bang. Hiding his contempt for the man, Joi smiled brightly as if he were seeing a long-lost friend.

"The news is good. The clinic has a spare slot for a test owing to a cancellation. Khun Gan can have an ultrasound scan and Nurse Flora will take her there now."

Joi made to follow Gan.

"No, best if you wait here, said Doctor Gop, there's not much room in the reception area. Your wife's in good hands. Let's sit and have a little chat while we wait for her return."

With an even broader smile, Joi said, "Sure." Noticing the chair he had been offered was much lower than the doctor's and having played the dominance game all his life, Joi declined the seat with the excuse that he had an old knee injury. Used to bullying people and intimidating them, the doctor, who was basically a coward, was not happy about Joi looking down on him, but there was little he could do.

"Oh, well," shrugged Doctor Gop, thinking, *what does it matter? This simple ex-boxer has to do what I want*, as he delivered his sales pitch in a pompous tone.

"Now, even if your wife has a benign tumour, it could still grow into cancer. Did you know that?"

Joi returned the doctor's smile, waiting for the tone

to change as the pitch continued.

"No, I didn't think you did. Although non-threatening tumours generally grow slowly, cases of fast-growing types have also been documented. Even if the tumour is benign, we will still need to operate as it might become cancerous. So, we must act fast. Unfortunately, there is the question of the waiting lists. Such a terrible thing, but, you see, so many people are badly affected by life's ills. Tell me, Khun … err?"

"Call me Joi," Joi suggested sardonically.

"Tell me, Joi, does your family have any savings? Perhaps you would like to donate to my foundation, and then I'm sure we can get Khun Gan's operation underway in no time at all. And we want to do what's best for your wife, don't we?"

With unconcealed contempt, Joi regarded Doctor Gop. "What do you mean?" he asked, his expression blank. With dread, he recalled the myriad of offers he had received over the years to make filthy lucre in the dark side of Muay Thai. Purposefully slowing down his breath and imagining iced water pouring over hot coals, he suppressed the urge to take two steps forward and break the doctor's nose.

"Well, of course, there's lots of extra work involved in speeding up operations now. I won't bore you."

Joi cut in, "I get it. I totally get it." Controlling his anger for the sake of Gan, he calmly replied, "Thank you, we understand each other."

"Good."

"I'm off to get a glass of water and wait in the

reception area," said Joi.

"Fine, fine," replied Doctor Gop, looking at his phone with a lascivious smile when it bleeped as a new message popped up. "Khun Gan will be another twenty minutes or so. We use a variety of techniques to diagnose tumours. Only laboratory tests can determine with certainty whether a tumour is harmful. Don't forget that further tests need to be done and about the fast-track solution I offered."

In the examination room, the nurse instructed Gan to lie back on a padded table so that the technologist could perform an ultrasound test. Gan showed the nurse where the pain and swelling were. The nurse applied a small amount of water-soluble gel to the skin. The gel felt freezing on her stomach and reminded Gan of the pregnancy scan. The memory of carrying Nong caused a pleasurable flush of warmth through her body. Suddenly, the examination room door flew open, and a female doctor with an open face and energetic manner rushed into the room, apologising for keeping her waiting. The doctor washed her hands, scrubbing them fastidiously with a soap that smelt like Dettol. Turning away from the small porcelain sink, she greeted the nurse, who handed her a wand-like device called a transducer, which she gently applied against Gan's low abdomen. The doctor asked Gan to hold her breath briefly several times. The test took about ten minutes to complete.

"You may dress yourself now," said the doctor. "Please return to the waiting room. We will pass the results to the radiologist immediately, but I can't promise when we will know the final outcome."

In the waiting room, Joi leant back in his chair, hands behind his head, staring at the ceiling. He pondered the problem of funding Gan's further tests. A six-month delay was not an option. Like a kid with a Rubik's Cube, he twisted and turned the conundrum, back and forth, over and around. He could ask Lucy for a loan, but the challenge there was that he could not afford to pay the money back. Nobody he knew had the money to cover private hospital fees. His salary was not going to suffice. Every penny he earned went to education, besides some savings for when he could no longer teach, and the family's living expenses. Leaning forward, he sunk his head in his hands. He would rather be knocked out in the ring than deal with Gan being ill. She was the trunk and roots of the family, while he and Nong were the branches. Pushing himself upright in the chair, he admired the portrait of the previous King Bhumibol and his unfailing image of kindly impassivity.

Taking inspiration from the King's ability to have a public face, Joi decided that he needed to do the same for the benefit of his own family. Doctor Gop who was more interested in self-enrichment than providing good medical care might be beyond his reach to tackle, but he had a profound belief in the power of the community to support one another.

Confident he had a plan that could turn around not just the medical bill problem for Gan but also restore the lost betting money to the community as well as the honour of the gym, Joi smiled to himself as he spotted Gan making her way down the hospital corridor. "Don't worry, Gan," he said under his breath, "Everything will be OK."

CHAPTER TWENTY-SIX

"NO. I'll go and work at the Seven-Eleven and leave school," Nong replied.

"What and break your mother's heart? That's not happening."

The conversation had been terse for some time, but Joi could wait. The boy was grieving for the loss of a friend, angry at being betrayed and feeling gullible for not having spotted Somchai's treachery.

"But what's the point?" muttered Nong tetchily. Beneath the banana tree, he continued to pull up grass by the roots, throwing the blades over his shoulder for the wind to carry past the old frangipani tree, where Joi leant on its lowest branch.

How come everything in my life hides something wicked? pondered Nong, picking up one of the white frangipani flowers with a yellow centre and waxy petals. *Even this flower if you cut it, has a sticky, poisonous sap!* Gan had told Nong that frangipani trees were once considered taboo in Thai homes because of superstitious associations with the plant's Thai name, *lantom,* which sounded similar to *ratom,* the Thai word for sorrow. And that in her grandma's time, frangipanis were thought to bring unhappiness, unlike now, when blossoms were presented as fragrant offerings to Buddha and women wore them in their hair during new year.

Somchai had not only been his teacher but an older brother too, someone Nong had respected and admired since he was a kid. Joi knew Nong had not given up on boxing despite his protestations to the contrary. Posters of great Muay Thai fighters still hung on his bedroom wall. Joi had left Nong alone to recover long enough. Now, his mother, the family, and the village needed him to get up and fight and fight he would. But Joi did not want to bully. Nong was no longer a child. What's more, he would never win unless he regained his former confidence.

"Nong, your mother's not well. Really not well, and we need you to pick up the gloves. The only person that's going to train you is me."

Self-absorbed and sullen, Nong didn't hear the mention of Gan's illness and retorted, "Yes, but you were supposed to protect me last time, and how did that work out?" The sharp note in his voice hit Joi harder than any strike an opponent had ever thrown at him.

Joi could not fail to notice his son's line of attack, but he did not immediately retaliate. Instead, he pressed forward his point, one that his opponent, in this case his own son, wouldn't guess. As a child, Nong had loved stories, and it was Nong's inner child and sense of wonder that he wanted to appeal to now, not this hurt, disillusioned young man.

"Nong, let me teach you a lesson that my grandfather taught me when I was let down by my trainer. Life is like this, and we have to either lie down and accept what is given or stand and fight to solve the problem. What passed with Somchai was unfortunate: the timing was *Khao Dai Khao Khem*, just as the moment when the thread was about to pass through the needle."

"Uhhhh?" replied Nong, his brow puzzled. Sitting up slightly, he stopped frowning.

"Well, it happened at that critical moment which determines whether one succeeds or fails. The first fight at Lumpinee was a golden opportunity, one which, if missed, doesn't come again. It's like threading a needle before sewing. Passing the thread through the needle takes perseverance and concentration. If someone or something interrupts at that moment, when the thread is about to go through the needle's eye, one might waver and have to start again. You need to start again. The opportunity to be a champion is still there for you to take. Don't be put off by what happened. The thread will pass through the needle."

Nong reflected on how like Tiger his father sounded. But Tiger had gone the way of Somchai. Up in smoke! Monkey appeared, but intermittently, as if checking in to see that he was OK. But the macaque never stayed long and scampered off when bored. Nong, feeling as flat as a leaf beneath the foot of an Asian buffalo, couldn't blame him. Nong knew he had been self-indulgent. It was time to pick up the thread again and stop feeling sorrow for himself. His father was right. He needed to dust himself down and stand up.

Joi sat next to Nong and relayed all that had happened over the past month: the hospital visit and the struggles of the villagers who had bet their savings. There was a golden opportunity for Nong to have a rematch against Agung in four weeks' time at Lumpinee. Joi had spoken to Desnee, Agung's coach. Tanawat had negotiated all the contracts and was ready to press the button. The fight purse was going to be the biggest in Muay Thai fight history at one million dollars, given the media interest and television rights he had negotiated. Images of Nong leaning over the ropes, sheet white and staggering, had gone global, with international media stations such as the BBC, Reuters and CNN covering the story. National and international live-streaming services had fought to win the rights to cover a rematch. But an exclusive had gone to TV8. The injustice had imploded like a mind bomb. People took to the streets, demanding that the Royal Thai Army must better protect boxers from the gamblers. Nong was going to top the bill with Agung, and the match was sure to draw record global television audiences. He had the support of Dragon's Gym, the promoter, Muay Thai aficionados, and the media. But would Nong fight?

Nong felt sick. Sick that his mother was unwell. He missed the competitive feel and lightness of fitness but wanted to talk to his mother before making any decision.

As Nong got up to leave, Joi pulled him back by his

left forearm. "Listen, Nong, we've received the doctor's report. Tumour shapes have been located in her stomach, but the full Magnetic Resonance Imaging (MRI) scan is going to take time. If we want to go to the Bangkok Lotus Thailand Hospital, we could have the appointment in forty-eight hours, but we don't have the money."

Not wanting to load more weight on his son's shoulders, Joi left out the details of the conversation with Doctor Gop, whom he knew would not make the much-needed referral if he did not receive a kickback. Nong slumped down and put his head in his hands. As father and son sat in silence, the sweet jasmine smell of the frangipani tree flowers floated around them. Nong's worried expression contrasted sharply with the calm veneer of Joi's face. So immersed were they in their own thoughts, they did not notice Gan standing in the doorway observing them. She was dressed in a light cotton t-shirt and jeans, which had been tight but were now baggy. *How alike they are in every way*, she thought. *A tiger and his cub*. It was clear her family was contemplating some deep decision and hoped that the cause for their consternation wasn't her illness. She had tried hard to hide how she felt, but it had been impossible when her husband noticed everything from the scurrying of a lizard along the wall to a downturned mouth expressing dissent.

Joi smiled at Gan as she approached, her feet cracking twigs in the yard. She raised one eyebrow at him and inclined her head in the direction of Nong, who was sitting cross-legged, staring at the sandy yard, stabbing at the leaves littering the ground with a stick. "Nong, are you trying to spear lizards for dinner?" asked Gan with a gentle smile.

"No."

"Is something up?" asked Gan.

"Dad wants me to box," replied Nong sulkily, jabbing the stick even harder and faster into the soil while somehow managing to avoid hurting the ants scuttling on the multitude of highways crisscrossing the sand. A number of ants dragged a small black butterfly between them like a fisherman pulling in a net. The bigger ants lugged animal particles so much larger than themselves at times, they veered off the path.

Joi observed Nong watching the ants.

"Son, even ants don't give up. Look at how some of them are weighed down by huge loads, but they make the best of it and carry on."

"It can't be all that bad, can it?" asked Gan, sitting down on the grass on the other side of her son and putting her arm around him.

Nong did not shrug her off and continued looking at the cheerfully working ants. Eventually, he said, "You know what? I bet we look like the three wise monkeys to the neighbours." He raised his head and smiled.

Joi grinned. "Maybe, but I think Gan is the one that sees no evil, speaks no evil and hears no evil. I'm not sure about us two!"

"You'll be at my back, Dad? There's not going to

be a repeat of last time, is there?"

"I promise there won't be. I'll support you just like those ants hold up those leaves."

"Hang on, Nong," said Gan, "you must make merit. Before any final decision is made, Nong has to see Abbot Anurak and offer to help do jobs around the temple every Sunday. No-one is fighting anyone without a blessing, and that's final."

"But every Sunday?"

"Nong, this is a fight you can't win," whispered Joi, giving him a slight nudge in the ribs with his elbow and overjoyed that Nong was now complaining about not being able to fight. There was one further hurdle: Lucy needed to be told, and her permission sought for him to clear his training schedule. *I probably should've asked her first,* thought Joi. *There'll be hell to pay if I have to tell Nong the fight's off.*

CHAPTER TWENTY-SEVEN

NONG trudged up the uneven path towards the forest *wat.* Either side of the path, the dense vegetation smelt earthy and fresh. A myriad of verdant leaves gleamed in the weak, early morning sunlight. The life that was the forest breathed with him as he went, singing to himself as he hopped over puddles and fallen branches. Gan always said that walking in the forest was like meditating in an herb bath. Suddenly, the birds and animals rustling in the woods fell silent. Goosebumps appeared along Nong's arms as his hair stood up. The very forest seemed to be listening, watching him as he continued his way upwards, now carefully picking his way around the rivulets of water as the path began to incline steeply.

Nong stopped. He turned round abruptly. *What's there?* he wondered, straining his ears to listen and scanning the canopy. To his left, he swore he heard the heavy pant of a large animal amongst the bulrushes, his eyes narrowing as he peered through the tall stems swaying gently.

Reminding himself not to run in case it could be one of the predators that roamed the ancient forest, he scanned the trees to select one suitable to climb. The breathing came closer. Fighting to calm himself, he veered off the path, cutting through the foliage. Vicious palm thorns scratched at his legs. Fifty metres in, the green wall stopped, revealing a small sunlit clearing where there stood a centuries-old Ta-khian. Around its massive, large trunk, a series of large blue, yellow, red, white, and orange satin cloths had been tied, all of which had faded with time. The colours symbolised the aura that Buddhists believed emanated from the body of the Buddha when he attained Enlightenment. Blue stood for the Spirit of Universal Compassion. Yellow, the Middle Way. Red, the Blessings of Practice—achievement, wisdom, virtue, fortune and dignity. White, the Purity of Dhamma—leading to liberation, timeless. Orange, the Wisdom of the Buddha's teachings. Lastly, there was another darker orange colour that was comprised of a combination of rectangular bands of the five other colours in the aura's spectrum. This compound colour was referred to as the Truth of the Buddha's teaching, as *Pabbhassara* or 'essence of light'.

The huge tree roots had grown into a natural bench, and there sat Lady Ta-khian, anthropomorphised from her tree form into a slender, long-haired, beautiful young woman. She was wearing a *pha tung,* a traditional long wraparound skirt. In her hands, she held a jar containing a golden liquid from which a sun bear sipped with its long tongue. The bear had short black fur and small triangular ears and was living up to its nickname, 'honey bear'. The bear lifted its head and sniffed the air as Nong approached to better sense him; its eyesight was very poor. The bear had yellowish crescent-shaped markings on its chest, which bore a resemblance to a rising sun.

Slowly, the bear turned to where the forest resounded with a series of twitters, chirps, songs and trills. A welcome chorus greeted the new arrival. Nong's heart soared when the thick reeds parted and Tiger padded nonchalantly into the clearing. Thrilled, he gingerly stepped forwards to greet the royal arrival. Her Majesty ignored him, however, and sauntered past in the direction of Lady Ta-khian, who was calming the bear with soft cooing noises. Tiger flicked her black ears with the white spots at the small bear as if saying, "You may go." She lowered her head for Lady Ta-khian to stroke, making chuffing sounds. Lady Ta-khian put down the earthenware honey pot, then cupped her hand to the sun bear's ear and whispered. The bear gave a grunt and ambled off in search of plants, fruits or insects. The long, curved, sharp claws, which the bear used to rip open termite mounds, rotten logs and honeybee nests, marked the ground as it walked away.

Lady Ta-Khian caressed the short fur on Tiger's forehead where there was a pattern in the exact formation of the Chinese character for king. The big cat closed her eyes in contentment. Tiger shifted her enormous size around to lay down on her haunches facing Nong. Looking every inch as royal as Cleopatra with a leopard, Lady Ta-Khian sat in silence.

Nong fell to his knees in the dirt before her and gave a *wai*, his palms pressed together in prayer, not raising his eyes. His heart pounded as he continued to stare at his knees with his hands in his lap, waiting for the spirit to speak. Counting his breath, he knelt calmly, closed his eyes and focused on his breathing. When he lifted his head, Elephant stood before him, with Monkey perched on the top of her head. Elated, Nong stood up to hug her while Monkey chattered and jumped up and down before running down her trunk to sit on his shoulder. Full of joy, he turned to face Lady Ta-khian. Tiger's amber eyes regarded him, a jury of one waiting for direction from the judge.

Smoothing her skirt, Lady Ta-khian scrutinised his face for tell-tale signs of negative emotions or doubt before asking, "Nong, what do you remember from your father's stories of Nai Khanom Tom?"

Confused, Nong tried to second-guess where the conversation was going. *Answer the question but be polite. Whatever you do*, Nong told himself, *don't sound cheeky. And be honest.* There were two sides to this spirit, and he did not want to experience the vengeful one. *She's testing me*, thought Nong as his mind raced *to see what I think is important. The guts, glory and showmanship or something else? What could it be?* A sense of panic started to tie his stomach in knots, and bile rose in his throat. Thinking back to his conversation with this father about the need for him to fight for the community, he hit upon the answer. "I can. Err… remember that what was special about Nai Khanom Tom… was his. Err… will win for an honour other than his own?"

“What else?”

“Well, it’s that and the big battles.”

“No, Nong, not the big battles. What about his character? Why do we remember him?”

“His bravery?” said Nong, looking up into the bright, endless blue sky and exhaling a long, drawn-out breath as he remembered.

Tiger yawned, showing her huge fangs, and flopped down on her side. Bored, she stretched out her four legs and flexed her paws. Pursing her lips, Lady Ta-khian leaned over and tweaked Tiger’s whiskers, admonishing her for the lack of patience and focus. Elephant shifted her weight from side-to-side as she swung her trunk with impatience. *Come on, Nong, come on,* he said to himself. Elephant decided to give him a bit more encouragement and prodded him so hard it almost knocked him over, causing Monkey to shriek in protest.

Nong shouted the answer as it hit him suddenly, “The readiness to face odds, odds in defence of fighting!”

Tiger opened one amber eye as if to say, “So you’re not a total idiot, but that’s not perfectly correct.” Rising, she moved her back legs to push her body up into a standing position and rubbed her head against the tree right next to where Lady Ta-khian sat.

Beaming with light and approval, the tree spirit said, “Yes, Nong, these are the very attributes of what it means to be truly Thai. The ancient warrior had the indomitable will to win for an honour other than his own and the readiness to face any odds in defence of the fighting art. Do you think, Nong, that you can do that? Can you put aside your own ego and fight for your friends, neighbours, the community and your mother? Will you fight like your hero both inside and outside the ring and show that you can be true?"

Silence. A cool breeze blew, gently lifting dry leaves and rustling the vegetation as every animal, insect, and plant waited.

"I'll fight," swore Nong, eager to return to the ring once more and no longer hesitant about the challenges he would face.

"Go then," Lady Ta-khian ordered, her form disappearing back into the bark of the tree. Her voice started to fade as she warned: "We'll be watching."

Tiger's eyes were alight with volcanic orange, red and yellow. Looking into them as she passed him by, not two feet away, Nong could feel the heat of her power and strength as he watched her go. At the perimeter of the clearing, Tiger stopped, looked over her right shoulder and waited. Together, the four friends left the clearing, with Monkey and Elephant following behind. Nong rested his hand on the top of Tiger's muscled back, absorbing her powerful energy, subconsciously raising his head higher as they climbed the path to the *wat*.

CHAPTER TWENTY-EIGHT

JOI went to the front porch to check that his motorbike had not fallen over in last night's storm. Briefly, he wondered where Sam had got to. It was unlike the dog not to be bounding around first thing in the morning, his head raised, sniffing the air in search of titbits.

Feeling a sense of unease, Joi poked his head into Nong's room. But the bed was empty, the crumpled sheets on the floor. Bending down, he picked up the bed linen, noting that it felt cool. Where has that boy gone? Joi wondered. Then he shouted, "Gan, have you seen Nong?"

"He's out running!" replied Gan poking her head between the kitchen beaded curtains with a cheerful expression. "Nong said he had to catch up with Mongkut and Panit at the lake."

"Running!" exclaimed Joi with a broad grin. "Well, it looks like we're back in business if the boy's put his champ training shoes on!" Gan's golden smile warmed his heart. For the first time in weeks, she wasn't looking tired. *It's about time we had a good start to the day*, Joi thought, returning her smile with a broad grin of his own as he followed Gan back into the kitchen.

"The month ahead isn't going to be easy, Gan. Nong'll get tired, and I'm not going to not let up," Joi confided. "You know the whole busy-body village will want to know how he's getting on. Let's try and keep the pressure off the boy a bit by not talking about the match when he's home. He's going to need some space somewhere. Nong went to make merit as you asked, didn't he?"

"He said he did, but I've no idea why it took him so long," Gan mused. "I'm going to see the abbot later."

"OK, I'd better get to the gym and have a few words with everyone. We've got a month to get Nong ready for the rematch!" he said, clapping his hands together, eager to get started. I'll get coffee later. Most likely, I'll be back late."

Adrenaline rushed with the amount of organisation that needed to be done, the calls he had to make, and how he would frame the conversation with Tanawat. He gave Gan an absent-minded hug, then walked through the beaded kitchen curtain without bothering to hold the strands of wooden balls aside, the force of his passing causing the threads of beads to rattle and swing erratically.

Alone at last, Gan bent over, clutching her stomach. The stabs of pain were worse. Sitting down for a moment to say a prayer, not for herself, but for the success of her son and the happiness of her husband, she began to feel a candle of hope glowing from within. Dispensing warmth and a sense of lightness that spread from the top of her head to the tips of her toes. As she felt the pain recede, her thoughts returned to Nong and Joi. The last month between them had been difficult, with Nong's recovery and Joi's remorse. But now they were like peas in a pod again. Desperately hoping everything would be well, she set about making an extra special offering for the spirit house.

* * *

At Dragon's Gym, Joi himself sparred with Nong.

"Sharper, Nong. Sharper. Remember, bees frighten elephants. No matter how big your opponent, if you can sting your assailant, you can cause him to panic," encouraged Joi. "Again. Come on, give me a double jab that's a bit tougher than that."

Joi had been perfecting Nong's timing all morning. Nong's kicks needed to be sharper and faster. In ballistics and martial arts, speed *is* power. Nong had not trained hard since Bangkok, and it showed. His moves were stilted as he had to think his way through the sparring session rather than feel each situation and rely on his muscle memory.

Mongkut and Panit hung over the ropes, egging Nong on, proffering advice which neither Nong nor Joi heeded. They were in their own world, working together in a space that no-one could enter. Mongkut and Panit had greeted the news of the rematch with hoots and hollers. The mood in the camp had been off now for a month, with Joi speaking to them with a tongue so sharp it cut. Mongkut and Panit had tried to stay out of his way whenever they could. The pressure on them had been intense, with the still angry villagers questioning their motives and darting black looks in their directions. It was as if the treachery of Somchai had tainted them both. Mongkut reckoned that Natcha would happily land a couple of punches in their faces too, if she even smelt the scent of foul play. The news of Nong's rematch gave them the opportunity to rebuild bridges Somchai had dynamited.

A carnival atmosphere was colouring the hopes of the villagers. Aunts, uncles, cousins and neighbours popped by Dragon's Gym to watch Nong training and offer words of encouragement. Nong thanked everyone for the support with a friendly nod or wave, even though, at times, he felt like a zoo animal. In the early mornings, unemployed older men came to watch the training. Puffing away on their fake Marlboro or Lucky Strike cigarettes, they arrived in small groups of three or four. The Dragon's Gym reception had posters of the fight plastered over the four walls. What is more, Lucy had given everyone the night off on fight night and happily agreed to host another screening in the gym.

Whenever Nong went on his training runs, cars hooted, and people shouted out of their windows, "*Chok dee!*" Nong always waved in acknowledgement or smiled as he pushed himself harder and harder, focusing every day on running around the lake at a quicker pace than the day before. As the time for the rematch drew nearer, Gan started to hear the rumours about the levels of betting. Villagers were putting their life savings on Nong and making merit at the forest temple daily. Abbot Anurak reported that he was drowning in a tide of fruit, vegetables and rice. A number of monks had been sighted hiding the overflowing food donations in the forest. Not being able to refuse the offerings, they had no choice but to dispose of the food somehow. Even the temple macaques had started to put on weight with all the extra food. Their bellies extended as they dozed in trees during the hot tropical days.

The eve before the Bangkok trip arrived at last. Nong was eager to step on the boxing stadium ramp and run into the ring, talking about the fight to anyone who would listen. There would be no training in Bangkok or trying to cut weight like previous occasions. To compete in the famous Lumpinee Stadium was but a dream for many boxers. To be the main event was even more difficult to achieve. But to win the main fight was to reach nirvana. Nong would fight in the welterweight division and maintain a comfortable 65 kilograms.

Joi had tried to book the MRI scan for Gan, and he suspected that the reason why the office had been incapable of finding a time was because Doctor Gop had not made the necessary referral. Not wanting to put pressure on their son, Joi kept quiet and thought of alternative options. He had considered asking Lucy to pay for private hospital treatment, but how could they ever repay her? They couldn't. Nong just had to win.

CHAPTER TWENTY-NINE

THE compressed air from the pneumatic braking system hissed as the battered bus parked outside Dragon's Gym. Eager to be on their way, Nong's neighbours and extended family paused their conversations and rushed to gather their belongings of brightly coloured four-foot by four-foot bags filled with clothes for the trip, slices of watermelon, cardboard boxes tied with string, bananas, as well as an assortment of food parcels. A few of the older folk had toothbrushes in their top pockets. The youngest travellers wore their smartest shorts and flip-flops. The teenagers were mostly dressed in jeans, as were the adults. Everyone sported an item of clothing in common. It was a yellow t-shirt emblazoned with a black silhouette of Nong in a classic Muay Thai stance on the front. Printed on the back was *Dragon's Gym, Khao Lak to Bangkok, Champion's Tour*. Everyone had enjoyed the secret planning of the excursion as much as the thought of visiting Bangkok. Joi and Nong had no idea they were coming, which made the trip even more exciting.

The old coach doors released a whoosh of air, and a Thai version of Yoda from *Star Wars*, wearing a back-to-front baseball cap and Ray-Bans, waved them onto the coach, causing a melee as the supporters swarmed as one to secure a window seat. Some grandparents sent their grandchildren ahead to guard a space. Warit passed a plastic washbag and change of clothes to Sert and ascended the coach steps while ordering those occupying the front seats behind the driver to move.

"You think this tin can will make it nearly eight-hundred kilometres to Bangkok?" asked Sert to no-one in particular.

Natcha frowned, her eyes scanning the 44-foot green and gold coach from back to front. Its tyres were old and worn. The tread had disappeared in some places. The coach's side panels were scratched, rusting over the wheel arches, and the windscreen had more than a few chips. "It'll be fine. But I'm so not looking forward to the eleven-hour journey there," she replied, putting her headphones firmly on her head with a note of finality and hitching her blue and white polka dot rucksack up. "Let's board this baby now. I'll tell you something else, Nong had better win. This crowd will be depressed for a year if he doesn't."

"Yeah," agreed Sert. "And the long journey home will be really, really shit."

"Come on, little brother," laughed Natcha, "Let's try to grab those back seats. Nong has trained as hard as he can. I know. I've been to the gym and seen the sessions, unlike you, shorty!"

"Less of the little," grumbled Sert, trailing behind Natcha as she disappeared into the coach. His phone bleeped. It was Nong text messaging him that they were boarding the plane. Sert's footsteps were heavy on the three metal steps. The last to enter, he couldn't see a spare seat, just rows of brown heads leading all the way to the back of the coach and the occasional hand fiddling with the overhead air-conditioning nozzle. There had been talk of inviting along the Dragon's Gym guests, but the coach was so oversubscribed that Lucy, who had hired it, informed all the guests that they would have to fly to Bangkok if they wanted to see the match or arrange another form of transport.

"I've saved you one," hollered Natcha, "here beside me."

Sert wavered as he walked down the aisle to the back, as the coach started reversing its way down the road leading up to Dragon's Gym. Then BOOM. The driver hit a particularly bad pothole, and there was a bang. The doors hissed open again, and the driver disembarked to check the right back wheel. Noses pressed to smeared glass windows, attempting to gauge the reaction of the driver. When he held his arms up in the air and started gesticulating that everyone should get off the bus, the passengers gave a collective groan.

To his surprise, Sert saw that Gan had joined the group trip. She was standing at the front, politely letting people disembark. "I wonder if Nong knows. Not once has his mum ever been to see him fight!"

"Get on with it," pressed Natcha from behind. "The quicker we all get off, the faster we can get going."

"I'm going!" snapped Sert with an angry glare at his sister.

The tyre was as flat as the lake surface on an arid afternoon.

"Bet this adds another two hours to our journey," sighed Natcha, plonking herself down on the grass verge next to Sert and shaking her head.

"Yeah, right!" said Sert, shaking his head in disbelief. "Wake me when we have to board again, will you? If it looks like the tyre is going to take forever to fix, then I'm off."

"Sert, get your arse over here. Can't you see we need more help?" shouted Warit, sweating with a group of men and women struggling to change the old wheel. Behind the flustered brigade of volunteers, mongrels of various sizes barked and chased one another. The more enterprising strays had approached the teenagers, who were now cheerfully handing the dogs food from the containers their mothers had prepared for the trip. Some of it was still warm from the wok. Gan picked up a stone and threw it in the direction of the kids, shouting at them to stop.

"It's me, it's always me," puffed Sert. "He just NEVER lets up."

"Run along, Daddy's favourite. You know he doesn't like to be kept waiting," teased Natcha, lying down to wait in the long grass and sighing in contentment. She loved being right. The trip was turning out to be just as she had expected. Utter chaos.

CHAPTER THIRTY

BANGKOK Suvarnabhumi Airport was as disorganised as Nong remembered. The domestic airlines terminal was mobbed, full of useless information about the airport but few exit signs. He recalled from the last ill-fated trip that the airport had the world's tallest control tower and the world's fourth-largest single terminal building. Fine, but how were they supposed to arrive at the pickup point? Then, in the distance, Nong spotted Tanawat and waved his hand in greeting.

"*Sabai dee mai*," said Tanawat. "Welcome back, Champion. You're looking terrific." Tanawat grasped their hands in both of his and shook them vigorously, first Joi, then Nong. "Journalists, the hotel, Agung—everyone's been asking when you're arriving. But I've kept my mouth shut. Guessed you didn't want to do media interviews as you stepped off the plane?" he joked, putting a friendly arm around Nong's shoulders. Tanawat did not bother to introduce the PR girl with the fixed smile, her forehead shiny with Botox and frazzled dyed red hair standing by his side.

"I'd have been fine," replied Nong, calmly hoisting his rucksack onto his shoulder and rolling his shoulder blades, itching to get to a quiet space where he could stretch more fully after the flight.

"That's the attitude I need! Right there! But you've gotta give a BIG smile in front of the camera. Amplify it! We need more excitement and energy for the press. We're saying this is the rematch of the century. Now, listen, as soon as we arrive at the hotel, you can check-in, and then it's straight to the ballroom where the media will be waiting. Cameras and all," said Tanawat, literally bouncing on his feet. He stood to make a lot of money from tomorrow night's fight regardless of whether Nong won or not and had made sure to have a series of lunches and dinners with the promoters from the online bookies that offered Muay Thai betting coverage almost every day of the year. With each meeting or meal, he had pretended that he was giving special, secretive insights to encourage them to cover the fight and stir up the excitement. Tanawat scrutinised Nong and asked Joi, "He's ready for the weigh-in, isn't he?"

Joi raised one eyebrow as if to say, "You're questioning me?" and nodded his affirmation.

Nong felt his stomach tense and took a slow breath in and out to steady himself. The fight he couldn't wait for, but he felt unprepared to deal with a room full of journalists and definitely had no desire to talk about the poisoning or his quick recovery, which his mother said was due to the infusion she had made from the small green plants. He hadn't been able to explain Monkey and his leaves to her. How was he supposed to tell a room full of journalists?

"Honey, give Nong the sponsors' gear, will you, in

case there are any journalists lurking? Nong, change in the lavatory over there behind the Maybank currency exchange booth. But hurry the car's outside."

Tanawat waited till Nong was out of earshot before asking in a low voice. "How's he really getting along, Khun Joi? He seems fine, but is he ready?"

"He's good. Listen, though, Khun Tanawat, if the media start asking about his recovery more than tomorrow night's fight, then I'm pulling him out of that ballroom," said Joi, his mouth set in a straight line and the former easy-going side of his nature gone as he held Tanawat's gaze. "Nong is going to focus on the fight and only the fight. Not the recovery. The next thirty-six hours are for us to prepare."

Accustomed to Joi's taciturn character, Tanawat replied, "Sure, sure," and held up his hands, palms upwards, to placate him before continuing to brief Joi in a machine gun fire manner, words hitting their mark in a short, sharp tone. "Let's finish this conversation before Nong's back. There's no need to overburden him with the plan, now is there? Agung, his trainer Desnee and Colonel Mongkol Siriparu are just a few of the people waiting at the hotel. We need to get some photos done today. Tomorrow's going to be a frenzy. Just thinking of Nong, you know?"

Tanawat's not listening, thought Joi, stepping forward and clapping his hand on Tanawat's back. "Old friend, I'm not joking. I'll pull Nong out of that ballroom and any other situation that I do not feel is right. And I don't care who you've got lined up.

There'll be no pretend trash-talking for the media; that's not Muay Thai, and that's not us. Nong told me about some TikTok stunts he was thinking about, but we're not doing that either. We're here to fight, not to perform tricks for the media circus."

"Easy. I've got it. Calm down. I've got Nong's best interests at heart," said Tanawat. "He has to stay in the hotel and NOT leave. Not until my car collects you. Don't even get in a taxi yourself or accept drinks or food from strangers. Some of these guys may even think they can get at Nong by getting to you. There's a shitload of money riding on the fight."

Tanawat recalled at times that Joi could be disturbingly calm and was always, always in control of his emotions. Thinking that perhaps he had overstepped the mark, Tanawat ceased the excited torrent of instructions, which even to his own ear sounded like babbling.

Joi knew that beneath all the camaraderie, it was the money that mattered most. At the moment, there were eleven promoters with responsibility for bringing fighters to challenge for the titles. The rules were the same as in Rajadamnern, with the boxers having to weigh more than 45.4 kilograms, be aged over fifteen years, and there could not be more than a two-point-three-kilogram weight difference between the boxers. The cost of tickets at that time ranged from 2,500 baht and upwards. Any visitor to Lumpinee would notice the frantic betting around the ring—every stadium applied for a special gambling licence, which enables the activity.

Joi gave Tanawat a beatific smile, eased his own body language, and relaxed his muscles as he did so. "Now just look at Nong, the joy of being young, eh!" For a few moments, the two men relived happy memories as they envied Nong gazing in awe as five stunning Singapore airline hostesses floated past. Dressed in the custom-made, distinctive sarong kebaya SIA uniforms that showcased their beautiful figures, each flight attendant was immaculately dressed. When one of them dazzled Nong with a smile, he blushed and attempted to return her gaze, but his features crumpled like Jenga bricks, and what was meant to be a sultry look was more like a grimace, causing the flight attendant to quickly turn away, giggling.

"Nong, you've no defences for such beauty," teased Tanawat as Joi chuckled beside him. "Win this match, and maybe one of those ladies might, just might, accept an invitation to dinner!"

"What? Don't know what you mean," denied Nong as he sauntered over like a cowboy who had been on his horse for too long, dressed in a crisp white cotton tracksuit with more than fifty logos covering the hooded top and the sides of his trousers.

Tilting his head to one side and narrowing his eyes, Joi turned to Tanawat with raised brows, "Really? Nong looks like some crazy ladyboy?"

"Ahh, come on. Nong loves his new gear. Don't you now?"

"Err…" stuttered Nong, unsure what to make of the

outfit and struggling to think of anything positive to say. "It's new. The trainers are a bit tight… I can't walk quite right. I'll be back in a second," he said, spying a full-length mirror outside a shop.

"Yeah, you do that, lover boy!" Turning back to Joi, Tanawat said, "Anyway, it's all in the contract that he'd advertise the sponsors for the duration of the fight. How was travelling business class?"

A smiling Joi said, "The flight was terrific. Thanks for that. Shame Nong couldn't enjoy the food, but on the way home, he can stuff himself!" Silently, Joi thought, *pick your battles, Joi. Pick your battles. You know you hate all this shit. The boxing world's not like it was. Ignore the Red Bull logo*. But then, he saw Nong and sighed. His son was adopting different poses in front of the fashion boutique's mirrored entrance to better admire his new look. Raising his face to the sky, Joi prayed for deliverance from the boy's rapidly expanding ego.

Nong was preening and standing with a swagger in his American-style logoed tracksuit. People glanced in his direction as they walked past, trying to recollect how they knew him. Boxing aficionados held out bits of paper for an autograph, wished him luck, and asked after his dad. The older men let him know that they planned to place bets on him winning. Nong smiled and chatted, thanked everyone and kept turning back to look at Joi, his eyes expressing the need for some help as he did not want to touch any paper or pens.

"Do your job!" snapped Tanawat at the PR woman

in a tone that was both familiar and sharp. Rolling his eyes at Joi, he said, "Sorry, we'll deal with this."

Joi lowered his head to hide his grin. He suspected that Tanawat and the girl had had a lover's tiff on the way to the airport.

The PR woman trotted off on her high heels and tapped Nong on the upper arm, telling him in a soft, breathy voice that they had a tight schedule and needed to go. Nong thanked her and stepped away from the old man with a face ravaged by too much tobacco and life in the sun, pestering him to sign a crumpled sheet of paper.

"Nong, we've got a fight to win!" said Joi, slapping Nong around the back of the head and eliciting a smirk from Tanawat. If they could win this fight, Nong would be up for a title fight. The glitz and glamour came and went; now was the time to work.

Tanawat's smugness had not escaped Joi, who warned, "Nong will do no more than an hour with the media, and then he's with us. He needs to sleep, rest, do some warm-ups and get his head in the right space for tomorrow."

"Give me an extra couple of hours, Joi. We've got the TV slots in the evening. And what else?" Tanawat asked, addressing the PR assistant who had returned from placating the autograph hunters.

"Tomorrow morning, there's—"

"Not happening," butted in Joi shaking his head.

Joi reminded Tanawat of the particularly cantankerous Asian male buffalo he had seen when he had last travelled south to Koh Samui to see the local sport of buffalo fights. There, too, millions of baht changed hands in betting. Tanawat was considering expanding his promotion business to include the buffalo fights as they drew lots of excitement. Crowds would gather to see a good battle of bulls in the dust. The more aggressive the buffalo, the greater the entertainment for the audience. The fight ended when one of the buffalos ran away, usually well before any of the animals were seriously hurt. Tanawat reckoned he could turn the fights that were banned on the mainland into a lucrative business.

The Bangkok traffic was chaotic as usual and their black limousine cruised into the Orchid Hotel's four-star lobby an hour later than planned. Bedlam greeted them, with rows of journalists pushing and shoving, waving microphones and shouting at Nong as soon as the doorman opened the Mercedes door. Unceremoniously, Joi sprung out of the car, leapt over the bonnet and pushed several of them back, striking them in the chest with the palm of his hand.

Other than the single doorman, the staff of the hotel were nowhere to be seen. A furious Tanawat shouted at the PR girl who refused to leave the safety of the air-conditioned car. Holding tightly onto Nong, Joi pulled him forwards, thanking people as he barged through them. Then he saw welcome familiar faces in the crowd. Hugely relieved that his friend had kept his word, he waved at Dang and beckoned him to hurry up. Together, the two of them shielded Nong, steering him up the hotel steps, past the doorman, through the revolving doors, and into the bright lobby with its cool pink faux Italian marble flooring and carved colonnades.

The traditional garb of the receptionists and doormen, with its nod to ancient modes of dressing, and the Central dialect the locals were speaking, which was also the standard for TV, were all that distinguished the interior of the lobby from any other place on earth. They could have been in Rome. Knowing Tanawat could manage himself, Joi marched to the hotel reception desk, gave the boxing promoter's name and handed over his own identity card. A breathless but unapologetic Tanawat appeared just in time to give the receptionist his credit card to secure against any unforeseen expenditures. Tanawat's magic card was a relief to Joi, as he did not own one and never had. Like most of the trainers at Dragon's Gym, he dealt very much in cash.

"Thanks," said Joi, never forgetting his manners and refraining from mentioning the shit show outside. His goal was to get Nong to the hotel room straightaway. Double-checking on the location of the elevators and that the room number was correct, he declined the staff's repeated offers to carry his small, shabby, but immaculately clean holdall and led the growing Nong entourage to the gilded elevator framed by reproduction Thai temple arches complete with *Nagas*. Tanawat, Joi, Nong, and Dang had ample space in the cavernous, air-conditioned lift interior to take a much-needed breath.

Tanawat spoke first. “Well, that was fun,” he said, attempting to make light of the bedlam.

“We’re missing your assistant,” said Nong. “She okay?”

Tanawat puffed in annoyance and tutted, “She’s gone home. The Royal Thai military communications officer is on his way over from the stadium. He’ll be with us in thirty minutes. The mess outside was on national TV and my left ear is still burning from his call. Thought it best that we blame the hotel. Luckily, Colonel Mongkol Siriparu couldn’t make it today. Otherwise, he’d have cancelled my fucking license,” growled Tanawat as the lift arrived at their floor.

“But how—”

“Nong, stop your worrying,” snapped Joi. *Nong’s kindness and concern were not needed right now,* he thought ruefully. He swore that his boy became more and more like his mother every day. Same care for every person, animal or plant. But now was not the time to be fussing around a girl who could clearly look after herself. “Khun Tanawat, you told the driver to take her home, didn’t you?” said Joi, knowing that the concern Nong felt would be like a scratch he couldn’t itch unless his mind was put at rest.

“Yeah, yeah. Sure I did,” said Tanawat, his eyes averted to avoid Joi’s direct look.

“There you go, Nong,” said Joi, giving Tanawat a sideways glance as he tapped the key card against the twin room door. The four of them entered the functional bedroom, with the standard city hotel décor of famous landmarks and panoramic views in cheap frames. Pure luxury compared to the cement square that Nong called home. Pushing past his father, Nong rushed to claim the bed nearest the window and furthest from the front door. Tanawat's eyes travelled around the room, checking everything was in order, opening and shutting the mini-fridge. Satisfied that it was empty and he wouldn't be receiving any unexpected bills, he said, "See you in a few hours," before heading back down to reception. Dang stood back to let Tanawat exit. The three boxers could hear him shouting into his phone as he waited for the elevator.

She needs to find a new job, mused Joi, shaking his head before turning to Dang and Nong. Joi said, "Okay, let's not waste time. In thirty-six hours, the fight starts."

CHAPTER THIRTY-ONE

JOI and Dang had switched off their phones, unplugged the hotel landline and stood leaning against the hotel bedroom wall, reminiscing. In the corridors and lobby, journalists continued to buzz like Asian hornets. Even the gym was not off limits for their questions. Nong had the bright idea of turning the two single beds onto their side to create a small training space. Joi had turned the air conditioning units off and shut the windows shut. The hotel floral scent had been replaced by the smell of sweat as Nong skipped in his sauna suit, going through the fight game plan and half listening to Joi chewing the fat with Dang. The conversation moved from Muay Thai gossip to technique, and now they chatted about the factors that affect striking power. His father was stressing the importance of the right mindset, using the famous boxer Saenchaí to illustrate his point.

"Yes, old friend, you've got to consider precision, technique, and the force delivered, but it's fight IQ that matters. Saenchaí's only five-feet-four-inches tall and used to fight around his walking weight of one-hundred-and-thirty pounds. But he was often made to give up weight during his peak, as much as over ten pounds when facing foreigners. The guy had perfect timing and footwork, and he could switch his stances and confuse opponents. Never been one like him! Who else can you think of who could throw scissor and cartwheel kicks and use Muay Thai strategies that most people don't even know? Tell me that?"

"Your boy? He's confident and obsessive too!"

Nong flashed Dang a grin, appreciating the compliment. Saenchaí had won his first super flyweight Lumpinee title at the age of sixteen and bantamweight at the age of eighteen.

There was a sharp rap at the door. "I'll get it," said Joi, checking the scratched Casio watch he'd purchased from the local gas station. "It'll be Tanawat on our case to hurry up for the weigh-in downstairs."

Nong paused his skipping and looked questioningly at Dang when the tone of his father changed to a formal manner, which he only used with people he either did not know, like or wanted to be particularly polite to. Joi had not fully opened the door and invited whoever it was in, so something was up. Joi waved his hand behind his back, beckoning. Nong, curious and eager to see who it was, dropped his skipping rope and made for the door.

Dang grabbed Nong by the upper arm, pushing him to one side, before following Joi outside and closing the door behind him. The sound of raised voices echoed in the hotel corridor. Nong put his ear against the wood and struggled to place the stranger's muffled speech. Then it hit him. It was in Chiang Mai where he had first heard that voice, and along with it, he could now distinguish Bhan as well. Nong yanked at the door handle, but someone was holding it shut from the other side. Looking through the spy hole, he cursed as he saw Aye and Bhan casually talking, as if they had nothing better to do than pass the time of day.

"He's resting right now," repeated Joi with a shrug of his shoulders while Dang smiled and nodded without saying anything. Joi's face was perfectly composed in a bland, polite expression, like a government bureaucrat who wanted to keep the tone of a conversation pleasant whilst lying. His eyes narrowed to stone black chips, which contrasted sharply with his buddha-esque smile. Not used to being denied, Bhan was struggling to keep his tone civil and avoid menace from entering his repeated request that Joi either send Nong out or he could enter and have a few words. Bhan kept insisting he just wanted to wish Nong well. Frustration showed as Bhan's irascible expression began to crack, but his manufactured charm made no dent in either Joi or Dang's countenance. Like benevolent *Yakshas*, nature spirits that guard the gates of Buddhist temples, they stood either side of the hotel bedroom door, not moving, not caring about anything either Bhan or Aye had to say. Joi's eyes flitted from first Aye to then Bhan, gauging whether they had got the message. Aye's pursed lips and Bhan's silence gave him the confirmation he needed.

With a broad smile, Joi said, "Well, thanks for stopping by. I'll let Nong know you came to see him. Please excuse us." Looking at his watch, he continued, "But we need to go over the fight plan. You know how it is." Joi gave a nod in the direction of the door to Dang and turned away from the unwanted visitors.

"Yep, we've got the weigh-in in half an hour, so see you then," added Dang, guessing the pair had already planned to attend, shaking first Aye's hand and then Bhan's goodbye.

"Yeah, right," said Aye, tapping Joi on the back, causing him to face his direction once again. "Be sure to pass on my regards. Here's the gift I've bought. Just a few snacks to keep the champ's energy levels up."

"Thanks. I'll give them to him," said Joi as he followed Dang back into the hotel room, firmly closing the door behind him and putting on the latch. He scrutinised the gaudy box with its numerous ribbons, no doubt purchased from a high-end store, and threw it into his rucksack. "I'll send that for testing," he snapped.

"What was all that about?" asked Nong, irritated at being treated like a child and having such simple decisions as greeting Bhan and Aye made for him. "What's going on with you?"

"Never you mind, Son. Let's get this room back into order. Then shower and get changed into your Elvis Presley pantsuit. The show's about to start," said Joi.

Chapter Thirty-Two

At the weigh-in-come-press-conference, shouts of anger and jeers greeted Agung's pushing and trash-talking. The oldest match official sharply pulled Agung back by the arm with a reprimand that this was not the Thai way. Still, Nong started to respond to the opponent's sneering and swearing in his face by shoving Agung in the chest. Hard. Nong cursed himself for rising to the bait when he caught sight of his father, shaking his head with both eyebrows raised.

At the back of the packed ballroom, Aye chatted with the other gambling bosses, pleased with himself for devising the scene for the media's entertainment and making Nong late for the media briefing. The delay they had staged at the hotel door was aimed at rattling the old coaches. Already, Aye could tell that Joi was seeing enemies everywhere. He was standing so close to Nong and intercepting anyone who approached. He could see the screens of the TV cameras from where he was standing, and unlike Agung, who appeared strong and confident, Nong's team were coming across as nervous. Joi's continual scanning of the room gave him a shifty, furtive appearance. *Perfect*, thought Aye, talking aside to Bhan in a hushed tone,

"This is what we want. Tension. I believe there's not much between these two fighters and the more friction we can create the better the show."

Bhan shrugged. What did he care about how the boxers felt? His expression unsure, he asked, "What more can we do? There's no way we can get near Nong's team this time. I tried to meet with Dang, but he's not having any of it."

"Shut up and listen," snapped Aye, impatient with Bhan's worrying. "Can't you see I'm watching the reports!"

The national TV news clips were as bad as Aye hoped. The boy who everyone had been touting as the wonder kid appeared weak and petulant on the big screen. The shove to Agung's chest and surprised look contrasted sharply with Agung's dominant stance.

Punters would soon be switching bets to Agung for the first round, which Aye believed Nong would win, given his fight record.

"What does it feel like being back here as the main event? Have you fully recovered from the alleged poisoning?" asked an overweight, bald, wrinkled journalist.

Tanawat cringed. He had been expecting that one of the hacks would ask this question, but he had briefed this particular journalist to focus on the excitement surrounding tomorrow night's match, which was why he gave him the opportunity to speak to Nong first. Concealing his anger at the use of the word *alleged*, he handed Nong the microphone.

Nong took a deep breath before answering in a calm tone, "Excited, really excited. I've got the best trainer in the world, in my dad. What more can I ask for?"

"Next question," barked Tanawat, grinning at Nong as he took back the microphone while ignoring the journalist waving for attention so he could continue his pointed line of questioning.

Nong fielded the enquiries into the poisoning like a professional. Moving the conversation back each time to the rematch, flashing a smile cheekily at the cameras and thanking the media for their interest. In sharp contrast, Agung kept up a combative, surly tone, insisting that he was the stronger and alluding to the perceived weakness of his opponent. Agung earned a thumbs-up from Aye and Bhan, but scowls from the officials, who did not appreciate his abrasive Western style.

The next morning, the newspapers questioned if the rematch hadn't been planned too soon and if Joi was the right coach for Nong. The *Bangkok Guardian* led with a full-page image of Joi with his arm around Nong's shoulders, given what appeared to be a spiteful sideways glance at Agung's coaching team. Someone in the photography department had digitally altered his hand so it appeared as if Joi was giving Agung's coach a one-fingered salute. *Boy Wonder Let Down by Doubtful Coach* screamed the headline.

Over breakfast in the hotel dining room, Joi took one look at the paper and tossed it aside. Leaning across the table, he spoke to Dang in a low voice, "Keep all the papers away from Nong, will you? The write-ups aren't good. Not only do the camera angles make

Agung look twice Nong's size, but the odds are also stacked against him. The journalists are saying he doesn't look confident, not like before he was poisoned. The less he knows about this bullshit, the better."

Dang frowned and retrieved the paper.

Joi raised his eyebrows at Dang's smug expression.

"Hey, I'm looking pretty good, aren't I?" Dang claimed. "When did you get so old? That's the problem, you old bastard, eh? You're not worried about Nong." Dang pointed a toast crust at Joi. "Your lovely Gan'll wonder what she's doing with such a fossil. I mean, what a shifty old man. No-one's going to think we're the same age now, are they?"

Joi slapped the broadsheet down with one hand. "Remind me why you're here?" he snarled. Quickly, though, a smile broke through his stormy expression as the pressure he had felt over the past few weeks lifted. The two old friends returned to the business of breakfast in companionable quiet.

Dang broke the silence, "I saw your boy fight in Chiang Mai. There's one thing I can say about him. He's determined! You're his father. You know what motivates him that I can't speak to. What I do know is that if he maintains his good form and wins tonight, he is going to have a shot at the Lumpinee title. Don't doubt your boy. You and I need to have 110 per cent confidence right now. We can worry about what goes on outside the ring once we've won this thing. Deal?"

Joi listened to his instincts before replying, "It's not

Nong that I'm worried about!" His eyes scanned the room for Nong while taking a sip of his coffee. Joi realised Nong had disappeared. *Most likely, he's gone back to his room*, he thought, gulping the too-hot beverage down and searching in his pockets for the key. Suddenly, shouts and cheers erupted in the hotel lobby. Joi's brow furrowed in an uneasy recognition of a particular sing-song timbre twinkling in the cacophony.

"Isn't that Gan?" Dang asked with a puzzled look.

"Can't be."

"But that's Gan's laughter."

"No way. She's back in the village. She's never been to see Nong fight before. She hates the idea of seeing him hurt almost as much as she hates Bangkok."

An excited shout of "*Mum*" echoed from the lobby, causing Joi to knock his coffee over and shoot out of his chair. Dang crumpled the newspaper into a ball, throwing it on top of his half-eaten fried eggs, rushing after Joi. The rubber sole of his flip-flops squeaked on the marble floor. *This should be a riot*, he thought, chuckling at his old friend's hurried walk. It was the first time in thirty years he had seen Joi rush anywhere. Even when he fought, he moved either slowly or lightning-fast with decisiveness.

Joi stopped at the dining room exit door, speechless for once. There wasn't a face he did not recognise in the coach party swarming throughout the lobby like a hum of bumble bees, buzzing and flitting around the sunflower that was Nong, whose face shone a golden colour in the soft glow of the hotel lobby chandeliers. Natcha and Sert were chatting and laughing next to Nong, who stood stock-still. His eyes fixed on Gan as she held his hands in hers, tears streaming down her face. The doorman uselessly flapped his arms, attempting to usher the rowdy crowd, who were not hotel guests, back to the main road outside, where the battered coach was parked on the forecourt, blocking the narrow entrance. Taxi drivers and private cars honked and bleeped in a chorus of protest, unaware that the coach driver was inside, making his way to Joi so he could shake his hand and wish him the best of luck for the big fight.

"Stop crying, will you? It's only a boxing match. I'll win or lose," soothed Nong, separating his hands from Gan's and staring with wide eyes at the hotel lobby, which had transformed into a village fiesta hall.

Gan inspected Nong with a mother's eye and thought, *how like Joi my son has become without my even noticing*! Memories flooded back of when Joi was his age. Even then, she reflected, he had a quiet composure and self-confidence that was different from other boys his age. Seeing how uncomfortable she was making Nong, Gan took a deep breath, clasped both hands together and said, "I'm not worried or sad, just happy to see you after such a long journey. We never thought we would make it to Bangkok in that tin can Where's your father, he should be with you!"

Before Nong could reply, Natcha pointed to where Joi stood on the other side of the marbled foyer next to

Dang. Both men wore bemused expressions as they watched the affray. Seeing Natcha and his father in the hotel lobby, an idea occurred to Nong. Since Somchai's betrayal, an important part of Nong's team had remained unfilled. There was no-one in his corner who knew Muay Thai as well as Somchai did and who was also a peer. Joi would always be Nong's anchor, but Somchai's presence had served a purpose too. Sometimes, a friend could sense a need where a father could not.

In a burst of enthusiasm, Nong pulled Natcha across the lobby towards Joi and Dan to ask if Natcha would form part of his corner team. Everyone knew what a sexist bunch some of the stadium organisers were. One of the reasons why Natcha had given up on boxing was that being female, it had been impossible for her to compete at the famous Bangkok boxing stadiums. She had argued that it was outdated and wrong but was repeatedly told it was part of Thai culture, a response she felt was bullshit.

"*Sabai dee mai,* Joi and Dang," she said, pressing her palms together, as did Sert, who stumbled up behind her and Nong. Joi returned their greetings, the expression in his eyes warm as he also shook hands and thanked other villagers who worked as street food vendors, waiters, fishermen, street cleaners, and housemaids. There wasn't a person amongst them who made more than $600 a month. Many of the villagers had sacrificed two days of much-needed pay to travel across half of Thailand.

As Nong looked at the optimistic faces of his friends and neighbours, most of whom had now begun to leave the hotel lobby to alight the bus, he pursed his lips in concern. Then he reminded himself that however bad their dilapidated hotel on the nearby backstreets was, most of these supporters would still find it luxurious compared to their own homes. At least there wouldn't be outdoor lavatories in which scorpions, snakes and spiders sheltered in the rainy season and a mildewed hose pipe serving as a shower. Natcha had already told him that she and Sert would join the other youngsters, who would sleep on the bus. Not everyone could afford hotel accommodation in Bangkok, and the coach would take the remaining supporters to Lumpinee Stadium, park up outside and provide free temporary overnight accommodation. The following morning, after a no doubt uncomfortable sleep, the bus would drive them to Benjasiri Park, with its shady trees, playground and central lake. Here, the whole group would reunite before making the long trip back to Khao Lak. Everyone had packed their swimming costumes for the public swimming pool visit, where the coach driver's uncle worked and had agreed to waive the normal fee and registration requirement of a Bangkok Hospital health certificate in return for a ticket to Nong's fight.

"When was all this planned, then?" asked Joi, still of two minds as to whether this surprise visit was a blessing or a curse. Looking down and seeing Nong's calm expression, he decided it was the former. *What harm could it possibly do to have so much goodwill in the audience?* he thought, turning his attention to pragmatic matters.

"Natcha, do you all have tickets, or do I need to speak with Tanawat, the promoter?" he asked, praying he would not have to sort out this unexpected fan club. It was part of Dragon's Gym's culture for everyone to work as a team and help care for one another, but he could do without additional administrative headaches.

"We're good," replied Natcha, patting her teacher's arm. "I saw the weigh-in interview on Facebook Live. What's going on with Agung?"

"I don't know and don't care."

"I'd like Natcha to help us at the fight," Nong blurted, desperate to make his point before the opportunity passed him by.

"What do you mean?" asked Joi. Natcha shifted nervously, not wanting Nong's request to be refused.

"Can she help tonight? Can she be in our corner?"

"I'd like that very much," Natcha said in support of Nong, putting her own desire on the scale.

Joi paused before answering. No fool, he knew that she and Nong were asking his permission to break the Lumpinee-biased rules against females. Like Natcha, he believed that Muay Thai would benefit from permitting professional female athletes to compete at Lumpinee. Women were banned from entering the Muay Thai ring due to the superstition that a female presence might destroy a Muay Thai fighter's skill, making him weak and prone to injury and jinxing the ring. The other boxing gyms with fighters competing would complain that Natcha was too near centre stage. Joi took a step closer to Natcha and Nong, and he signalled to Dang and Sert to move nearer. "Dang, you know we have had men dressed as women fighting in the rings. How about Natcha disguises herself as a man for our corner?"

Dang gave a sideways glance at his old friend to check if he was joking. One look at his old friend's serious expression told him Joi wasn't. "I'm fine with it." He shrugged.

"I am too," Nong added. Joi smiled wryly, enlivened by his son's enthusiasm.

"But," piped up Sert, "she's a female."

"Sert, your powers of observation are superior to your Muay Thai skills," responded Joi, laughing. "We need you to keep our secret. Can you do that?"

"Yes, sure."

"Good. If Natcha agrees to dress as a man and work Nong's corner, we can never say anything. Do you all understand me? People show up to help the corner men, so no-one's going to question why a couple of extras are with Nong during the warm-up and waiting for the main event in the back room. Women coming into the prefight space isn't a big deal, but a female doing the fight prep and touching the boxing ring will cause all hell to break loose. And worse, they might give the judges award to Agung in spite." Joi turned to look into the eyes of first Natcha, then Nong, then Dang, followed by Sert to see if they agreed before continuing his team talk. "Do we want to take this risk?"

“No, no, it’s okay,” said Natcha, waving her palms to signal that there was no way she was prepared to risk Nong not winning because of her.

“Natcha, you asked to do something that has consequences. There is always going to be an element of risk when you try to make changes to centuries-old rulings. I believe that you can keep it together and not let us down. You’re in!”

Natcha opened her mouth to argue but snapped her jaws shut again. Since she was six, she had been at the receiving end of Joi’s rich brown gaze. Every time she had doubted herself or needed to train even harder, the force of his nature had given her the confidence to fight with greater courage. “Thank you. I won’t disappoint you,” she promised, giving a quick *Wai.* Stomach churning, she held her head high as she thought about how she was going to make Muay Thai history. Natcha knew from her father, Warit, that the so-called tradition argument was invented. At the age of ten, she had asked her dad why it was fine for trans women boxers like Angie Petchrungruang to fight at Lumpinee Stadium but not *Nak Muay Ying,* female boxers. As with a lot of what was bad about boxing, the taint of gambling reared its ugly head here too. Thai women had not fought professionally at Lumpinee since the late sixties when efforts were made to promote the sport by holding female bouts at the famed old stadium. But the efforts were abandoned after three years because the predominantly male Thai fans refused to watch or bet on the matches. In the ensuing four decades, the only place to see women boxing was at provincial temple fairs and festivals. It was true that *Nak Muay Ying* was gaining acceptance. But not all Lumpinee female fighters were welcome, and the Ayes and Bhans of this world, with their strong connections in the military, resisted any change. Natcha welcomed the chance to fool them.

"Good, that's settled." With a nod to Dang to continue the conversation with Natcha, Joi hurried to welcome Gan. "Can a husband get a word in?" he teased, edging through the crowd to enfold Gan in his arms. Sensing that Nong had followed him, Joi leaned in to whisper in Gan's left ear, "You shouldn't have come."

"It's about time I saw Nong fight, wouldn't you say?" responded Gan, leaning back her head and holding Joi's face in her hands. Looking at his thin visage, his steady eyes bright with intelligence and finding solace in his strength, Gan let him know she felt fine with a calm smile. The decision to travel to Bangkok had not been taken lightly, and she did not want to be in the chaotic city or experience the anguish of seeing her son fight, but she could hardly stay at home when her friends and family had travelled hundreds of miles to support Nong. She was under no illusion that her presence positively impacted Joi. He had no need for her support. If anything, he might think her joining the group was a distraction. Although she knew he would never tell her that in so many words. It was Nong she had come to support in any way she could. Joi gave a tight smile in disagreement but asked, “Where are you staying?”

Gan snorted with laughter, slapping Joi lightly on his left cheek. The man she loved so much and knew so well. Raising her eyebrows and putting her hands on her hips, she gave her sassiest smile. “If you win, then with you, but if not, then the bedroom door is locked, and I’ll see you back in the village! Don’t worry, I’m not going to disturb the pre-fight preparations.”

“Oh, women: always a problem. First, they show up wanting you, then they lock the door!” laughed Joi, turning his head for support. For better or worse, no-one was watching their exchange. Behind Gan, Nong was making a great show of studying a semi-abstract painting in burnt primary colours to avoid witnessing his parents' cringeworthy flirting. Outside, the coach blared its horn in short, sharp, loud bursts, warning any last stragglers it was leaving.

“Gan, stop joking. Where are you staying?” persisted Joi, wanting to know where his wife would be. “You know I’m sharing with Nong and Dang.”

“With Natcha and Sert. I’ll call you later, off with you. And best of luck,” Gan replied, kissing him goodbye, conscious that in less than twelve hours, Nong would meet his opponent and needed to win the most important fight of his life.

CHAPTER THIRTY-THREE

NONG found waiting for the fight to start boring. Outside the dressing room, he could hear the *Samara* music playing and the shouts of the crowds cheering on a fighter as he kneed his opponent in the ribs. "Aiyee, Aiyee, Aiyee," they roared in time, with the fighter's knee striking his opponent just below the ribcage, in the kidneys. *Better him than me,* thought Nong ruefully as he shadow-boxed and ran through one of the boxing sequences he had treasured learning from Joi, which incorporated elements of Muay Boran and Muay Thai.

As a child, Nong would lie in bed listening to his father, Warit, and Kritsada reminisce about the golden era of Muay Thai that existed from the 1980s to the mid-1990s. The rich sound of their laughter was audible through the bedroom window as they ruminated on the fifteen-year period when Thailand's best and most revered boxers competed. As they debated many finer points, such as if the training was harder, the talent pool larger, or the match-ups well paired, the teachers all agreed that apart from a few exceptions, the quality of fights and athletes has never again been able to reach the same heights. The acrid smell of cigarette smoke mingled with the musty scent of the forest as they relived their own careers and swapped stories late into the night to the accompaniment of squeaking bats, mosquito whines and the occasional cicada. They would suggest, but just as easily also dismiss, ideas as to how Muay Thai could escape the scourge of corruption and gambling. Eventually, at long last, Nong would hear the scraping of metal chair legs on the cement porch, signalling it was late and time to sleep.

Sad that traditional Muay Thai techniques were no longer taught, Nong asked Joi if the art was fading. He felt sorry to hear that in the past, judges awarded points based on a demonstrated mastery of technique, not strength, unlike now. Nong studied and memorised as many Muay Thai moves as possible. Each time he fought, when he knew he had won a match, he would show the skills he preferred to use, rapidly moving around the ring, imagining he was Nai Khanom Tom, using flying knees, backward elbows and reverse kicks to the roar of the crowd. His old-school techniques interfered with the gamblers' ability to predict a fight. If he had started in the first round with a show of his mastery, he would win no points, causing the gamblers to lose money. Tonight, he would follow the fight strategy until he won; then, there was fun to be had. In truth, not many people understand the points system today.

The sweet scent of flora, summer breezes and a sharp prod in the ribcage jolted Nong from his reverie. Moving around from behind him, Natcha, dressed in a backward Red Bull baseball cap, baggy jeans and an old palm leaf green sweater, said in a low, hushed voice, her eyes sparkling with mischief, "It's time."

"Ok, boss," grinned Nong, with a sideways glance at Dang standing by the door scrutinising everyone entering and leaving the changing room.

Joi, with the help of Sert, who had nagged his way into joining Nong's corner team, had administered his pre-fight massage with Namman Muay. Nong always disliked the hard downward massage strokes on his stomach muscles both before and during each fight, but to refuse help would be very rude. He had no choice but to lie still, keep his mouth shut and appear grateful for the pair's attention. Once the massage was finished, Natcha had liberally covered his face and the back of his neck with Vaseline until Nong had slapped her hand away, telling her enough was enough and that he was going to break out in sweats because of the thickness of the layers. But she had only given a parody of a deep male laugh and applied more.

Nong adjusted the red cape Tanawat's new PR assistant had sent to the hotel room earlier that day, took a deep breath and joined his father and Dang. "Let's get this done," he said, leading his corner team down the narrow corridor to the stage. Shouts of "*Chok dee"* greeted him as he made his way, slowly shadow-boxing and continuing to limber up and replay his fight strategy. He only stepped aside to let the bloodied form of an unconscious fighter on a stretcher be wheeled past. From behind the black curtain, he bounced on the soles of his feet, shaking his arms and energising himself for his appearance on the ring runway. Aware of Natcha, Dang, Joi and Sert behind him, he felt grateful for the wall of support their presence provided. Livelihoods depended on him winning. Nong thought, *I'm going to win this fight*, and thanked his parents, Dragon's Gym, Abbot Anurak, Lady Ta-khian and the spirit animals. He rolled back his shoulders and stood up straight. To Nong's right, Agung's team waited. Dressed in blue shorts and similarly covered in oils and Vaseline, Agung stared straight ahead, the muscles in his jaw twitching.

"Best of luck," called Nong. But Agung only snarled in his direction, earning himself a clip around the back of his head from his trainer and a sharp rebuke not to embarrass the gym two days in a row.

Nong wore red crimson shorts embroidered with a gold fringe and silver and gold writing. The shorts had the logo of Dragon's Gym on one side and his name on the other. When the villagers had presented him with the flashy attire, he had struggled to contain his laughter at the huge gold bows attached to the waistband. Still, he had solemnly accepted the gift with both hands and a nod of thanks. It was only later that Joi told him the ribbons, which were 50 centimetres long, were detachable.

The few minutes wait seemed to drag for hours, and Nong shot through the curtain like a greyhound from a trap when his name was called, startling Dang, who had not anticipated having to rush after him. In the rehearsal, they had all moved as one team and followed the carefully choreographed steps, even including the slapping of at least three imaginary audience hands as Nong travelled up the ramp to the ringside corner. Now, in performance, not rehearsal, spotlights swirled in blues, whites and reds, giving the stadium the appearance of a high-tech nightclub. When he reached the boxing ring, he saluted the crowd, not needing to look back to check if his team was there. As he climbed over the ropes, already people who may or may not have been supporters were shouting advice. Joi had given him strict instructions to listen only to his advice. As soon as Nong moved back to the red corner, he felt a sharp tug on the waist of his shorts, causing him to start. He looked down to see Joi holding up one of the big gold ribbons.

"I think we can do without the gift wrapping, don't you?" Joi climbed into the ring to detach the now limp bow on Nong's left hip and readjust the blue, yellow, green, and pink *Pra Jiads* on his upper arms.

All warm-ups and salutations complete, the downward slice of the referee's arm was greeted with a roar. Nerves dominated as Nong and Agung circled with their gloves up. Both boxers led with their left foot forward and right back, no more than a hip's distance apart. They moved towards one another, tapping their front left feet, shifting their weight back and forth and feigning strikes and kicks, probing with jabs, crosses, and kicks with their chins down. A swift low kick by Agung failed to strike Nong's outer right left thigh because he pre-empted it with a small step back. Agung stepped forward and jabbed Nong in the stomach, causing him to take a sharp intake of breath. Nong retaliated with a sharp kick, which smashed just below Agung's ribcage. Resetting, Agung aimed a swift jab cross to Nong's head, but failed to land a right hook. Agung came on again, but Nong kicked him in the stomach with a toe jab between the ribs. The kick caused Agung to open his eyes in shocked surprise. Nong advanced, chasing him in a flurry of jabs and crosses. By a kitten's whisker, Agung's uppercut failed to contact the underside of Nong's chin. Next, Nong attacked Agung, who met his forward moves with a block followed by a roundhouse kick, which Nong failed to shield himself from. Ignoring the sharp pain in his ribs, he struck out with a left kick, which clipped the side of Agung's head, followed by a low kick to his outer thigh.

Sweat poured down their faces. Their eyes focused on one another's chest in order to spot the tell-tale signs of the brain committing to a line of attack. The crowd roared again and again as the fighters feigned and struck out, testing each other's lines of defence and speed of attack. It was only a minute into the first round, and already the Muay Thai aficionados could tell that the fight was special.

Nong wrapped his arms around Agung's shoulders, aiming not just for a clinch but also the judges' approval. Nong crossed his wrists at the nape of Agung's neck. Their muscled stomachs pressed against one another as their bodies moved from side to side, seeking dominance. Suddenly, Nong twisted Agung around to the left while swiping his foot from underneath him in a show of skill. Agung crashed to the mat, landing on his right side. Within five seconds, however, Agung was back on his feet, ready to challenge Nong again. His expression of frustration caused Nong's corner to shout even louder.

Nong stood back, appraising Agung before moving in like a lion not yet committed to chasing his kill. Nong blocked Agung's low kick, lifting his leg up with his shin bone pointing outwards so his opponent would feel even more pain than he would from the attack. Agung had made the mistake of letting his guard drop, and Nong missed the opportunity to take advantage of the defensive gap, his attention caught by the coach party wearing yellow t-shirts with his name emblazoned on the front. The villagers held up placards and cheered him on. Gan covered her face with both hands, causing Nong to give the briefest of grins before re-engaging with Agung with a deft low kick followed by a sharp jab, which only managed to skim Agung's glove.

Agung attempted to hold Nong back with a series of *teeps* to the stomach. With perfect timing, though, Nong moved in with a combination jab and cross-double low kick, swiftly followed by a kick to Agung's left side, forcing Agung into the corner. He tried to defend himself but failed to make contact as Nong stepped one move back, quickly retaliating with a kick, keeping up the pressure. The two fighters exchanged a flurry of blows. Agung found himself on the ropes again. Nong purposefully slowed the tempo of the fight down so he could look for gaps in Agung's defence. Nong opted to attack with a knee to the stomach, but Agung stepped aside and caught Nong with a left hook that sent him reeling. Shaking his head, he re-engaged with Agung, and he landed a perfectly timed jab, his glove smashing into Agung's nose just as the bell rang. Joi jumped into the ring as Natcha and Dang pushed the battleship grey round metal tray into his corner and a chair on top.

Blocking out every sound but his father's voice, Nong sipped water and spat into the spittoon.

"Time to stop playing, Son. You need to finish this and go for the knockout, so there's no doubt as to who's the winner."

Just as his father spoke, Nong saw Tiger moving past the other side of the ring, her shoulders rising and falling as she walked stealthily, the tip of her tail flicking. Hunting.

Her mouth open and upper lip fixed in a slight snarl, she turned to look at him, her amber eyes supernaturally glowing as if letting him know she had business of her own to settle. Then she disappeared. Nong looked at his prey on the other side of the ring, locking eyes with Agung, who couldn't quite hold his gaze. "You are going down," swore Nong, getting to his feet before the bell had rung and moving into the ring centre.

The music picked up a fast pace, and Agung started

the second round with a swift kick to Nong's side, followed by a combination of jabs and kicks as he sought to dominate from the outset. With his gloves held up, Nong defended himself and stepped back to avoid a low kick and give himself a second to breathe. *This fight is going to be fought at my pace*, he vowed as he moved in to attack. The crowd roared in approval and stamped their feet, egging the boxers on.

Gan, who had lowered her hands during the match, now hid her face in her handbag as she covered her ears with her hands to block out the sound of the fight. Four times, Nong lifted his right knee to distract and threaten Agung with a knee strike before striking him with another toe jab that didn't find its mark but still caused Agung to falter. Nong maintained his defences, shielding his head from Agung's punches as he continued to advance. Then Agung delivered such a hard, low kick to his outer left thigh that he almost fell Agung followed through with yet another low kick to exactly the same spot, numbing his left leg with searing pain. But Nong fought on, taking jab after jab, cross punch after cross punch, and uppercuts to his sides. As he gained confidence, Agung's defence became sloppy, and that's when Nong threw a perfectly timed cross that hit Agung square on the face, knocking him flat on his back. Shaking his head, Agung rolled over onto his hands and knees while Nong circled the ring without taking his eyes off his opponent, steadying his breath as he planned his next line of attack.

Ignoring the exhaustion that was starting to set in,

Nong walked straight up to Agung and re-engaged in the fight, knee first. Nong jabbed with his right and threw a left straight elbow followed by a low kick. Agung was on his back foot as he moved away from the onslaught, blood pouring down his bruised face. Nong's right front kick smashed into Agung's sternum, sending him flying backwards onto the ropes. Collecting himself, Agung attempted a roundhouse kick but missed Nong completely and almost fell over again. Like a shark scenting blood, Nong moved in to finish the fight. Agung was now in the corner just where Nong wanted him. Left foot forward, he jabbed Agung hard in the jaw, clinched him and smashed into his ribs with knee strike after knee strike.

The crowd met each punishing blow with a deafening "AIYEE, AIYEE," egging Nong on to finish the fight. The referee, his black shirt soaked in sweat, yanked their arms from around each other's necks. Once separated, he gave them the order to continue. Nong, now the aggressor, charged to engage Agung in a clinch and sledgehammer him with his knee strikes. Agung struggled to regain the strength to fight back. The referee raised his knee and pushed it between their tired bodies while hauling them apart. Once separated, he gave the downward hand signal.

Barely able to keep his guard up, Agung stumbled backwards, almost crashing into an over-eager journalist resting his camera on the ringside. Nong punched Agung, who was starting to swing wildly, his punches ill-timed and no longer as straight. Then,

Agung stepped back to deliver a roundhouse kick with his right foot. The pain exploded into Nong's head and knocked him onto his hands and knees, but Agung also slipped on the sweat-soaked ring floor, crashing backwards. Grinning manically at seeing Nong struggle to get up, he sprung to his feet and roared at Nong, pulling back his right arm to jab him in the face. A sense of unexpected victory gave him a surge in strength. However, Nong met his attack with a straight left elbow to his jaw, followed by a right cross, which sent him flying backwards four feet and crashing onto the mat. The referee pushed Nong aside with a shove to the chest so he could check Agung was not concussed.

Permission was given to carry on. Now, it was Nong who sensed victory. Reaching out to a dazed Agung, Nong rested his left glove on his opponent's forehead and smashed into his jaw with an uppercut that jerked his head up, and blood sprayed in a wave, splattering Nong's cheek. As Agung slumped, the referee intervened to prevent Nong from kneeing Agung in the face. A move which could have broken Agung's neck. Nong's knee caught the referee's leg instead. Wincing and clutching at his own leg, he urged the fighters on. It was not only the boxers who would be suffering from bruised legs and arms the following day.

The iron scent of blood filled Nong's nostrils as he twisted a hook into Agung's face. The pain and frustration of the past month exploded in a powerful lower right kick. Agung struggled to stand up straight, his body swaying to and fro as he tried to focus. Nong gripped the back of Agung's neck with his glove, simultaneously giving an uppercut to his jaw and moving back his right foot. The Muay Thai aficionados who knew what was coming next roared in appreciation. Nong thrust his knee into Agung's face, and while he did instantly go down, he was finished. Everyone knew it. His neighbours, his friends, his father. Every single person in the audience apart from one. Gan. She still had her head in her handbag, her muffled shouts for news of the fight ignored by the jubilant Khao Lak coach party.

"Nong, Nong, Nong," went up the shout as Agung collapsed. The referee managed to signal an end to the fight while catching the back of Agung's head like a baby and gently laying him to rest on the floor. Nong ran around the ring, his arms about his head and tears streaming down his face, against a backdrop of medics, media and his fans in the corner.

"Go pay your respects to Agung," ordered Joi as he grabbed Nong's arm.

"Not before I pay them to you, I won't," said Nong, kneeling. Smiling up at Joi, he touched his forehead to the mat, then jumped up and hugged him.

Joi fought back tears as he pushed his son towards Agung, but not before raising an eyebrow at Natcha, whose excited voice was becoming higher pitched by the second. Joi scanned the crowd to see Gan. From where he stood, he could see her surrounded by a group of their friends and extended family. This weekend, loan sharks would be paid, rice farmers could survive another season, much-needed household repairs completed, food put on the table, and school uniforms purchased. And above all, medical bills could be covered.

CHAPTER THIRTY-FOUR

"WHAT the fuck were you doing, Bhan?" screamed Aye, his face purple with rage as he stomped up and down the tiger skin rug, its back-right paw mangled from where it had been caught in a snare, a cigarette burn visible on its left ear. "You were supposed to stop Nong, you shit."

Aye believed you win some, you lose some, but last night, they would not have lost if it had not been for Bhan's stupidity. He claimed he had had to fight off a macaque in the men's lavatory, but the idea was nuts. More likely, he thought, the scratches on Bhan's face had been caused by a girl not wanting to be groped.

"You just think with your dick, don't you?"

"I'm telling you; it was a frigging monkey. I took the drugs out of my pocket to check them when this monkey appeared out of nowhere and grabbed the packet. Then it attacked me. Its evil face all fangs. His incisors BIT my ear!"

"Yeah, right," snarled Aye, shaking his head. Leaning against the heavily carved, gilded rosewood desk behind which was hung an oil painting of King Rama X in a white military uniform with the Queen Consort. "More likely, you tried to get some poor girl shoved into a cubicle against her will, didn't you? You're just some kid running around being a playboy on Daddy's money. You don't know how to work. You're a parasite around here. And I've started to wonder what value you add," screamed Aye, appraising Bhan through slitted eyes.

"*Do*? *What do I do?* I've done everything you asked. And more... I spiked that drink the first time around… I arranged that man's fall, I—"

"Shut up!"

"Well…"

"I said shut up. Now get the fuck out!"

The fight had cost Aye millions. But that was not what was really bothering him. There were always other boxers; many ways to earn the cash back. Ringside judges could almost always be bribed. A military friend could lend a hand with a little persuasion. Still, he had the feeling that he was being watched, stalked. Since the first bell, he couldn't shake the sensation that there was someone or something hunting him. Slowly and methodically. Not in a hurry, not hungry.

"You're going mad," Aye muttered to himself, reaching behind to retrieve a Cuban cigar from a lacquered hand-carved box. "I'm not perfect, but no-one knows what a fucker I am, do they?" he said, addressing the king's portrait.

Drawing in the acrid smoke, Aye studied the fine, lively brush marks of the oil painting. He never tired of the way the artist had managed to illuminate the subject's face as if the divine right of kings shone from heaven. The queen's serene expression always caused a bit of a chuckle. Rumours circulated of a different story about the couple's relationship, reporting on how enraged she was at the king for keeping a harem. So engrossed was Aye in the painting, his fantasies running wild with what he would do if he were king and how many wives he would have, that he momentarily forgot his fear.

The rug's dusty orange was intensifying into a vivid hue. The grey fur became brighter, a diamond white. Its black stripes were as dark as the deepest depths of an ancient forest on a clouded night. Fur was growing back in the areas where the carpet had been worn down by human footsteps, and the glassy blue eyes were enkindled to a living, fiery amber. If Aye had turned around, he would have seen that the tiger skin rug, which Aye believed gave him manly strength, riches and good luck, was no longer a pallid, pitiful imitation of the creature it once was. There was a Queen of the Forest coming to life, ready to administer justice. In the wild, tigers creep slowly forward, keeping low to the ground, and use their striped coat as camouflage in the vegetation. When close enough, they spring from cover, killing their prey with a bite to the neck. But Tiger had no need to hide in Aye's office, and the ten-foot leap to rip out his thorax would be easier than changing her gait.

The goosebumps on Aye's skin told him he was not alone, that behind him stood the reason for his disquiet, waiting patiently. Watching. Assessing. Enjoying his fear. Petrified, he crept towards the door to his left, fighting the urge to run. Blinking away the sweat from his eyes, he slowly lowered one hand to retrieve the loaded SIG Sauer P226 semi-automatic pistol from the desk's middle drawer. Behind him, Tiger snarled, showing her sabre canines, her head lowered as she fixed her eyes on Aye. Her tail lashed from side to side, her pupils fully dilated. Tiger wanted to look him in the eye when she attacked. She wanted Aye to meet his death face-on.

Perspiration soaking through his black Gucci shirt, Aye clenched his jaw as he forced himself to turn around. Terror caused him to retch as he saw the huge Tiger, its fangs dripping saliva. Recalling that you should never look a Tiger in the eye but back away slowly and fight the urge to run, he raised the pistol, his hand trembling. Then he fired between the coals of fire that were her eyes.

The bullet slammed into a blue and white Ming vase; chips of fine porcelain flew. Tiger crouched, watching the blood drain from Aye's already pale face as he fell to his knees, the pistol clattering onto the floor. He understood that what burned so brightly before him was not a fire any human could extinguish. He pressed his sweaty palms together in supplication. "Please, no." Playing with his pain, Tiger stretched out her muscular front legs, scratched deep grooves into the polished mahogany floor, and roared to display her razor-sharp teeth. Aye whimpered and shunted backwards into his chair. Then she leapt.

Her claws tore into his chest as her fangs sunk into

Aye's throat just below the junction of the jaw and neck, crushing the trachea and suffocating him. She held the bite long after Aye had ceased to struggle, relishing the sensation of ending his life. Satisfied, she sat back down on her haunches and slowly licked the blood first from her right front paw with the black scar tissue caused by the poachers. Dark red splatters marred the king's portrait. Her tread was silent as she padded back to the centre of the room, where she lay down and rested her beautiful, symmetrically patterned head on her paws. As her brilliant colours started to fade to a flat orange, she chuffed, sniffing the air as the scent of forest breezes filled the room, and a young woman's voice sang a lilting song describing the wonderous forests of yesteryear.

CHAPTER THIRTY-FIVE

BRIGHT yellow, green and blue pennants hung on strings tied to the Dragon's Gym's corrugated iron roof. Multicoloured balloons framed a greyed, slightly frayed bedsheet that had been draped across the external wall facing the car park. The words 'Welcome Home, Champ' were written across the sheet in ivy green paint. Vegetable crates had been arranged into makeshift trestle tables by the gym's reception team in a circle formation facing two loudspeakers, a microphone and a karaoke machine. Each crate had been covered in a thick blue tarpaulin weighed down at the edges by stones in case a tropical storm hit. Soi dogs barked in warning as the dusty coach parked outside the gym only to crowd around its slowly opening door moments later in a semi-circle, their noses raised in the air, searching for the scent of the humans they recognised. Tails began wagging furiously, and their loud, deep woofs changed to excited barks.

Lucy came out from reception along with Warit and Kritsada, grins as wide as watermelon slices. Lucy encased Natcha and Sert in a wide hug.

"Come here," said Warit, pride evident in his voice as he opened his arms to embrace her.

"Watch the match then, did you? See anything

special?" asked Natcha, smiling up at her father and relaxing in the warmth of his sinewy arms. The familiar scents of Tiger Balm on his shoulders proof he had been coaching that morning.

"Nong fought well," said Warit. "I sat on Kritsada's front porch to watch the fight instead of in the gym with the rest of the village so we could see it without being deafened. You must've heard the racket they made from Bangkok!"

"What about Nong's corner team," said Natcha, stepping back and playfully punching her father in the arm. "Anyone new there?"

Warit held his daughter's slim face in his calloused hands. "I have never felt so proud of my beautiful girl," he said, tears in his eyes. "You fight and fight, no matter where you are, always standing up for yourself." Pausing to check that Sert could hear, he said, winking at Natcha with a grin, "If only your broth—"

"Ahh, come on," said Sert, adjusting his backwards-facing baseball cap and looking at the small group smiling at him. Their faces lit with amusement as they waited to see if he would rise to the bait. Sert rolled his eyes and shrugged. The days had long since passed that he needed to run at the very mention of Muay Thai. Over the last few years, he had worked almost as hard as Natcha at his schoolwork. Neuy said that if he continued trying, he might be the second person in the family to enrol at university, Natcha having been the first. And now, with the money his father had bet on Nong winning the match, they would have enough for him to at least finish college.

Ahead of Nong, weary, crumpled travellers descended the uneven, rusted metal coach steps. Glad to be home, they put their bags on the ground, stretched their limbs, and greeted friends and family, eager to hear all the gossip of the trip. Nong, Joi and Gan were last off the bus. Tanawat had tried to persuade them to fly back home, but they would have none of it, preferring to travel with the people whose fortunes had been reversed by Nong's win.

"You must be tired," said Joi to Gan, glancing to the motorbike parking area to check that his moped was still where he had left it a few days ago.

Gan smiled weakly and said, "We all are." She stroked her husband's cheek in a quick caress. Joi scrutinised her with narrowed eyes and pursed lips as she went to give a cordial greeting to his boss. Last night, Joi had given Nong a cold stare when he had commented that Gan's jeans made her look like she had an elephant's bum. Loose folds of material hung down like excess skin. The greeting shouts, whining of dogs and diesel fumes from the bus faded away as Joi said a prayer, asking Buddha to protect Gan from the disease that seemed to be rotting away her body and thanking him again for protecting Nong in Bangkok. Then he sighed and exhaled slowly, expelling the stress from the past few days in one long breath. Joi had excused himself from the post-fight celebration in Bangkok to slip around the back of the street food stands outside the stadium and call the 24-hour medical hotline to book an appointment for next Friday. Tomorrow, he would drive to Phuket to pay the deposit the clinic demanded before Gan's MRI scan could go ahead.

The news of Aye's murder had made the afternoon news. It was Sert, with his interest in current affairs, who had shared the coverage with the rest of the coach as it streamed into his phone. The police were mystified. All the forensic evidence pointed to the cause of death being an enormous predator, but that was impossible. The last person seen leaving the room was known as a small-time playboy, a bespectacled, suited news reporter announced. The newsreader stated that he was nicknamed Bhan and that his father had several nefarious links to crime organisations. The television journalist went on to say that Bhan was the chief suspect.

"Even if he's not guilty, knowing how the police work cases, it's likely that he's going to jail. Unless his parents can persuade their connections with a fat bribe that the boy should walk," Sert had opined to his coach mates.

"Too right," Joi agreed from the seat behind, wondering how the murder had been executed, and asking himself, *What machine, knife or sharp instrument could tear someone's throat out like that? How come there was fresh blood on the fangs and claws of the tiger skin rug?*

"Nong, wasn't that the boy at the forest *wat* when you were there?" Gan had asked.

"Yeah, that's right," said Nong, his face pale.

The other passengers continued to argue how the brutal murder had been executed. Each explanation was wilder and more improbable than the last.

"You okay, Nong?" asked Natcha. A small electronic fan was blowing in her face to try and counteract the stifling air of the bus. The sun was at its zenith, and even the grimy windows of the coach were hot. Natcha swung one leg over the other to turn and face Nong, who sat in silence, slumped back in his seat, staring at the tobacco-stained coach interior ceiling, refusing to be drawn into conversation.

"A shaman claims it's a tiger attack!" said Sert, looking around excitedly for an audience.

"Shut it, Sert," said Natcha. Athletic, she was not used to sitting still for long periods of time. The journey, with its stale food, constant chatter, and people bumping her as they walked up and down the aisle, was irritating, to say the least. "I hate buses," she sighed, turning her attention back to Nong. "You knew this guy?"

"Yeah, I met both of them."

"Where?"

"I met Bhan when I was a kid at the *wat*. In Chiang Mai, a few years later, he was there with Aye, the gangster that was murdered last night."

Natcha fell silent, considering the answers, then shrugged. "Well, who knows what went on? I certainly don't care," she said, considering the conversation closed. She turned back to face the front of the coach and her fan.

Nong knew, though. Tiger had let him know that she was hunting. She had appeared in the stadium to let him see that she was after prey. But why? Why had she taken the decision to kill?

Throughout the journey home, the conversation returned to the circumstances of Aye's gruesome death. The murder was forensically analysed on social media and every news channel. Anchor men and women interviewed witch doctors and monks on the powers of supernatural beings. These experts in the paranormal claimed it was a *Suea Saming*, a male or female who transformed into a tiger by black magic. So horrific and gruesome became the stories that Joi told everybody to shut up. For her part, though, Gan had only laughed. Her husband had more chance of stopping the sea. There was no way the conversation would die down. Everyone was delighting far too much in the macabre story, inventing and elaborating with scenes from popular horror films and television shows.

Glad to be back home, Gan rode pillion on Joi's bike while Nong jogged behind along the dirt road to their house. Dogs rushed out to greet him, and he waved in acknowledgement of the shouts of congratulations from the villagers along the way. His body ached, and he slowed down to a walk before veering to the left into the old rubber plantation so he could walk in the shade. Birds flitted overhead, and small geckos darted around tree trunks, protecting their territories and love interests.

Nong's shoulders relaxed for the first time in what

felt like a century. Sunbeams danced amongst the long grass as if a humongous disco ball twirled in the canopy overhead, illuminating the abandoned plantation with sparkles of light. As Nong ambled along the narrow path between the rubber trees, some of which still had half-coconut shells tied to their lower trunks, he thought about getting a *Sak Yan* tattoo. Smiling ruefully, he thought *I'd better get a tiger, given its associations with healing, luck, strength and protection against evil.* The breeze was desert hot, but the humidity gave a dampness to the air. In the canopy above, a troop of monkeys chattered and crashed along the branches. Looking up, he could see the mothers leaping amongst the foliage, their young grasping their stomachs and backs. One of the macaques landed on all fours in front of him, a cigarette tucked behind its left ear.

Monkey meandered forwards to greet him, tail held high. "I guess thanks are in order," Nong said, kneeling down so he could gaze directly into the monkey's perennial old man's face. Then Monkey leapt onto Nong's shoulder. Nong stood up and continued walking along the path fringed by long green grass; amongst the blades flitted small yellow butterflies. The macaque chattered into his ear, re-enacting the lavatory scene and his set-to with Bhan and his poisons.

"I know, I know," said Nong. "I'm grateful, but—"

Then he saw her. Beautiful and regal lying in the sun. As he approached, Tiger rolled onto her stomach and turned her head to face him, her amber eyes assessing him from ten metres away. As Nong and Tiger stood regarding each other, Monkey leapt off Nong's shoulder and scampered over to where she reposed. He gave a quick bow of his head and sat back on his haunches. His mischievous eyes caught sight of the white tip of Tiger's tail. One paw slowly reached out to grab the pale fur, and when Tiger let out a low growl, Monkey quickly whipped his arm away.

Laughter bubbled up from Nong's chest, grateful for Monkey's antics. Nong approached Tiger. "Why?" he asked, wanting to hear the truth first-hand after the hours of speculation and strain at having to keep his emotions in check. Since childhood, he had played alongside these beautiful spirit animals, and he prayed she had not murdered Aye.

"Do you not know my nature?" said Tiger, her eyes open in an almost human expression of surprise.

"Yes, but do you have the right to be both judge and jury?"

"I have the right to protect a cub," said Tiger, daring Nong to challenge her as she regarded him with a hunter's steadfast gaze. "When and as I see fit. That's the law of the forest. You humans seem to have forgotten that."

"Nong," said Lady Ta-khian, stepping out from amongst the trees. "When you were a child, I asked you to learn about the forest and our ways. Do you remember *Tham lai pa khue ahm lai chat*—'to destroy the forest is to destroy life'? Aye was destroying life. Our life. His thirst for money led him to corruption far beyond trying to ruin you. He was involved in destroying ancient forests illegally, trafficking of rare animals and many, many crimes. Come and sit with us. We have much to celebrate and your future to think of. Let us not make a man who did not deserve to be on this earth matter anymore."

Nong shrieked as he was suddenly lifted into the air by a powerful force. Elephant picked him up as if he were a leaf by wrapping her trunk around his waist and placed him where Tiger, Monkey and Lady Ta-khian waited. Tiger chuffed, a warm gleam in her eyes, while Monkey leapt up in the air, causing his cigarette to go flying into the leaf mounds at the foot of a nearby tree. In a flash, he dived into the pile to retrieve his cigarette. Shaking her head with a soft smile, Lady Ta-khian gracefully knelt on the grass, resting one hand on Tiger's back.

Two hours later, Nong awoke. All the stiffness had gone from his body, and the cuts and bruises had disappeared from his limbs. Nong sat up and looked around for traces of his animal friends. Suddenly, however, he felt the difference. He was alone, apart from the myriad of small creatures scurrying through the vegetation as they went about their chores. Nong stood, removed his shirt to shake off the forest debris and brushed down the back of his shorts. Whistling to himself, he followed the path in the direction of his parents' house, feeling every inch the ancient hero.

The End

GLOSSARY

Ajahn – A Thai- and Lao-derived term that translates as 'professor' or 'teacher'. It is used as a title of address for high school and university teachers and for Buddhist monks who have passed ten *vassa*—in other words, those who have maintained their monastic precepts unbroken for a period of ten years. The term *Luang Por*, 'Venerable father', signifies an Ajahn of acknowledged seniority in Thai Buddhism.

Kuman Thong – A household divinity of Thai folk religion. It is believed to bring luck and fortune to the owner if properly revered. Kuman or Kumara means 'Sanctified young boy'; thong means golden.

Mongkhon – A type of headgear worn by Muay Thai athletes. The Mongkhon is given to a boxer after their trainer sees that the student has become an experienced fighter and learned a great deal about Muay Thai. The Mongkhon is never be placed on for fear it would lose its worth and is unique to Thai boxing. It must be worn during the *Ram Muay* and should be handled only by the fighter and teacher so as not to lose its perceived special powers.

Muay Thai – A combat sport from Thailand that uses stand-up striking along with various clinching techniques. It is similar to other Indochinese styles, namely *pradal serey* from Cambodia, *tomoi* from Malaysia, *lethwei* from Myanmar and *Muay Lao* from Laos. Descended from Muay Boran, Muay Thai is Thailand's national sport. The word *muay* derives from the Sanskrit *mavya*. Muay Thai is referred to as the 'Art of Eight Limbs' or the 'Science of Eight Limbs' because it makes use of punches, kicks, elbows and knee strikes, thus using eight 'points of contact', as opposed to 'two points' (fists) in boxing and 'four points' (hands and feet) used in other more regulated martial arts sports, such as kickboxing, boxing, and *savate*. A practitioner of Muay Thai is known as a *nak muay*. Western practitioners are sometimes called *nak muay farang*, meaning 'foreign boxer'.

Namman Muay – The main ingredients in Namman Muay are methyl salicylate and menthol. The methyl salicylate is a salicylate similar to Aspirin. Both ingredients together provide temporary relief of muscle or joint pain caused by strains, sprains, arthritis, and bruising. They also create a warming effect on the muscles.

Pi Javea – A Javanese clarinet.

Pha Tung – A traditional, long wraparound skirt.

Phuang Malai – The *phuang malai* is a floral arrangement given to a fighter as a token of good luck. These flowers, usually made of jasmine, are tied together, making the bouquet long enough for the fighter to wear over their neck. In Buddhist tradition, the flowers symbolise life and death and the impermanence of existence.

Pra Jiad – These are armbands which are often worn into the ring. They originated when Siam was in a constant state of war. Young men would tear off pieces of a loved one's clothing, often a mother's sarong, and wear it in battle for good luck as well as to ward off harmful spirits.

Wai Khru and Ram Muay – The *Wai Khru* is the first part of the dance one sees the fighter perform prior to the start of the bout. The fighter will seal the ring by walking along the inside perimeter of the ropes while stopping in each corner to say a quick prayer. The act of sealing off the ring is said to keep bad luck out and protect the fighter throughout the course of their bout. Next, the fighter goes to the centre of the ring and circles about three times. After which, the fighter will lower themselves to their knees and bow three times. Many gestures in Buddhism are done in threes as a sign of imperfection. Each time they bow, they will give respect to their trainer and their spiritual beliefs and ask for luck and an honourable performance. Following the *Wai Khru,* a fighter will begin to perform the *Ram Muay*. The *Ram Muay* does not have set routines, like the *Wai Khru,* and is more personal and fighter-specific. However, there are recognisable movements that can be seen. The ceremonial *Ram Muay* dance is taken from the *Ramakien* (a Thai epic closely based on the Hindu *Ramayana*).

Nai Khanom Tom – In 1767, a notorious fighter by the name of Nai Khanom Tom was captured by the Burmese during a battle. As a sign of respect for his capabilities in hand-to-hand combat, he was given the chance to fight for his freedom. He prevailed and was allowed to return to his native Siam. He was heralded as a hero by his people upon his return. His fighting style was christened as Siamese-style boxing. It would later become known as Muay Thai.

Sarama – This is the exciting yet haunting music of Muay Thai. It starts quietly and slowly during the Ram Muay and picks up pace as the fight progresses. The musicians increase the tempo and volume as the action picks up in a fight. The four instruments are the Pi Java (Javanese Clarinet), Klong Kaak (set of drums), Ching (cymbals) and Kong Mong (heavy drum).

Sawadee kap/Sawadee kaa – Women say *"ka",* and men say *"kap"* at the end of greetings, phrases, and sentences. They are polite words used to show respect. *Sawadee K*a is simply 'hello' in Thai as said by a woman, and *sawadee kap* is a similar greeting said by a male.

Songkran – An annual event that marks the beginning

of the Thai New Year. It is the largest celebration throughout the whole country and is also famous for being one of the wildest water fights you may ever participate in.

Suea Saming – A male or female human transformed into a tiger by black magic.

Sabai dee mai – "How are you?"

Wat – Thai monastery or temple.

Printed in Japan
落丁、乱丁本のお問い合わせは
Amazon.co.jp カスタマーサービスへ

12125929R00222